Sport Management, Innovation and the COVID-19 Crisis

This book looks at how sport and sports organisations have had to innovate during the COVID-19 pandemic.

Against a backdrop of lockdowns, empty stadia and a fast-moving public health crisis, the book presents fascinating case studies of innovation and crisis management in sport, with valuable lessons to be learned for preparedness and resilience in future crises. The book explores how managerial processes have evolved during the pandemic in areas as diverse as sports communication, youth sport, sports events, esports, sports tourism, and physical activity, in both professional and community settings. It considers the fundamental importance of technology as a tool of innovation and considers how different stakeholder groups, from governing bodies to athletes to fans, have developed new pathways of engagement and what that might mean for the future development of the sport industry.

This book is fascinating reading for any student, researcher, practitioner or policy maker looking to better understand this profound moment in the history of sport and society, and to anybody with an interest in key themes in sport business and management, such as innovation, crisis management or consumer behaviour.

Gözde Ersöz is an Associate Professor at the Department of Sport Management at Fenerbahçe University who specializes in sport management, behaviour science, sport, and exercise behaviour. Dr. Ersöz has published 30 research articles and 6 book chapters, and also presented more than 100 papers in scientific congress. Dr. Ersöz is the co-editor of the *Journal of Sport and Social Sciences* and *The Journal of Eurasia Sport Sciences Medicine*. She also serves on the editorial board of many journals published in the fields of Sport and Exercise Psychology, Sport Sciences and Recreation. Dr. Ersöz has served on the committees and boards of institutions and organizations such as the Basketball Federation, the Triathlon Federation, the Exercise and Sports Psychology Association, the Sports Sciences Association, and the Sports and Physical Activity Association for Women.

Meltem Ince Yenilmez is an Associate Professor at the Department of Economics at Izmir Democracy University who specializes in economics of gender and labour economics. She was a Visiting Researcher at the University of California, Berkeley between 2014 and 2015 and was at Georg-Universität-Gottingen during the summer school of 2015–2016. She is currently a visiting researcher at the University of Massachusetts, Amherst, Visiting Faculty at IIM Rohtak, India and a Visiting Professor at the University of Tohoku, Japan. She is an economist focused on gender, feminist theory, discrimination and care work. She has four books published by Routledge and Palgrave, and her next book projects income equality, cyberfeminism and women's participation in the sports market.

Routledge Research in Sport Business and Management

Sport and the Pandemic
Perspectives on Covid-19's Impact on the Sport Industry
Edited by Paul M. Pedersen, Brody J. Ruihley and Bo Li

Embedded Multi-Level Leadership in Elite Sport
Edited by Svein S. Andersen, Per Øystein Hansen and Barrie Houlihan

Good Governance in Sport
Critical Reflections
Edited by Arnout Geeraert and Frank van Eekeren

Stakeholder Analysis and Sport Organisations
Edited by Anna-Maria Strittmatter, Josef Fahlén and Barrie Houlihan

Sport and Brexit
Regulatory Challenges and Legacies
Edited by Jacob Kornbeck

Sport Management Education
Global Perspectives and Implications for Practice
Edited by Mike Rayner and Tom Webb

Digital Business Models in Sport
Edited by Mateusz Tomanek, Wojciech Cieśliński and Michał Polasik

Sport Management, Innovation and the COVID-19 Crisis
Edited by Gözde Ersöz and Meltem Ince Yenilmez

For more information about this series, please visit https://www.routledge.com/
Routledge-Research-in-Sport-Business-and-Management/book-series/RRSBM

Sport Management, Innovation and the COVID-19 Crisis

Edited by
Gözde Ersöz and
Meltem Ince Yenilmez

Routledge
Taylor & Francis Group

LONDON AND NEW YORK

First published 2023
by Routledge
4 Park Square, Milton Park, Abingdon, Oxon OX14 4RN

and by Routledge
605 Third Avenue, New York, NY 10158

Routledge is an imprint of the Taylor & Francis Group, an informa business

British Library Cataloguing-in-Publication Data
A catalogue record for this book is available from the British Library

Library of Congress Cataloging-in-Publication Data
Names: Ersöz, Gözde, editor. | Yenilmez, Meltem Ince, editor.
Title: Sport exercise during the covid-19 catastrophe
Identifiers: LCCN 2022006791 (print) | LCCN 2022006792 (ebook) |
ISBN 9781032182926 (hardback) | ISBN 9781032182933 (paperback) |
ISBN 9781003253891 (ebook)
Subjects: LCSH: Sports administration. | Sports—Health aspects. |
Sports—Safety measures. | COVID-19 Pandemic, 2020-
Classification: LCC GV713 .S67756 2022 (print) | LCC GV713 (ebook) |
DDC 796.06/9—dc23/eng/20220408
LC record available at https://lccn.loc.gov/2022006791
LC ebook record available at https://lccn.loc.gov/2022006792

ISBN: 978-1-032-18292-6 (hbk)
ISBN: 978-1-032-18293-3 (pbk)
ISBN: 978-1-003-25389-1 (ebk)

DOI: 10.4324/9781003253891

Typeset in Goudy
by codeMantra

The book is dedicated to my mother, Nilgün; my father, Mehmet; my sister, Hande; and my brother, Yasin. The book is also dedicated to our many wonderful teachers and students, past and present, from whom we have drawn inspiration and learned so much. I am also grateful to my friend Meltem Ince Yenilmez, one of the editors of this book. Finally, I am indebted to the reviewers who contributed suggestions and feedback to ensure that the book is a success.

Gözde Ersöz

Words cannot express how grateful I am to my mother, father, mother-in-law and father-in-law for all of the sacrifices that they have made on my behalf and whose love and guidance are with me in whatever I pursue. They are the ultimate role models. I wish to thank my sisters. I have no words to describe the meaning of your love and support. Most importantly, I owe my deepest gratitude to my loving and supportive husband, Özgür, and my wonderful beloved son, Bryan Poyraz who provides unending inspiration and being such a good boy always cheering me up. You are the best thing that is still happening to me. Last but not least, I am so grateful to my dear friend and colleague Gözde Ersöz whose supportive approach and encouragement have guided me throughout the process.

Meltem Ince Yenilmez

This book is for all the women in the world who are the foundation stone and the architect of the society.

From Editors
Gözde Ersöz
Meltem Ince Yenilmez

Contents

Figures

Tables

Contributors

Murat Yalçın Beşıktaş (orcid.org/0000-0002-0260-1526) started his doctorate education at Marmara University Institute of Health Sciences in 2010 and became a doctor of sports sciences in 2013. Yalçın Beşıktaş, who worked as a trainer and manager in various sports clubs and centres, worked as a lecturer in the Department of Sports Management at Istanbul Okan University School of Applied Sciences between 2009 and 2018. Since 2018, he has been continuing his academic career as a faculty member at Fenerbahçe University Faculty of Sport Sciences.

Selçuk Bora Çavuşoğlu (orcid.org/0000-0003-4163-9655) is serving as Assistant Dean of Istanbul University – Cerrahpaşa, Faculty of Sport Sciences. Specialized his doctorate in the fields of Communication Sciences and Public Relations, Assoc. Prof. Çavuşoğlu has conducted academic studies in Vancouver, Canada; Boston and North Carolina, United States in 2013 and 2014. He is a member of the Turkish National Olympic Committee Fair Play Commission and a board member of the Turkish Triathlon Federation.

Pero Duygu Dumangöz (orcid.org/0000-0002-2827-5538) started her doctoral education in the Department of Sport Management Sciences at Istanbul University with her thesis titled "Examination of the Relationship of the Athletes Participating in the European Tennis Championships with Their Coaches and the Effects of Leadership Perceptions on Communication Skills". She has taught at Istanbul Aydın University, and currently is a lecturer at Istanbul Technical University. She mainly works on communication, coach-athlete relationship, leadership and sports philosophy within the scope of sports management sciences.

Yasin Ersöz (orcid.org/0000-0001-5116-3246) is currently working at Mersin University, Faculty of Sport Sciences, Department of Sport Recreation, and is also the co-editor of the *Turkish Journal of Sports Science* and language editor of the *International Journal of Recreation and Sports Science*. Working in the field of Sport and Exercise Physiology, Dr. Ersöz conducts research on subjects such as exercise physiology and health and sport performance.

Mustafa Selçuk Özaydin (orcid.org/0000-0003-3935-8790) graduated from Boğaziçi University, Faculty of Economics and Administrative Sciences, Department of Economics in 2012. In 2014, he completed his master's degree in Project Management at the University of Warwick (UK), and in 2020, he received his PhD from Yıldız Technical University in Economics. He is currently working as an Assistant Professor in the Sports Management Department at Haliç University. His research focuses on the economics of football.

Aylin Seçkın (orcid.org/0000-0003-4139-2728) completed her undergraduate education at Boğaziçi University in 1991. She completed her MA at Université Libre de Bruxelles and PhD at Carleton University, Ottawa. Throughout her career, she took part in various international and national projects, gave lectures, participated in seminars and workshops, and also tries to expand the awareness to art economics and sports economics. She serves as a Professor at Istanbul Bilgi University.

H. Neyir Tekeli (orcid.org/0000-0002-4627-2840) is an Assistant Proffessor at the Istanbul Kültür Univesity, Vocational School. She is also the Head of Civil Air Transportation Management and Civil Aviation Cabin Service Departments. Neyir Tekeli holds bachelor's, master's and PhD degrees in art history, economics, tourism management and project management from Istanbul University. Her areas of research are tourism, tourism management and tourism economics. Dr. Tekeli has published 20 research articles and 5 book chapters, and also presented more than 50 papers in scientific congress. She also has 20 years of experience in the academic sector.

Cem Tinaz (orcid.org/0000-0002-9595-4995) is the Director of the School of Sports Sciences and Technology at Istanbul Bilgi University in Turkiye. He is also an esteemed board member and Vice President of the Turkish Tennis Federation. Dr. Tinaz's research interests include sports policy and development, administration, legacies and impacts of sports mega-events – all integrated with his primary area of expertise in sport management. He was awarded a 2016/2017 Advanced Olympic Research Grant by the IOC Olympic Studies Centre for the project "Examining Positive Outcomes of Unsuccessful Olympic Bids".

Burcu Turkcan (orcid.org/0000-0002-7494-5897) is an Associate Professor in the division of Economic Policy in the Department of Economics at Ege University. Currently, she gives lectures on economic complexity theory, network economics, tourism economics and statistics at both undergraduate and graduate levels. Her current research interests include economic policy, regional economics, economic complexity and tourism economics.

Merve Üsküplü (orcid.org/0000-0001-5916-1288) is a PhD student at Istanbul University, Cerrahpaşa Institute of Graduate Programs, Department of Sports Management Sciences, and is currently working at Istanbul Gedik University,

Faculty of Sport Sciences, Department of Sport Management as a research assistant. Working in the field of Sport Management, Üsküplü conducts research on subjects such as sports management, gender and media.

Tuna Uslu (orcid.org/ 0000-0002-5616-2987) started his doctoral programme in Cognitive Sciences and completed his doctorate in I/O Psychology after completing his master's degree in TQM. Since 2016, he has served as the Head of the Sports Management Department at Fenerbahçe University. He still conducts scientific studies in the field of development through sports and works as an editor and referee in international journals. Uslu has participated in hundreds of national and international congresses, publications and scientific boards.

Preface

Sport has a significant economic and social impact on society, which is constantly discussed in the news. Sport is rapidly being acknowledged as a powerful tool for enhancing people's quality of life. However, little is known about how sport may impact society's expectations of its role in corporate growth and creating technology from the position of innovation. More understanding about how to create it effectively is needed to realize sport's promise in the global economy. Sport may be found in a wide range of businesses, including tourism, fitness, health, entertainment, and education, illustrating its interdisciplinary nature both practically and intellectually. Sport innovation may also be seen in for-profit, non-profit, and hybrid companies, making it a challenging phenomenon to study.

As a result of a greater understanding of the context variation of sport, further research on the function of innovation in sport is required. This has to do with the importance of sports organizations in the global economy, as they look for new ways to maintain their long-term sustainability. The relevance of the idea of innovation in sports arises from the scarcity of research on the topic. Gözde Ersöz and Meltem Ince Yenilmez's numerous papers have contributed to the growth of research on these subjects. Academics have expanded on their work by infusing sports research with more entrepreneurial and innovative concepts.

In the ten chapters of this book, there is a lot of discussion to assist readers in understanding how innovation is connected to other strategies, especially those at the organizational level. This entails developing a more innovative sports organizational structure and management system that incorporates contemporary technologies to improve the sports sector. The book also highlights the need for growing human capital, particularly through a transformational leadership strategy that links sports and creativity. This is because players are more integrated, allowing for greater sports innovation and the role of innovation in providing organizational, cultural, and sporting values.

This book examines how the worldwide coronavirus epidemic has influenced the sport business, including how entire seasons have been cut short, events have been cancelled, players have been infected, and sport studies programmes have shifted online. Importantly, the book also considers how the sector could progress in the future. The book presents commentary, instances and informed analysis across a wide variety of issues and practical areas within sport business and management, from crisis communication and marketing to event management and finance, with contributions from sport studies experts. While COVID-19 will undoubtedly throw a long shadow over sport for years to come, and despite the fact that the situation is rapidly changing and the future is unpredictable, this book provides some critical early observations and reflections that will educate discussion and influence policy and practice. This is an essential resource for scholars, students, practitioners, the media, policymakers and everyone concerned about the future of sport. It is a timely contribution to the body of information surrounding the epidemic.

Gözde Ersöz
Meltem Ince Yenilmez

Chapter 1

Innovation in Physical Activity and Exercise during the COVID-19 Catastrophe

Yasin Ersöz and Gözde Ersöz

Introduction

The COVID-19 pandemic, which is a huge worldwide health disaster, has spread swiftly since March 2020, with 5.2 million deaths (December 5, 2021) compared to past pandemics. The number of cases has risen to the top of the list. This has had an impact on everyone in the globe practically, resulting in the isolation and quarantine of billions of individuals throughout the planet. Working from home has grown more common as a result of the epidemic, and the divide between personal and professional life has reduced. Home confinement, which was utilized to avoid pandemic transmission, resulted in a decrease in physical activity, an increase in sitting, and poor food habits. COVID-19 limitations have been found to have a detrimental influence on social involvement, life satisfaction, mental health, sleep quality, psychological, and emotional issues in recent global investigations (Ammar et al., 2020; Brindal et al., 2021; Kaur, Singh, Arya, & Mittal, 2020). With the pandemic, such a shift in people's habits has resulted in a significant deterioration of their mental health, manifesting as increased worry, stress, and sadness. The decline in physical activity and exercise habits, which is one of the lifestyle modifications, has major repercussions in this process, and the impacts are ongoing (Dai, Zhou, Li, Zhang, & Ma, 2021).

Physically active lifestyles and exercise habits not only safeguard physical and mental health but also assist individuals in avoiding diseases like diabetes, hypertension, cardiovascular disease, and respiratory disease by reducing the harmful repercussions of these disorders (Owen et al., 2010). Exercise helps to maintain not only the respiratory, circulatory, muscular, neurological, and skeletal systems but also the endocrine, digestive, immunological, and renal systems, all of which are vital in countering any known or unknown threat to our bodies (Lavie et al., 2019). Regular exercise has been shown in studies to minimize the risk of acute respiratory distress syndrome (ARDS), which is one of the leading causes of mortality in COVID-19 patients and will also help with stress management, psychological well-being, and good mental health throughout the pandemic (Yan & Spaulding, 2020). People have been compelled to

DOI: 10.4324/9781003253891-1

stay at home due to the closing of fitness facilities and public parks, which has hampered their workout routines. Long-term house confinement, which has harmed physical fitness and social communication, as well as the feeling of uncertainty and powerlessness, has resulted in psychological and physical health issues (Bentlage et al., 2020).

Physical Activity and Exercise during the COVID-19 Outbreak

People of all ages have limited their physical activities because of the COVID-19 epidemic. Indoor and outdoor sports and recreational facilities, such as fitness centers, gymnasiums, public swimming pools, playgrounds, and parks, have been shut down in numerous nations. Work, pleasure, physical activity, exercise, and shopping have all been done in online spaces. During the COVID-19 epidemic, people's physical activity patterns, as well as many everyday behaviors, were altered by the quarantine procedure, which was often launched with the phrase "stay at home" (Pinto, Dunstan, Owen, Bonfá, & Gualano, 2020).

When looking at the research on physical activity during the COVID-19 epidemic, it is clear that the results are largely comparable. Tison et al. (2020) used the smartphone application Argus to compare the step counts of 455,404 people from 187 different nations before the pandemic, 10 days after the pandemic, and 30 days after the pandemic (Azumio). When compared to the pre-pandemic era, the number of steps decreased by 5.5% 10 days after the pandemic and by 27.3% after 30 days, according to the findings of this study. Physical activity levels varied throughout the nations in this study based on quarantine time and duration, socioeconomic status, and population. Italy saw a maximum decrease in the number of steps of 48.7% after declaring a nationwide lockdown on March 9, 2020, whereas Sweden did not declare a nationwide lockdown and instead managed the process more with social distance and restrictions, resulting in a maximum decrease in the number of steps of 6.9%. In general, Tison et al. (2020) report a global and worrying drop in physical activity levels.

A countrywide study was done by the French National Observatory for Physical Activity and Sedentary Behaviors to investigate the possible impacts of quarantine on the population's physical activity and sedentary behaviors. The French Ministry of Sports surveyed children, adolescents, adults, and the elderly to learn more about their physical exercise habits. Physical activity levels and exercise practices have reduced among 42% of children, 59% of adolescents, 36% of adults, and 39% of the elderly, according to new research. While physical activity and endurance workouts for transportation decreased significantly, indoor muscle strengthening and flexibility activities rose. Children spent 36% of their time sitting, 27% of their time as teens, 26% of their time as adults, and 36% of their time as the elderly; screen time increased by 62% in children, 69% in adolescents, 41% in adults, and 32% in the elderly (Genin et al., 2021).

During the COVID-19 epidemic, the Spanish adult population, notably youth, students, and males, lowered their physical activity levels, walking times, and rate of intense physical activity, according to a research by Castaeda-Babarro, Arbillaga-Etxarri, Gutiérrez-Santamara, and Coca (2020). According to a study conducted in France with eight professionals and six elderly individuals, a total of ten people in the study, the elderly's physical activity levels decreased, they did not want to be in the exercise environment due to the risk of transmission of the virus, and they were not willing to do physical activity at home or participate in online exercise activities (Goethals et al., 2020).

FitBit customers reported substantial declines in their daily step count on March 22, 2020, as compared to the same period the previous year (FitBit Staff, 2020). In March, the number of steps taken by individuals decreased by 38% in Spain and 25% in Italy, where the epidemic was felt most acutely, and by 12% in the United States and 8% in the United Kingdom, where the pandemic was less effective at the time. Other nations whose physical activity has reduced during the epidemic include Australia, Canada, France, and Kuwait (Goethals et al., 2020; Husain & Ashkanani, 2020; Moore et al., 2020; Phillipou et al., 2020).

The following demographic, psychological, and environmental elements are beneficial in the process of adopting an active lifestyle, according to studies evaluating the factors impacting physical activity and exercise behavior in the COVID-19 epidemic. The following is a list of these factors (Alomari, Khabour, & Alzoubi, 2020; Kaushal, Keith, Aguiñaga, & Hagger, 2020; Ingram, Maciejewski, & Hand, 2020; Meyer et al., 2020; Rhodes, Liu, Lithopoulos, Zhang, & Garcia-Barrera, 2020; Robinson et al., 2020; Rogers et al., 2020; Yang & Koenigstorfer, 2020):

Age
Income
Gender
Education
Ethnicity
Body mass index
Working status
Marital status
Owning a garden
Owning a dog
Having children at school age
Availability of household supplies
Use of physical activity and exercise mobile application
Social distancing practices of the living area
Physical and mental health status
Infection status
Previous level of physical activity
Personality characteristics

Exercise identify
Goal orientation
Strategic planning
Attitudes
Perceptions of risk related to COVID.

Young People's Physical Activity and Sporting Activities during the COVID-19 Outbreak

In terms of youth sports during the pandemic, public health specialists indicated that kid obesity rose in the months following the viral epidemic, and that teenage mental health deteriorated significantly (Robert Pearl, 2020). The National Center for Chronic Diseases in the United States has outlined issues for youth sports organizations targeted at safeguarding individuals and groups against COVID-19's sluggish spread. To govern these groups, the United States has devised a risk assessment framework. Low risk, increased risk, higher risk, even greater risk, and high risk are the five levels of risk (CDC, 2022).

This rule covered the following topics:

- Type of physical activity (individual/group activity, contact/non-contact activity)
- Level of interaction with equipment in physical exercise
- Demographic characteristics of the participants (ages of the participants)
- Structural elements of the activity (individual/group activity, contact/non-contact activity) (local, interregional)
- The audience's age and demographics.

The fact that the sporting event is completed as a team is a key component in COVID-19's spread. One of the elements determining the spread is the existence or lack of physical contact in team sports. While there is physical contact between young people in basketball, it is less harmful in volleyball since there is a net between them and no one-on-one battle. Tennis, another activity with a net in the middle, is considered low-risk since it is played alone. The degree of interaction in physical activity activities and the sharing of sports equipment are two elements that influence viral transmission. While there is less contact with the tennis racket, more ball contact with the basketball may have a dangerous impact. The higher the potential for COVID-19 to spread, the more the danger for shared sports equipment or spaces. Because COVID-19 has a greater impact on older people, mingling with young people and watching sports activities is also a factor that raises the risk. Furthermore, executing these activities locally or between areas is regarded as an additional risk factor. Traveling across cities or nations will enhance the danger level because it is a factor that increases the spread. As a result, sports organizations for young people were designed based on the COVID-19 pandemic's spread level, taking into account all of these risk categories (Pierce, Stas, Feller, & Knox, 2020; Sanderson & Brown, 2020; Watson & Koontz, 2021).

Management and Organization in Fitness Centers during COVID-19

Following discussions with 324 fitness managers, the Importance-Performance Analysis (IPA) approach was used to analyze what was done in terms of crisis management at fitness centers in Korea during the COVID-19, and a crisis management plan was produced. In order to manage the epidemic issue in fitness facilities, six titles were formed as a consequence of this analysis: business, financial, preventative, social distancing, disinfection, and cleanliness management.

Each topic's connected items were identified. Figure 1.1 shows the items linked to the subjects (Kim & Park, 2021).

The relevance of the following aspects in the COVID-19 crisis management of fitness facilities was stressed by fitness managers in this study:

- Providing a non-contact thermometer,
- Finding a means to lower the monthly rent,
- Disinfecting the gym on a regular basis,
- Maintaining a social space between staff and customers,
- Teaching employees how to wash their hands,
- Customers are notified ahead of time when the store will be closed.

They also stated that risk management and preventative management are the most important activities in their businesses. In order to manage the process during the pandemic, spare masks were given in fitness facilities in Korea, toilet ventilation was increased for cleaning management, face-to-face meeting hours were reduced for remote management, and customer concerns were addressed over the phone. State incentives helped with financial management, while quarantine planning helped with disinfection management. When it comes to crisis management at fitness facilities during a pandemic, the following suggestions have been made (Central Defense Countermeasure Headquarters Response Guidelines, 2020; He & Harris, 2020; León-Quismondo, García-Unanue, & Burillo, 2020).

- Social distance should be ensured between employees and customers.
- A non-contact thermometer should be provided on-site.
- It should be ensured that hand disinfectants are available in suitable places.
- It should be ensured that the furniture is kept clean.
- Regular disinfection of the gym should be provided.
- Equipment should be disinfected.
- Working hours should be well planned and notified to customers.
- It should be ensured that the employees pay attention to the hygiene issue.

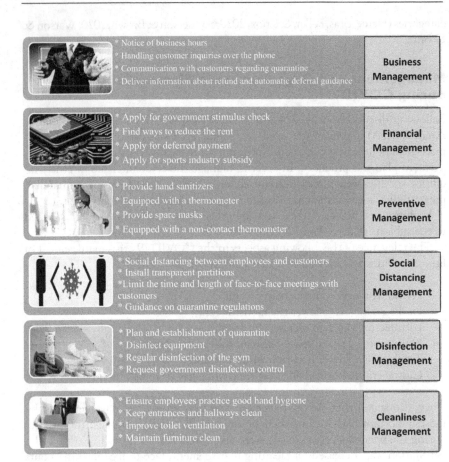

Figure 1.1 Importance-performance analysis of crisis management of fitness center during the COVID-19 pandemic.
Source: Author's own design.

- Applications should be made for government incentive programs to provide financial support.
- Ways to reduce rent must be found.
- Application for deferred payment can be made.
- An application can be made for a sports industry subsidy.
- Continuity of communication with members during the quarantine process should be ensured.
- Face-to-face meeting time with members should be limited.
- Customer questions can be resolved by phone or video conference.
- Spare masks should be provided.
- Indoor and toilet ventilation should be improved.

During the COVID-19 Outbreak, Management and Organization of Sports Facilities

Sports facilities, which are places where people engage in physical activity and exercise, are physical spaces with cultural, economic, and social features that benefit people's physical, psychological, and social health and vitality. Fitness centers, which are large-scale facilities dedicated to the provision of exercise services, are where we primarily carry out our physical activity and exercise activities. Outdoor gyms, smaller boutique gyms, and retail outlet gyms are just a few of the innovative exercise concepts that are popping up. Large and medium chains, tiny individual firms, and franchise brands are frequently in charge of fitness centers. Swimming, football, tennis, squash, badminton, mixed martial arts, jogging, and basketball are among the sports offered at these facilities (Fried & Kastel, 2020; Grieve & Sherry, 2012).

Fitness facilities are purposefully built, selectively offered facilities that are typically suited to users' needs in order to promote health, fitness, and endurance. Members also use these amenities to unwind, socialize, and get away from job stress. These facilities are also available to athletes who want to improve their sports performance. Individuals who desire to develop and preserve their physical appearance might benefit from fitness facilities that are active and motivating. In order to safeguard their revenue, the owners and management of these facilities strive to fulfill the changing demands of their members while also contributing to social welfare and sustainability. Fitness facility managers are in charge of keeping the facility clean and safe for members, instructors, and all personnel (Batrakoulis, 2019; Fried & Kastel, 2020; Glasgow, Mastrich, & Geller, 2021; IHRSA, 2019).

It is vital to keep up with emerging technology, create training methodologies, enhance support services, and provide a healthy atmosphere in order to assure excellence in the fitness industry. With the spread of COVID-19 expected in 2020, several of these facilities have re-examined their operational and holistic policies in light of the pandemic's implications. Many sports facilities throughout the world were closed for a period of time in response to health authorities' recommendations and punishments, and when they returned, they maintained their operations by implementing new pandemic-specific laws (Komańda, 2020; Piotrowski & Piotrowska, 2021).

Following the commencement of the COVID-19 process, many studies on the technical aspects, management, and organization of fitness facilities were conducted, and nations developed recommendations for sports, physical activity, and exercise settings. During the COVID-19 era, the UK government has issued particular instructions for the operation of sporting facilities. The purpose of this guide is to help facility managers in providing the appropriate security for indoor and outdoor sports facilities. In a closed sports facility, a minimum of 9.3 m^2 per participant is permitted. According to the recommendations, a COVID-19 risk assessment is essential to properly establish the necessary activities to improve health and safety preventative measures in sports facilities. For mitigating pandemic risks, operational records, protections, signs, and briefings are said to be crucial (DBEIS, 2020).

With the control measures brought by the Hong Kong government, the spread of the virus in Asian countries such as Macau, Taiwan, Singapore, and Hong Kong was partially prevented. In Hong Kong, all public sports and leisure facilities were closed on January 25, 2020, and the disease prevention and control regulation called CAP599 was issued. In March 2020, while imposing temperature controls at the entrance to all public spaces, all private fitness centers prohibited the gathering of more than four people, and in mid-July 2020, public sports facilities were completely closed. The return to normal public services took place in September 2020, following a large-scale case study by the Hong Kong government (Ibrahim & Hassanain, 2021). Following the publishing of a revised and modified COVID-19 rule (CAP599G) in late September 2020, both indoor and outdoor sporting facilities (e.g. gyms, massage parlors, badminton courts, ice skating courts, bowling, and table tennis courts) were reopened (e.g. bike parks, riding schools, golf courses, and outdoor tracks) (Ho & Chan, 2021).

Saudi Arabia's Ministry of Sports has developed a reference protocol to administer the COVID-19 procedure, which is divided into six sections. The following themes were covered in general at fitness facilities (Ibrahim & Hassanain, 2021):

1   Environment, protection, and social distance regulations,
2   Sports facilities regulations,
3   Arrangements of playing fields,
4   Sports requiring additional precautions and protective regulations,
5   Reporting and monitoring of symptoms,
6   Awareness and communication arrangements.

Abu Dhabi sports council has gathered the COVID-19 measures around three different dimensions and outlined the necessary measures for the reopening of its facilities as follows (Ibrahim & Hassanain, 2021):

1   Physical regulation precautionary measures,
2   Regulations for the technical sector and training teams,
3   Measures regarding members and athletes.

Based on focus group talks conducted over the internet, the International Association of Sports and Entertainment Facilities (IAKS) in Germany has established the actions to be implemented for various types of facilities. During the COVID-19 period, the German Federal Environment Agency issued a statement stating that swimming pools can be utilized as long as disinfection (chlorine) is applied to the water according to established regulations (German Federal Environment Agency, 2020).

The employees were advised to make sure that swimmers maintain proper distances and do not collide during training in order to avoid contamination. On

April 21, 2021, sports facilities in Denmark were progressively reopened around the country. Individuals in Denmark are permitted to use the facilities based on their vaccination passports. The following papers are used to create the vaccination passport (IAKS, 2020):

1   Test (negative test within the last 72 hours),
2   Vaccination (two weeks after full vaccination),
3   Prior infection (positive test completed within the last 14–180 days).

Clubs and athletic activities performed inside in gyms, fitness centers, climbing areas, ice rinks, and pools were accessible to children and youth under the age of 18 with a maximum restriction of 25 individuals during the re-normalization process in Denmark. In addition, sports and recreational activity centers for individuals over 70 possessing a Corona passport were opened, with a limit of 10 persons participating. During the COVID-19 era, participation in athletic activities involving more than 50 persons is restricted across Europe. Outdoor physical activities conducted by governmental authorities, organizations, associations, corporations, or cultural institutions in groups of no more than 50 individuals are authorized (including coaches and parents). Furthermore, professional football matches in Denmark are permitted to be observed if the COVID passport is presented and the spectators are separated by 1 m and separated by separate entrance and exit gates, according to a unique plan with a maximum distance of 500 m (IAKS, 2021).

Guo et al. studied and analyzed the operating guidelines of heating, ventilation, and air-conditioning systems in different fitness facilities in light of the COVID-19 pandemic's airborne propagation, and made suggestions for these systems.

According to the findings, the insufficient use of ventilation systems and the limiting of closed spaces were the primary factors influencing the spread of respiratory infections in the facilities. Because COVID-19 droplets travel through buildings via airflows, air supply, and drainage systems, dilution of airflows in these facilities aids in particle containment. Researchers working in heating, cooling, and air-conditioning organizations of various countries reviewed the measures against airborne transmission of COVID-19 in heating, ventilation, and air-conditioning systems in buildings. As a result of this review, they explained the following measures for ventilation:

• To increase the amount of external ventilation and the opening of the dampers to full capacity as much as possible,
• To improve central air filters with minimum efficiency reporting value (MERV-13),
• To keep the HVAC system running for 24 hours,
• To ensure the use of portable air cleaners with HEPA filters, seven days a week,
• Increasing the use of ultraviolet germicidal irradiation for higher risk areas.

Workforce in the Fitness Industry during the COVID-19 Outbreak

Workers in the fitness industry are encouraged to improve soft skills such as digital technology skills, communication, and customer service as a result of numerous trends such as technical, social, health, and economic. Furthermore, it is becoming increasingly clear that fitness experts must be trained to work with the special population. Employees in the fitness industry should be prepared for new trends such as technosports, online exercise, and remote customer tracking, which focus on specific customer demands, as well as the increased use of technology throughout the COVID-19 pandemic process (Moustakas, Szumilewicz, Mayo, Thienemann, & Grant, 2020; UK Active, 2018).

Fitness sector customers have increased by 72% in the previous ten years, and about 10% of all European adults utilize fitness services. Emerging developments in the fitness sector have been addressed in studies on the industry, as well as the industry's continued professionalization. Despite the fitness industry's expansion, employers indicate that substantial skill shortages and mismatches in the workforce limit service delivery, and they struggle to locate people with the proper abilities to fulfill the industry's increasing demands. One in five employers reported having difficulty hiring the coaches they wanted to work with at their club. Additionally, fitness employers are considering how their current and future workforce will need to evolve to support changing public health needs. In order to continue the growth of the fitness industry and contribute to public health, it is necessary to be prepared for the sectoral challenges in the future and to train and develop the employees accordingly (Deloitte, 2019; EuropeActive, 2019; Jimenez et al., 2018).

EuropeActive (EA), an organization for the fitness industry in Europe, has launched the Sector Skills Alliance for Active Leisure (SSA), according to the European Union Council's declaration of the European Apprenticeship Alliance. The Active Leisure Skills Partnership and Employment Plan project intends to produce a fitness sector skills development plan in collaboration with major European organizations representing fitness industry stakeholders (EuropeActive, 2019).

Moustakas et al. (2020) interviewed 104 people in order to conduct a study to determine the skills expected of those working in the fitness industry in the future, in order to understand new trends in the fitness industry in 2030, how the fitness industry will change after the COVID-19 epidemic, and how to manage these changes. According to the findings, fitness practitioners should be better integrated with the health sector in order to contribute to the fitness industry's rising public health agenda. For example, it has been demonstrated in this study that a predominantly life coach-style approach to special populations such as hypokinetic diseases (non-communicable diseases) and the elderly will be a dominant trend in future fitness consultations.

Exercise and a healthy lifestyle not only help to avoid obesity and the diseases of sedentary living, but they also help to mitigate the effects of COVID-19. Physical activity is useful in lowering COVID-19-related mortality, strengthening the immune system, and improving psychological well-being that was negatively affected by the pandemic, thus health and exercise sectors should establish conditions where they will work together in the future (Abdelbasset, 2020; Hagiu, 2021).

Fitness activities are commonly used in the health industry to prevent a disease from progressing or to manage an existing ailment. However, the new tendency in this area is toward preventative medicine and empowering individuals before problems emerge. In this regard, it is consistent with the fact that the physical activity guide for healthcare workers is deficient in areas such as training science (Lavie, Sanchis-Gomar, & Arena, 2021). According to Füzéki, Weber, Groneberg, and Banzer (2020), it strongly recommends adding physical activity and health and physical activity counseling topics to the medical curriculum and strengthening education on this subject. On the other hand, it is essential for public health that employees in the health sector work in collaboration with fitness experts.

Innovation and New Trends in Physical Activity and Exercise during the COVID-19 Outbreak

Wearable technology assists fitness enthusiasts in keeping track of their training progress. It helps them to get more involved in their training and is a useful tool for defining quantifiable objectives. People may measure the number of steps they take, the number of calories they burn, their heart rate, blood pressure, blood oxygen level, body temperature, and sleep patterns using wearable technology. This device is currently being set up to identify abnormal heartbeats or diabetic symptoms that might lead to a new stroke. Wearables may soon be able to connect to your electronic medical records, giving you a comprehensive picture of a person's profile. Mobile applications that encourage physical activity and fitness also help to motivate users by awarding points based on the amount of movement they make. These smart wearables are made to track how you're progressing or exercising (Best, 2021; Capodilupo & Miller, 2021).

The gadgets will allow exercise participants to simply share this data with their personal trainer, and they will soon be able to deliver even more detailed directions to their customers in the form of a virtual assistant. It will be able to advise you on the number of repetitions you should do, for example. In other words, they will be able to provide more detailed and individualized advice for correcting particular behaviors that need to be altered. Smart fitness equipment: It is not only wearable technology that records and directs exercise participants, but also smart fitness equipment. These devices can give real-time training analysis, as well as feedback on how you move and the equipment you utilize (Gross, Wenner, & Lackes, 2021; Saifee & Kapoor, 2021).

Big data is frequently a modern and free product of digital exchanges. Artificial intelligence, which employs descriptive statistics of high information-density data to measure things, may lead us through data, according to an increasingly developed notion. Artificial intelligence can help you design personalized fitness regimens for your training objectives, eating habits, and current fitness level using wearable devices or manually supplied data. Simultaneously, artificial intelligence is being used to construct software that can regulate your training form and correct you, much like a personal trainer (Farrokhi, Farahbakhsh, Rezazadeh, & Minerva, 2021; Yong et al., 2018).

Exercise participants may obtain real-time feedback on their exercise postures by using their phone's camera to make one-to-one changes. Classes are being streamed live: People may pick and practice lessons from their favorite personal trainers while preserving social distance at home, thanks to the rise in popularity of online and virtual exercises during the COVID-19 epidemic. Online and virtual training environments allow individuals to exercise at home by participating in live-streamed or pre-recorded training sessions (Ai, 2021; Mann et al., 2018).

Due to its entertaining nature, increasing mobility via exercising or playing games with virtual reality (VR) technology has grown popular among individuals. A fitness game, sometimes known as an exergame, is a type of video game that uses technology to detect body movement to help people exercise. Body movements may be monitored by VR sensors, which can also impact the user's emotions, making exercise games using VR technology a new trend. The VR business has exploded in recent years, with the market predicted to rise from 6.2 billion dollars in 2019 to over 16 billion dollars by 2022. Virtual reality exercise games are expected to become increasingly popular in the future. Although this technology is new, there is a greater level of participation of many people in virtual exercises; the increase in exercise motivation due to the high level of enjoymentin performing these activities is promising in terms of the prevalence of virtual exercises. Many game consoles such as Xbox, PlayStation, and Nintendo are programs used in exergame activities (Khundam & Nöel, 2021; Molina & Myrick, 2020).

Many mobile applications used in the sectors of physical activity, exercise, and health not only instruct exercise participants and fitness advisors but also assist them in setting measurable objectives and tracking whether they are met. Mobile applications have been shown to increase people's motivation to exercise in studies. Because this is such a young topic, it is also noted in the literature that more research is needed to fully evaluate the impact of mobile applications on exercise participants (Khundam & Nöel, 2021; Kim & Biocca, 2018).

A mechanism in the form of a leaderboard is used in various apps to allow individuals to compete and compare themselves. A leaderboard may be constructed in the Strava program, for example, by comparing the distance and time run by participants jogging on the same track. According to studies, applications with such comparisons improve the motivation of exercisers with strong accomplishment motivation (Östlund, 2020).

Technology is cited as a critical driver for change in the fitness industry. Almost 80% of gym managers report that online training and technology use are emerging trends in the European region (EuropeActive, 2018). However, with the impact of the COVID-19 pandemic, we can predict some directions the technology could take in the fitness industry. Research indicates that digital exercise or the use of digital technologies in physical activities has become a prominent application area for the use of routine and innovative forms of information and communication technology (Angosto, García-Fernández, Valantine, & Grimaldi-Puyana, 2020).

In this regard, "digital physical fitness" or "mFitness" can be included in the concept of mobile health (mHealth), which is defined as "the use of mobile wireless technologies for health". COVID-19 has changed the way consumers exercise, just as it has changed the way healthcare is delivered. While fitness facilities and exercise classes provide a sense of community and personalized training, they're also crowded areas with lots of surface areas that can spread infections (Dolezel & Smutny, 2021; Moustakas et al., 2020). During maximum exercise, ventilation can increase from 5 L/min to over 100 L/min. Therefore, even an asymptomatic, infectious individual is likely to spread SARS-CoV-2 during high-intensity exercise. This situation has caused gyms and fitness centers in many countries to close during the COVID-19 process to ensure the safety of their customers, and individuals have turned to technology-based physical activity and exercise environments (Piotrowski & Piotrowska, 2021). Although it was gradually opened later, it seems that it may take a little longer for people to fully return to these facilities during the ongoing pandemic process. Therefore, even if the pandemic process is over, people can prefer homes, open spaces, and online exercise environments.

Before the pandemic, the usage of home fitness items grew in popularity owing to convenience and safety, and after the pandemic, products including toilet paper, disposable gloves, freezer, bread machine, puzzles, coloring books, air cleaner, and refrigerator were among the most purchased online. Peloton, treadmill, stationary cycle, yoga mat, kettlebells, exercise ball, and other workout equipment for use at home or in public spaces. Peloton offers internet-connected stationary cycles and treadmills that allow monthly users to participate in lessons remotely via an interactive environment (Andrienko, 2020). Home fitness programs that use interactive gym equipment such as peloton (e.g. treadmill, bicycle, mirror) and fitness apps that offer various exercise options without the need for interactive gym equipment are among the exercise instruments that my individuals will tend to in this process. Some examples of interactive health home fitness apps that require home fitness equipment include Mirror, Zwift, Tonal, iFit, and Nordic Track, each with different membership and pricing structures (Nyenhuis, Greiwe, Zeiger, Nanda, & Cooke, 2020; Parker et al., 2021).

These interactive platforms use real-time personalized health data to encourage users to take more active care of their own health. In addition, these equipment can provide a social connection with other users of the platform, making exercise more attractive for those who need social motivation and responsibility, and the data provided by these equipment can be combined with wearable technologies to monitor activities over time. However, for a variety of activities that can be done from home, there are activities ranging from cycling to running, from Cross-fit to yoga and dance classes (Nyenhuis et al., 2020; Saifee & Kapoor, 2021).

Many home-based hobbies need a variety of expenditures, ranging from costly stationary cycles and treadmills to more modest choices such as yoga or body-weight-strengthening sessions. Investing in home gym equipment can be costly, and some individuals prefer to work out outside rather than indoors. There are entertaining, on-demand, and live-streaming exercises accessible online via You-Tube, Instagram, and free smartphone applications for folks who wish to exercise indoors without incurring equipment expenditures or monthly/annual fees. Virtual courses and personal training sessions are offered by many gyms and fitness experts and may be completed in the privacy of one's own home (Cortis, Giancotti, Rodio, Bianco, & Fusco, 2020; Iannaccone et al., 2020).

Some fitness apps, such as Aaptiv, Strava, Peloton, Nike, and Zombies Run, offer a virtual community and health metrics tracking to accompany more traditional types of exercise that do not require extra home exercise equipment such as walking, jogging, walking, and yoga. In this process, it is important for people with every aspect of healthy living to offer the most suitable options for their individual fitness goals, budgets, and physical abilities. Quarantine is considered the best option to protect health and stay away from viruses during the pandemic process (Iqbal & Faiz, 2020; Schweizer et al., 2021).

Quarantine, on the other hand, has a significant detrimental impact on health, particularly in persons with a frail structure owing to old age or chronic conditions (65 years old and those with serious heart diseases, chronic lung disease, diabetes, obesity, and chronic kidney and liver disease). It is critical for people with these qualities to exercise on a regular basis in order to avoid health hazards. Furthermore, throughout the COVID-19 process, exercise may have a protective impact on the immune system (Flanagan et al., 2021).

Exercise at home within the scope of certain criteria is one of the most effective solutions for increasing physical activity in this process without negatively affecting health under quarantine settings. Wilke et al. (2020) surveyed 15,261 people in 14 countries affected by COVID-19 to determine their preferences for digital home workout programs. More than two-thirds of the sample (68.4%, n = 10,433) stated that they were interested in home exercise. Even if the quarantine process is over, it is also risky for individuals in this situation to exercise in crowded and closed areas as some precautions during the ongoing pandemic process.

In a study of 44,000 persons infected with COVID-19, the Chinese Center for Illness Control and Prevention discovered that advanced age, cardiovascular disease, diabetes, chronic pulmonary disease, hypertension, and cancer all enhance the chance of mortality from COVID-19. As a result, it appears that exercising at home or in open settings where one may separate oneself is preferable. Due to curfews or other limitations, it has become important to convert regular workout routines from outside to inside settings (Wu & McGoogan, 2020). Following the recommendations of scientific institutions, health organizations, and specialists is critical. Some health institutes have made recommendations in this area, including the use of home exercise in this process (Figure 1.2).

	Cardio	Resistance	Stretching
World Health Organization	Walk around the house Dance Do an online exercise class Knee to elbow Side knee lifts	Plank Back extensions Squat Superman Bridge Chair dips	Stretching exercises
American Heart Association	Jumping jacks Jumping ropes Jogging/marching in place Stair climbing or step-ups High knees Mountain climbers Star jumps Burpees	Plank and side plank Push-ups Sit-ups or crunches Hip-lift or bridge position Triceps dips on a chair Lunges Squats or chair position Wall sits	Stretching exercises Balance exercises
AMERICAN COLLEGE of SPORTS MEDICINE	Walk briskly around the house, or up and down the stairs (10-15 min x 2-3 times/d) Dance Jump ropes Do an exercise video Cardio machines (if available)	Strength workout app (eg, 7-min workout) Do a strength training video Strength training around the house (eg, squats from a sturdy chair, push-ups against a wall, lunges)	Yoga

Figure 1.2 Home-based exercise programs recommended by health institutions (ACSM, 2021; AHA, 2021; WHO, 2020).
Source: Author's own design.

Conclusion

Regular physical exercise benefits people's health and is a preventive factor against a variety of chronic conditions. Adults should engage in 150 minutes of moderate-intensity or 75 minutes of vigorous-intensity physical activity each week, or 500–1000 MET/min per week, according to the World Health Organization. Despite the benefits of physical activity, about one-third of people do not engage in enough of it. It further claims that just 20%–60% of older persons engage in acceptable amounts of physical exercise, and that their engagement decreases as they become older. It is estimated that 37%–79% of persons over 50 do not engage in regular physical activity. The COVID-19 epidemic has resulted in even lower levels of physical activity and a substantial shift in societal health practices, particularly sedentary behavior. It also influenced the motivation of those who exercise for health to discover new methods to continue their workouts. Given that physical inactivity is one of the leading causes of chronic illness and mortality from any cause, mobility limitations, such as house confinement, can have long-term health consequences (Haley & Andel, 2010; Kohl et al., 2012; Warburton, Nicol, & Bredin, 2006; WHO, 2021).

As a result, another issue that the COVID-19 epidemic reminds consumers and business people in the fitness industry is the necessity to find alternate solutions for circumstances where physical activity and exercise habits will need people to stay at home. The suspension of events and competitions, as well as the closure of buildings and firms in the sports sector, has brought the multibillion-dollar global industry to a halt. Solutions for management and organization in the fitness industry were sought during this phase, and the crisis was attempted to be solved. They sought to handle the problem on six topics: business, financial, preventative, social distance, disinfection, and cleanliness management in order to manage physical activity and exercise in a healthy way during the pandemic phase. The fitness center managers assisted in this process by assisting persons working in the field of fitness in adapting to new workout trends (Alomari, Khabour, & Alzoubi, 2020; Ho & Chan, 2021; Kim & Park, 2021).

Using the possibilities of developing technology, many innovative systems have been developed in physical activity and exercise setting in recent years. The new-generation information technology, including internet-supported, cloud computing, internet of things, and big data, offered great convenience for smart exercise. Technologically based new trends in physical activity and exercise settings are stated as wearable technology, smart fitness equipment, artificial intelligence, live-streaming classes, virtual reality, and mobile applications. It seems that technology-based exercise will develop more in the future and it is predicted that more individuals will use it. The important thing here is that people gain the habit of adopting and using these new trends. In the future, it is very important for the fitness industry to train and develop the fitness consultants' technology-based physical activity and exercise practices (Cortis et al., 2020; Iannaccone et al., 2020; Nyenhuis et al., 2020; Saifee & Kapoor, 2021).

References

Abdelbasset, W. K. (2020). Stay home: Role of physical exercise training in elderly individuals' ability to face the COVID-19 infection. *Journal of Immunology Research*, 2020, 1–5, Article ID 8375096, https://doi.org/10.1155/2020/8375096

Ai, L. (2021). Artificial Intelligence System for College Students' Physical Fitness and Health Management Based on Physical Measurement Big Data. Wireless Communications and Mobile Computing.

Alomari, M. A., Khabour, O. F., & Alzoubi, K. H. (2020). Changes in physical activity and sedentary behavior amid confinement: The BKSQ-COVID-19 project. *Risk Management and Healthcare Policy*, 13, 1757–1764. https://doi.org/10.2147/RMHP.S268320.

American College of Sports Medicine (ACSM). (2021). Staying Active during Covid-19. Available at https://www.exerciseismedicine.org/staying-active-during-covid-191/. Accessed December 10, 2021.

American Heart Association (AHA). (2021). Create a Circuit Home Workout Infographic. Available at https://www.heart.org/en/healthy-living/fitness/getting-active/create-a-circuit-home-workout. Accessed December 3, 2021.

Ammar, A., Trabelsi, K., Brach, M., Chtourou, H., Boukhris, O., Masmoudi, L., et al. (2020). Effects of home confinement on mental health and lifestyle behaviours during the COVID-19 outbreak: Insight from the "ECLB-COVID19" multi countries survey. medRxiv Preprint

Andrienko, O. (2020). Ecommerce & Consumer Trends during Coronavirus, 2020. Available at https://www. semrush. com/blog/ecommerce-covid-19/. Accessed December 13, 2021.

Angosto, S., García-Fernández, J., Valantine, I., & Grimaldi-Puyana, M. (2020). The intention to use fitness and physical activity apps: A systematic review. *Sustainability*, 12(16), 6641.

Batrakoulis, A. (2019). European Survey of Fitness Trends for 2020. *ACSM's Health & Fitness Journal*, 23, 28–35.

Bentlage, E., Ammar, A., How, D., Ahmed, M., Trabelsi, K., Chtourou, H., et al. (2020). Practical recommendations for maintaining active lifestyle during the COVID-19 pandemic: A systematic literature review. *International Journal of Environmental Research and Public Health*, 17, 6265, https://doi.org/10.3390/ijerph17176265

Best, J. (2021). Wearable technology: Covid-19 and the rise of remote clinical monitoring. *BMJ*, 372–413, https://doi.org/10.1136/bmj.n413

Brindal, E., Ryan, J. C., Kakoschke, N., Golley, S., Zajac, I. T., & Wiggins, B. (2021). Individual differences and changes in lifestyle behaviours predict decreased subjective well-being during COVID-19 restrictions in an Australian sample. *Journal of Public Health*, 43(1), 1–7, https://doi.org/10.1093/pubmed/fdab040

Capodilupo, E. R., & Miller, D. J. (2021). Changes in health promoting behavior during COVID-19 physical distancing: Utilizing wearable technology to examine trends in sleep, activity, and cardiovascular indicators of health. *Plos One*, 16(8), e0256063.

Castañeda-Babarro, A., Arbillaga-Etxarri, A., Gutiérrez-Santamaria, B., & Coca, A. (2020). Impact of COVID-19 confinement on the time and intensity of physical activity in the Spanish population.

Center for Disease Control and Prevention (CDC). (2019). Considerations for Youth Sports. Atlanta, GA.

Central Defense Countermeasure Headquarters Response Guidelines. (2020). Corona 19 collective facility multi-sue facility response guidelines (2nd edition). http://ncov.mohw.go.kr/guide

Centers for Disease Control and Prevention (CDC, 2022). *Considerations for youth sports*, https://cdc.gov/coronavirus/2019-ncov/community/schools-childcare/youth-sports.html. Updated January 13, 2022. Accessed February 2, 2022.

Cortis, C., Giancotti, G., Rodio, A., Bianco, A., & Fusco, A. (2020). Home is the new gym: Exergame as a potential tool to maintain adequate fitness levels also during quarantine. *Human Movement*, 21(4), 79–87.

Dai, W., Zhou, J., Li, G., Zhang, B., & Ma, N. (2021). Maintaining normal sleep patterns, lifestyles and emotion during the COVID-19 pandemic: The stabilizing effect of daytime napping. *Journal of Sleep Research*, e13259.

Deloitte. (2019). European Health & Fitness Market Report 2019; Deloitte: London, UK.

Department for Business EIS (DBEIS). (2020). Working Safely during Coronavirus (COVID-19). Available at https://www.gov.uk/guidance/working-safely-during-coronaviruscovid-19/offices-and-contact-centres#offices-3-3. Accessed May 17, 2020.

Dolezel, M., & Smutny, Z. (2021). Usage of eHealth/mHealth services among Young Czech Adults and the impact of COVID-19: An explorative survey. *International Journal of Environmental Research and Public Health*, 18(13), 7147.

EuropeActive. (2019). European Employers Skills Survey 2019; EuropeActive: Brussels, Belgium.

Farrokhi, A., Farahbakhsh, R., Rezazadeh, J., & Minerva, R. (2021). Application of internet of things and artificial intelligence for smart fitness: A survey. *Computer Networks*, 189, 107859, https://doi.org/10.1016/j.comnet.2021.107859

FitBit Staff. (2020, March 23). *The Impact of Coronavirus on Global Activity*. Available at https://blog.fitbit.com/covid-19-global-activity/

Flanagan, E. W., Beyl, R. A., Fearnbach, S. N., Altazan, A. D., Martin, C. K., & Redman, L. M. (2021). The impact of COVID-19 stay-at-home orders on health behaviors in adults. *Obesity*, 29(2), 438–445.

Fried, G., & Kastel, M. (2020). *Managing sport facilities*. Human Kinetics: Champaign, IL.

Füzéki, E., Weber, T., Groneberg, D. A., & Banzer, W. (2020). Physical activity counseling in primary care in Germany—An integrative review. *International Journal of Environmental Research and Public Health*, 17(15), 5625.

Genin, P. M., Lambert, C., Larras, B., Pereira, B., Toussaint, J. F., Baker, J. S.,... & Duclos, M. (2021). How did the COVID-19 confinement period affect our physical activity level and sedentary behaviors? Methodology and first results from the french national ON-APS survey. *Journal of Physical Activity and Health*, 18(3), 296–303.

German Federal Environment Agency. (2020). Coronavirus SARS-CoV-2 and Visits to Swimming and Bathing Pools. https://www.aquanale.com/news/magazine/statement-of-the-german-federal-environment-agency-after-hearing-the-swimming-and-bathing-pool-committee.php

Glasgow, T. E., Mastrich, Z. H., & Geller, E. S. (2021). The utility of university fitness facilities: Environmental vs. psychological determinants of their use. *Journal of American College Health*, 67(8), 1–8.

Goethals, L., Barth, N., Guyot, J., Hupin, D., Celarier, T., & Bongue, B. (2020). Impact of home quarantine on physical activity among older adults living at home during the COVID-19 pandemic: qualitative interview study. *JMIR aging*, 3(1), e19007. Grieve, J., & Sherry, E. (2012). Community benefits of major sport facilities: The Darebin international sports centre. *Sport Management Review*, 15(2), 218–229.

Gross, C., Wenner, W., & Lackes, R. (2021, September). Using Wearable Fitness Trackers to Detect COVID-19?! In International Conference on Business Informatics Research (pp. 51–65). Springer, Cham.

Guo, M., Xu, P., Xiao, T., He, R., Dai, M., & Miller, S. L. (2021). Review and comparison of HVAC operation guidelines in different countries during the COVID-19 pandemic. *Building and Environment*, 187, 107368.

Hagiu, B. A. (2021). Moderate exercise may prevent the development of severe forms of COVID-19, whereas high-intensity exercise may result in the opposite. *Medical Hypotheses*, 157, 110705.

Haley, C., & Andel, R. (2010). Correlates of physical activity participation in community-dwelling older adults. *Journal of Aging and Physical Activity*, 18(4), 375–389.

He, H., & Harris, L. (2020). The impact of Covid-19 pandemic on corporate social responsibility and marketing philosophy. *Journal of Business Research*, 116, 176–182.

Ho, K. K. L., & Chan, Y. T. (2021). Hong Kong's response to COVID-19: A glance to the control measures and their enforcement. *Social Transformations in Chinese Societies*, 17(2), 80–91.

Husain, W., & Ashkanani, F. (2020). Does COVID-19 change dietary habits and lifestyle behaviours in Kuwait: A community-based cross-sectional study. *Environmental Health and Preventive Medicine*, 25(1), 1–13. https://doi.org/10.1186/s12199-020-00901-5

Iannaccone, A., Fusco, A., Jaime, S. J., Baldassano, S., Cooper, J., Proia, P., & Cortis, C. (2020). Stay home, stay active with superjump®: A home-based activity to prevent sedentary lifestyle during covid-19 outbreak. *Sustainability*, 12(23), 10135.

Ibrahim, A. M., & Hassanain, M. A. (2021). Assessment of COVID-19 precautionary measures in sports facilities: A case study on a health club in Saudi Arabia. *Journal of Building Engineering*, 46, 103662.

IHRSA. (2019). Fitness Industry Trends Shed Light on 2020 & beyond. Available at https://www.ihrsa.org/improve-your-club/industry-news/2019-fitness-industry-trends-shed-light-on-2020-beyond/. Accessed November 25, 2020).

Ingram, J., Maciejewski, G., & Hand, C. J. (2020). Changes in diet, sleep, and physical activity are associated with differences in negative mood during COVID-19 lockdown. *Frontiers in Psychology*, 11, 2328. https://doi.org/10.3389/fpsyg.2020.588604

International Association for Sports and Leisure Facilities (IAKS). (2020). COVID-19 Easing the Restrictions for Physical Activities, 2020. Cologne, Germany.

International Association for Sports and Leisure Facilities (IAKS). (2021). Re-Opening Sports and Leisure Facilities in Denmark. https://iaks.sport/news/re-opening-sports-and-leisure-facilities-denmark

Iqbal, M. Z., & Faiz, M. F. I. (2020, September 28–30). Active Surveillance for COVID-19 through Artificial Intelligence Using Real-Time Speech-Recognition Mobile Application. In 2020 IEEE International Conference on Consumer Electronics-Taiwan (ICCE-Taiwan) (pp. 1–2), Institute of Electrical and Electronics Engineers, https://doi.org/10.1109/ICCE-Taiwan49838.2020.9258276.

Jimenez, A., Berriman, J., Collins, C., Thienemann, E., Szumilewicz, A., & Smulders, H. (2018). The Relevance of the Active Leisure Sector and International Qualification Framework to the EQF (SIQAF): Final Report. EuropeActive: Brussels, Belgium.

Kaur, H., Singh, T., Arya, Y. K., & Mittal, S. (2020). Physical fitness and exercise during the COVID-19 pandemic: A qualitative enquiry. *Frontiers in Psychology*, 11, 2943.

Kaushal, N., Keith, N., Aguinaga, S., & Hagger, M. S. (2020). Social cognition and socioecological predictors of home-based physical activity intentions, planning, and habits during the COVID-19 pandemic. *Behavioral Sciences*, 10, 133. https://doi.org/10.3390/bs10090133

Khundam, C., & Nöel, F. (2021). A study of physical fitness and enjoyment on virtual running for exergames. *International Journal of Computer Games Technology*, Article ID 6668280, 2021, 1–16.

Kim, G., & Biocca, F. (2018, July). Immersion in virtual reality can increase exercise motivation and physical performance. In International conference on virtual, augmented and mixed reality (pp. 94–102). Springer, Cham.

Kim, J. S., & Park, T. S. (2021). Analysis of Crisis Management of a Korean Fitness Center during the COVID-19 Pandemic, Preprints 2021, 2021040731 (doi: 10.20944/preprints202104.0731.v1).Kohl 3rd, H. W., Craig, C. L., Lambert, E. V., Inoue, S., Alkandari, J. R., Leetongin, G.,... & Lancet Physical Activity Series Working Group. (2012). The pandemic of physical inactivity: Global action for public health. *The Lancet*, 380(9838), 294–305.

Komańda, M. (2020). Fitness Clubs Facing Covid-19 Lockdown. Zeszyty Naukowe Wyższej Szkoły Humanitas. *Zarządzanie*, (specjalny), 21(5), 159–172.

Kowalski, D., Zysiak-Christ, B., Skalski, D., & Brzoskowska, K. (2021). Swimming sport in during the COVID-19 pandemic. *Scientific Journal of the Military University of Land Forces*, 53(2), 272–284.

Lavie, C. J., Ozemek, C., Carbone, S., Katzmarzyk, P. T., & Blair, S. N. (2019). Sedentary behavior, exercise, and cardiovascular health. *Circulation Research*, 124, 799–815. https://doi.org/10.1161/CIRCRESAHA.118.312669

León-Quismondo, J., García-Unanue, J., & Burillo, P. (2020). Best practices for fitness center business sustainability: A qualitative vision. *Sustainability*, 12(12), 5067.

Mann, S., Hao, M. L., Tsai, M. C., Hafezi, M., Azad, A., & Keramatimoezabad, F. (2018, August 15–17). *Effectiveness of integral kinesiology feedback for fitness-based games*. IEEE Games, Entertainment, Media Conference (GEM) pp. 1–9, Galway, Ireland.

Meyer, J., McDowell, C., Lansing, J., Brower, C., Smith, L., Tully, M. A., & Herring, M. (2020). Changes in physical activity and sedentary behavior in response to COVID-19 and their associations with mental health in 3,052 US adults. *International Journal of Environmental Research and Public Health*, 17, 6469. https://doi.org/10.3390/ijerph17186469.

Molina, M. D., & Myrick, J. G. (2020). The 'how'and 'why'of fitness app use: Investigating user motivations to gain insights into the nexus of technology and fitness. *Sport in Society*, 24(7), 1–16.

Moore, S. A., Faulkner, G., Rhodes, R. E., Brussoni, M., Chulak-Bozzer, T., Ferguson, L. J., & Tremblay, M. S. (2020). Impact of the COVID-19 virus outbreak on movement and play behaviours of Canadian children and youth: A national survey. *International Journal of Behavioral Nutrition and Physical Activity*, 17, 85. https://doi.org/10.1186/s12966-020-00987-8.

Moustakas, L., Szumilewicz, A., Mayo, X., Thienemann, E., & Grant, A. (2020). Foresight for the fitness sector: Results from a European Delphi Study and its relevance in the time of COVID-19. *International Journal of Environmental Research and Public Health*, 17(23), 8941.

Nyenhuis, S. M., Greiwe, J., Zeiger, J. S., Nanda, A., & Cooke, A. (2020). Exercise and fitness in the age of social distancing during the COVID-19 pandemic. *The Journal of Allergy and Clinical Immunology*. In practice, 8(7), 2152.

Östlund, F. (2020, January). Leaderboards in Fitness Applications and Their Effect on Motivation. Proceedings of the 18th Student Conference in Interaction Technology and Design and the 6th Student Conference in Electronics and Mechatronics, (pp. 64–68).

Owen, N., Sparling, P. B., Healy, G. N., Dunstan, D. W., & Matthews, C. E. (2010). Sedentary behavior: Emerging evidence for a new health risk. Mayo Clinic Proceedings, 85, 1138–1141. https://doi.org/10.4065/mcp.2010.0444

Parker, K., Uddin, R., Ridgers, N. D., Brown, H., Veitch, J., Salmon, J.,... & Arundell, L. (2021). The use of digital platforms for adults' and adolescents' physical activity during the COVID-19 pandemic (Our Life at Home): Survey study. *Journal of Medical Internet Research*, 23(2), e23389.

Phillipou, A., Meyer, D., Neill, E., Tan, E. J., Toh, W. L., Van Rheenen, T. E., & Rossell, S. L. (2020). Eating and exercise behaviors in eating disorders and the general population during the COVID-19 pandemic in Australia: Initial results from the COLLATE project. *International Journal of Eating Disorders*, 3, 1158–1165. https://doi.org/10.1002/eat.23317

Pierce, D., Stas, J., Feller, K., & Knox, W. (2020). COVID-19: Return to Youth Sports: Preparing Sports Venues and Events for the Return of Youth Sports, *Sports Innovation Journal*, 1, 62–80. https://doi.org/10.18060/24144

Pinto, A. J., Dunstan, D. W., Owen, N., Bonfá, E., & Gualano, B. (2020). Combating physical inactivity during the COVID-19 pandemic. *Nature Reviews Rheumatology*, 16(7), 347–348.

Piotrowski, D., & Piotrowska, A. I. (2021). Operation of gyms and fitness clubs during the COVID-19 pandemic-financial, legal, and organisational conditions. *Journal of Physical Education and Sport*, 21, 1021–1028.

Rhodes, R. E., Liu, S., Lithopoulos, A., Zhang, C. Q., & Garcia-Barrera, M. A. (2020). Correlates of perceived physical activity transitions during the COVID-19 pandemic among Canadian adults. *Applied Psychology: Health and Well-Being*, 12(4), 1157–1182.

Robert Pearl, M. D. (2020). Coronavirus Poses 5 Huge Threats to the Future of Sports. *Forbes*. Available at https://www.forbes.com/sites/robertpearl/ A662020/08/25/coronavirus-future-of-sports/#38727941792a. Accessed August 25, 2020.

Robinson, E., Boyland, E., Chisholm, A., Harrold, J., Maloney, N. G., Marty, L.,... & Hardman, C. A. (2020). Obesity, eating behavior and physical activity during COVID-19 lockdown: A study ofUK adults. *Appetite*, 156, 104853. https://doi.org/10.1016/j.appet.2020.104853

Rogers, N. T., Waterlow, N. R., Brindle, H., Enria, L., Eggo, R. M., Lees, S., & Roberts, C. H. (2020). Behavioral change towards reduced intensity physical activity is disproportionately prevalent among adults with serious health issues or self-perception of high risk during the UK COVID-19 lockdown. *Frontiers in Public Health*, 8, Article 575091. https://doi.org/10.3389/fpubh.2020.575091

Saifee, S. S., & Kapoor, A. (2021). Guidelines for maintaining physical fitness during COVID-19 pandemic. *Indian Journal of Forensic Medicine & Toxicology*, 15(1), 1495–1498.

Sanderson, J., & Brown, K. (2020). COVID-19 and youth sports: Psychological, developmental, and economic impacts. *International Journal of Sport Communication*, 1(aop), 1–11.

Schweizer, A. M., Leiderer, A., Mitterwallner, V., Walentowitz, A., Mathes, G. H., & Steinbauer, M. J. (2021). Outdoor cycling activity affected by COVID-19 related epidemic-control-decisions. *Plos One*, 16(5), e0249268.

Tison, G. H., Avram, R., Kuhar, P., Abreau, S., Marcus, G. M., Pletcher, M. J., & Olgin, J. E. (2020). Worldwide Effect of COVID-19 on physical activity: A descriptive study. *Annals of Internal Medicine*, 173, 767–770. https://doi.org/10.7326/M20-2665

UK Active (2018). Going the Distance: Exercise Professionals in the Wider Public Health Workforce; UK Active: London, UK.

Warburton, D. E., Nicol, C. W., & Bredin, S. S. (2006). Health benefits of physical activity: the evidence. *CMAJ*, 174(6), 801–809.

Watson, A., & Koontz, J. S. (2021). Youth sports in the wake of COVID-19: A call for change, *British Journal of Sports Medicine*, 55(14), 764–765.

Wilke, J., Mohr, L., Tenforde, A. S., Edouard, P., Fossati, C., González-Gross, M.,... & Yuki, G. (2020). Restrictercise! Preferences regarding digital home training programs during confinements associated with the COVID-19 pandemic. *International Journal of Environmental Research and Public Health*, 17(18), 6515.

World Health Organization (WHO). (2020). Stay Physically Active during Self-Quarantine. Available at http://www.euro.who.int/en/health-topics/health-emergencies/coronavirus-covid-19/novel-coronavirus-2019-ncov-technical-guidance/ stay-physically-active-during-self-quarantine. Accessed December 3, 2020.

World Health Organization. (2021). Physical Activity. Available at https://www. who.int/news-room/fact-sheets/detail/physical-activity. Accessibility verified December 8, 2021.

Wu, Z., & McGoogan, J. M. (2020). Characteristics of and important lessons from the coronavirus disease 2019 (COVID-19) outbreak in China: Summary of a report of 72 314 cases from the Chinese Center for Disease Control and Prevention. *JAMA*, 323(13), 1239–1242.

Yan, Z., & Spaulding, H. R. (2020). Extracellular superoxide dismutase, a molecular trans-ducer of health benefits of exercise. *Redox Biology*, 32, 101508. https://doi.org/10.1016/j.redox.2020.101508

Yang, Y., & Koenigstorfer, J. (2020). Determinants of physical activity maintenance during the Covid-19 pandemic: A focus on fitness apps. *Translational Behavioral Medicine*, 10, 835–842. https://doi.org/10.1093/tbm/ibaa086

Yong, B., Xu, Z., Wang, X., Cheng, L., Li, X., Wu, X., & Zhou, Q. (2018). IoT-based intelligent fitness system. *Journal of Parallel and Distributed Computing*, 118, 14–21.

Chapter 2

The Economic Impacts of Coronavirus and Innovation in Sports

Meltem Ince Yenilmez

Introduction

COVID-19 nearly flipped and turned the sports world upside down instantly, resulting in a severe setback commercially for this sector. The pandemic has taken a a heavy toll on world sports for the first time in 2020, and it will almost surely lead to a global economic catastrophe, according to preliminary estimates (Mohr et al., 2020). Professional and recreational sports throughout the world came to a halt in March 2020 when large gatherings, whether for music, religious reasons, or sports, led to the spread of COVID-19 (Memish et al., 2019). The World Health Organization verified that COVID-19 had attained pandemic status in that month (WHO, 2020). COVID-19 has created a new set of unknowns and concerns in the sports world, as there has been no effective vaccination for a long time (Ludvigsen and Hayton, 2020). As a result, COVID-19 has had an influence on sports at all levels, including elite, community, and grassroots (Parnell et al., 2020), with many (big) sporting events throughout the world being cancelled or postponed to limit transmission through close contact between fans or participants (Clarkson et al., 2020; Toresdahl and Asif, 2020). The Olympic Games were postponed for the first time in history to the following year. Even during World Wars I and II, sports and (particularly) football came to a halt in just a few nations for brief periods of time (Tovar, 2020). In addition, owing to the COVID-19 epidemic, non-profit amateur athletic clubs were forced to close down immediately, in many cases in the middle of the season, in order to comply with physical distance and shelter-in-place rules (Doherty et al., 2020). Due to the risk of infection, the sports world in Germany, as in other nations or areas, came to a halt for many weeks, beginning on March 13.

The first shutdown, on the other hand, had disastrous (commercial) effects on sports stakeholders. All physical sports in clubs or leagues were halted, resulting in the sports clubs' inability to produce any revenue. While some professional sports leagues (e.g., the German handball and ice hockey leagues, and the French football league) suspended their competition for the season, the German Football League (DFL) organized a restart of the Bundesliga without spectators due to the amount of money generated from sponsorship and television rights (Huth and

DOI: 10.4324/9781003253891-2

Kraus, 2021; Webb, 2020). However, this measure was the most effective technique to carry out the social distance strategy (Duarte Muñoz and Meyer, 2020). Economic despondency, on the other hand, was widely prevalent among grassroots sports. Sports clubs with large fixed costs are disproportionately affected. Golf courses are among them.

Despite COVID-19's detrimental (economic) impact on sports, early indications suggest that, at least in the medium to long term, sports can benefit from the existing limitations (Weed, 2020). Many individuals are becoming increasingly desirous of being "outside" and active there in addition to their daily activities, which have been severely limited. Second, according to Weed (2020), there is a rising political recognition of the relevance of sports – both active and passive sports – for human wellness.

COVID-19's economic influence on the sports industry

Since the end of 2019, the COVID-19 epidemic has been spreading over the world, affecting practically every facet of public and private life. Sports have always been an important aspect of social life. Isolated athletic events throughout Asia have been postponed or cancelled since mid-January 2020. Pandemic-related postponements or cancellations eventually spread to all levels of organized sports in practically every country. The Olympic Games in Tokyo, which were scheduled for 2020, were postponed until 2021, and soccer was no exception. The European Soccer Championship, which was supposed to take place in 2020, was postponed to 2021. Many European soccer matches were either played behind closed doors, such as two UEFA Champions League matches in France and Spain, or were cancelled between February and March. Matches played behind closed doors were solely used to discipline teams or their fans prior to the COVID-19 epidemic. Many major soccer leagues postponed or even cancelled matches as a result of the incident. No matches were played in any European soccer league at the end of March 2020. Despite the break, several leagues have been seeking ways to continue the season. Many leagues were allowed to restart play depending on the extent of political backing.

Many concerns remain unresolved regarding how spectator sports demand will return to pre-pandemic levels and patterns. The problem of expressed vs revealed preferences and demand will be an essential distinction for future study (ticket sales versus actual attendance). When assessing the behavioural response of German football fans to the 2015 Paris terrorist attacks, one research highlighted how this may have been largely hidden if merely looking at ticket sales (Frevel and Schreyer, 2020). In future demand studies, it will be crucial to distinguish between casual and dedicated sports fans. Becker and Rubinstein (2011) demonstrated in a different but comparable context that the demand responses for goods and services affected by terrorism in Israel were solely accounted for by occasional users; frequent users (season ticket holders) did not change their demand for bus travel or coffee shops in response to related terrorist activity in the country.

Sports research without the social pressure of a crowd has just scratched the surface thus far. For example, the data so far suggest that the lack of a crowd affects primarily referee bias, rather than the various match outcomes being a result of differences in player behaviour as well. Future research might untangle this by examining the in-game match environment when referees made their rulings. Do referees, for example, "level things up" less when there is not a crowd? Are they less likely to give one team a penalty or a red card after giving the other one? Do officials add less stoppage time at the conclusion of the game when the home side is losing when there is not a crowd? Football was the first sport to resurface with a considerable number of events after COVID-19.

In recent weeks, a rising number of games have been postponed due to players contracting COVID-19. This may result in a backlog of fixtures, which will hurt certain people more than others. Soon, there will be enough data to examine these impacts in sports and generate conclusions that may be applied to other markets and situations. With "extended COVID," several professional teams have had players out of action for weeks. The long-term consequences of what may be considered a random draw on the quantity of talent available on a team's performance could be investigated. The lack of social pressure on behaviour and outcomes in other sports, notably individual sports performed in quite different situations than football, is likely to provide opportunities (e.g. golf, snooker, and darts).

COVID 19's impact on the sports industry

Despite the fact that matches had been postponed and no date for the resumption of play had been determined, speculations and rumours have regularly surfaced that individual clubs in the first and second divisions were in grave danger of going bankrupt (Zülch et al., 2020). As a result, the Bundesliga's wealthier teams began to cross-subsidize other clubs through a solidarity fund (Follert and Daumann, 2021). The four German teams in the UEFA Champions League responded by pledging to contribute a total of 20 million euros to the Bundesliga's remaining clubs.

Consequences on a broad scale as well as in terms of money

If soccer leagues resumed play after the COVID-19 required sabbatical, the majority of matches were staged behind closed doors with no spectators in the stands. When the spectators' ban on entering the stadium will be lifted and when this "new normality" will cease is currently unknown. Critics may argue that even continuing under these conditions is too drastic, but a political decision must weigh the benefits of health-protection measures against the costs of suspending the "team sports industry" in accordance with the principle of proportionality so that the decision can be understood at least in the context of soccer (Follert and Daumann, 2021). When fights are placed behind closed doors, the spirit of the game suffers. Until COVID-19, one of the most essential features of professional soccer was the normal stadium environment, with spectators clapping, booing, chanting, and so on (Flatau and Emrich, 2016). The traditional stadium atmosphere is entirely lost when matches are held behind closed doors. Every sound they make and every word they say may be heard, therefore players and coaches must keep this in mind. The game's long-term consequences will need to be investigated.

Closed-door matches, on the other hand, significantly change the nature of the game. The regular stadium environment, which featured supporters clapping, booing, chanting, and so on, was one of the most defining elements of professional soccer prior to COVID-19 (Flatau and Emrich, 2016). When games are played behind closed doors, the mood in the stadium is very different. Every sound they make and every word they utter must be clearly understood by players and coaches. It is yet unknown what long-term consequences this will have on the game. However, the lack of fans at the stadium, and hence the loss of the customary stadium atmosphere, has changed the character of the broadcast, even if some TV stations try to compensate for the mood by employing recorded crowd sounds (Drewes et al., 2020).

If armchair viewers miss the extra flavour of stadium supporters, interest for televised matches is likely to fall. It's uncertain whether or not this will have an empirical impact on television demand. Industry representatives had heard, even before the COVID-19 virus broke out, that the mood in the stadium had little influence on the marketability of broadcast rights. If, as a result, TV viewers' demand, and hence the desire to pay for television, drops, interest in the transmission of behind-closed-doors matches is likely to wane. As a result, the value of time-delayed television rights may be altered.

Soccer clubs, on the other hand, were compelled to forego ticket sales and catering revenue if they were to go it alone. Apart from sports concerns, the game's continuing survival was mostly driven by the need to generate some form of revenue, most notably through television advertising and sponsorship money. The fact that major soccer leagues, unlike leagues in other sports such as hockey or handball, were keen to get started as soon as possible is likely owing to the fact that in soccer, revenue from ticket sales comes second to revenue from television marketing (Follert, 2018).

Is there a connection between COVID-19 and athletic events?

Surprisingly, there was minimal indication that athletic activities caused an airborne virus to spread (notable exceptions are Stoecker et al., 2016 and Cardazzi et al., 2020, both studying seasonal influenza in North America). In North

America, the first study to see if huge athletic events can spread COVID-19 was done (Ahammer et al., 2020). By utilizing volatility in the scheduling of NBA and NHL games over a 12-day period in early March 2020, the study looked at the effects of these large indoor gatherings on later COVID-19 transmission and mortality. The authors found that between the end of April 2019 and the end of April 2020, each of these huge gatherings increased the overall number of fatalities in the areas around the events by 9%.

Another study used a similar empirical technique to investigate the influence of large-audience English football matches on the spread of the pandemic (Olczak et al., 2020). Despite the fact that these events were hosted outside, the researchers observed that participation at matches resulted in local increases in COVID-19 transmission when compared to indoor events evaluated in North America. Six COVID-19 cases, two COVID-19 fatalities, and three extra deaths per 100,000 adjacent people were recorded in each match. Because there is so little information on how the virus spreads through sporting activities, governments should proceed with caution when deciding when and how to reopen sports facilities to spectators.

Is the virus preventing sports enthusiasts from attending games?

Sport is crucial to both economic and social growth. Governments recognize its value, as seen by the Political Declaration of the 2030 Agenda, which emphasizes sports' contribution to women's and young people's empowerment, as well as individual and community health, education, and social inclusion goals.

The COVID-19 pandemic has spread practically to every country on the planet since it began. As a consequence of social and physical distancing measures, corporate and school lockdowns, and general social life, many parts of everyday living, including sport and physical exercise, have been affected in the fight against the disease's spread. This policy brief focuses on the issues that COVID-19 has caused in the sports sector, as well as physical exercise and well-being, particularly for disadvantaged or vulnerable individuals. It also makes suggestions to governments, other stakeholders, and the United Nations system on how to promote the safe reopening of athletic events and physical activity during and after the epidemic.

The demand for tickets to athletic events during the outbreak may show something about how people react to a public health disaster, especially one that requires social isolation. It might provide a broader picture of how individuals react to risk and uncertainty. Due to high demand, most governments unexpectedly shut down professional sports in spring 2020 and limited the number of viewers allowed to return, limiting the opportunities to get new insights from stadium attendances. Pre-scheduled football matches in Europe's major leagues in early 2020 were used by Reade and Singleton (2020) to investigate if public announcements regarding domestic or worldwide virus illnesses and mortality impacted stadium attendance. There was no evidence of a negative demand association between international news about the outbreak's progression and stadium attendance demand, according to the study. Only England, Germany, and Italy appeared to be hit by the new confirmed domestic cases or fatalities the day before.

Demand for tickets to Belarussian stadiums plunged during the first time of greatest uncertainty regarding the virus and its severity in the only European professional football league that did not shut down due to COVID-19 (Reade et al., 2021). Despite the persistent threats, interest in this league has grown steadily. This would be in line with a survey of North American sports fans conducted in August-September 2020, which found that while most were still willing to accept COVID-19 risks in order to attend stadiums, they would be more willing to pay if safety restrictions were implemented, particularly for mask-wearing fans (Humphreys et al., 2020).

COVID-19's influence on athletic events and the ramifications for social development

From marathons to football tournaments, athletics championships to basketball games, handball to ice hockey, rugby, cricket, sailing, skiing, weightlifting to wrestling, and more, most major sporting events at the international, regional, and national levels have been cancelled or postponed to protect the health of athletes and others involved. For the first time in modern history, the Olympics and Paralympics have been postponed. The worldwide sports industry is projected to be worth US$756 billion each year.

COVID-19 threatens millions of employment, not just for athletes, but also for those in associated retail and athletic services sectors like travel, tourism, infrastructure, transportation, catering, and media broadcasting, which are all tied to leagues and tournaments. Professional athletes must also reschedule their training in order to stay in shape at home.

Aside from the financial implications, game cancellations have an impact on many of the social benefits of global and regional sporting events, such as strengthening social bonds, contributing to fans' social and emotional excitement, and increasing their identification with athletes, all of which can lead to increased physical activity. Sport has long been regarded as an effective means of boosting communication and overcoming generational divides. Sport allows many social groups to have a bigger part in social change and advancement, which is especially important in divided countries. Sport is utilized in this context to provide chances for learning and to reach out to underrepresented or at-risk communities.

Major sports leagues have pledged their support in the fight against the virus's spread. For example, FIFA and the World Health Organization have launched a 13-language "Pass the message to kick out coronavirus" campaign, urging people to follow five key steps to prevent the disease from spreading, including handwashing, coughing etiquette, not touching one's face, maintaining physical distance, and staying at home if sick. More worldwide sport for development and peace groups have joined together at this time to provide mutual help, such as through regular online community forums where individuals may voice their issues and challenges.

Participants in online discussions have also attempted to find novel solutions to larger social issues, such as determining how sporting organizations can respond to issues faced by vulnerable people who would normally participate in sporting programmes in low-income communities but are now unable to do so due to movement restrictions. COVID-19 has had an impact on the sports education sector, which includes national and local governments, public and private educational institutions, sports organizations and athletes, NGOs and the business community, teachers, scholars and coaches, parents, and, most importantly, the – primarily young – learners. While the current crisis has had a big impact on our organization, it also has the potential to play a key role in defining how to manage and overcome it, as well as promoting rights and values in crisis circumstances.

As the globe heals from COVID-19, major issues must be addressed in order to maintain the safety of athletic events at all levels, as well as the financial survival of sporting organizations. In the medium term, this will entail, among other things, event adjustments to safeguard the safety of athletes, fans, and merchants. Given the likelihood of a worldwide recession in the near future, it may be critical to promote sports club membership, particularly among youngsters.

There are several organizations in the sports industry

In the first half of 2020, the worldwide sports industry was thrown into turmoil by COVID-19-related lockdown (i.e., stay at home) and other social distancing rules. Sport has, for all intents and purposes, come to an end. A number of reasons have contributed to this. Sports facilities were ordered to close by local, regional, and national governments. Even non-facility-dependent sports were banned because they typically required close proximity body-to-body contact and other interpersonal interactions. People who watch athletic events sit close to one another for extended periods of time. Even after legalization, the sport was played in empty (or ghost) stadiums, resulting in a loss of revenue from ticket sales. Regulations reducing unnecessary travel to events limited domestic and international travel to events. Sports organizations were essentially shut down, whether they were neighbourhood clubs, professional sports teams, or international athletic events. Regardless of their differences, and while the immediate impact varied depending on the organization, sports organizations' revenue streams are ultimately determined by the sport being performed. Regardless of the nuances of the commercial strategy, the virus strangled the underlying business of every sports company.

Organizations responded by launching a slew of initiatives aimed at fixing the situation. Take a look at the following examples from the Australian sports business. Employees have had their employment terminated by their employers.

Several firms implemented compensation cutbacks (or reduced employee hours), as well as voluntary and involuntary layoffs. Employees were laid off or furloughed. Employees were required to take yearly or long-term vacations by others. Employees were moved to different departments. Government programmes were available to non-profits. Financial institutions and government bodies were contacted by organizations in need of assistance. Other companies have cut back on capital spending, hiring, and non-essential spending. Regardless of their peculiarities, and despite the fact that the immediate impact differed per organization, the sport being played eventually determines the income streams of sports organizations. The virus suffocated every sports organization's main business, regardless of how complicated the finance strategy was.

As a result, a spate of projects were launched to assist ease the situation. Consider the following instances from Australia's sports industry. Organizations have terminated the employment of employees. Many businesses lowered salaries (or reduced the number of hours employees worked), as well as forced and voluntary layoffs. Employees were either furloughed or stood down from their jobs. Employees in some other companies were given annual or long-term vacations. In some other cases, employees were transferred to various departments. Businesses took advantage of government programmes. To borrow money, financial institutions and regulatory bodies were addressed. Other businesses have cut back on capital expenditures, recruitment, and other non-essential costs.

Sports organizations' reputations were tarnished during the crisis. Anxious authorities found (desperate) strategies to allow top sports to be practiced while minimizing financial losses. These initiatives were not always warmly received. The broad agreement was that money drove the decision-makers' decisions rather than common sense. Elite players were perceived as greedy and "out of touch" when their player organizations refused to lower their (very) high salaries at a time when millions were unemployed. Organizations and athletes were able to maintain and/or improve their reputations by participating in COVID-related social responsibility initiatives. The strategy included food delivery, assistance to isolated individuals, fundraising, contributions, and public health messaging. Let us not forget that when sports organizations were knocked off their feet, they helped others get back on their feet as well.

The COVID tragedy impacted every aspect of every sports organization on the planet. The problem may be seen from a variety of perspectives and viewpoints. In the remainder of this part, I'd want to concentrate on three topics: business continuity, organizational reliance, and creativity. Operational consistency. The International Standards Organizations define business continuity as an organization's ability to continue supplying its products or services at acceptable defined levels after a disruptive event, whether natural or planned (1). Business continuity management is a technique for supporting businesses in detecting risk factors and being prepared to respond to them. Despite the fact that the majority of sports organizations survived the crisis, several were on life support and their businesses were unable to continue delivering services.

Sponsors are reducing spending as a result of the impending global recession. More than the virus, the global recession will have a long-term impact on the industry. And it is the recession that will compel businesses to change their business strategies. Some will be more successful than others. Only time will tell which aspects of these new business models will endure in the post-pandemic climate.

Sporting events

The COVID-19 outbreak has had a worldwide influence on sport, particularly sporting activities at all levels, from mega-events to small local ones. This situation in spring 2020 is an excellent example of today's instability, and it has created havoc on the athletic event industry. Games and competitions have been rescheduled or cancelled as a result of the weather. This affects not just event organizers, but also visitors. Sports tourism is becoming increasingly popular across the world, and it has the potential to help the hosting city or nation both monetarily and in terms of brand image. As a result of social distancing measures and precautions to prevent the transmission of the disease, several big events, including the Formula One Grand Prix and the World Athletics Championships, have been postponed or cancelled. The Tokyo 2020 Olympic Games (OG), which have already been postponed to summer 2021, are the most talked-about event.

The impact of COVID-19 on major and mega sporting events throughout the world, as well as national leagues, has been widely reported in the international media, with repeated cancellations and postponements. After a brief sabbatical, certain major leagues, including the NBA, NHL, Premier League, and other national leagues, have been allowed to continue play, initially without supporters and subsequently with fewer spectators in the summer. Local sports clubs and national leagues, on the other hand, have suffered enormous financial losses, and many have indicated that they will be unable to endure a possible second wave of the virus. Because sport is a spectator-driven business, the loss of matchday income combined with broadcast rights earnings encourages the idea of playing the series behind closed doors, even if the atmosphere is dreadful.

Sporting organizations and event planners aren't the only ones that are affected. One of the fastest-growing areas is sports tourism, and there is a great desire to attend athletic events (Maglovska, 2020). Non-mega or medium-sized sporting events can have a significant economic and social influence on the town they are held in (Battistini and Stoevsky, 2020). Small and medium-sized cities, as well as various economic sectors and the tourism industry as a whole, have been hurt by sporting event cancellations. Several wealthy countries' governments have already established funding strategies to aid the sports industry's COVID-19 effects, allowing certain sporting teams to exist until spring 2020. However, this form of short-term assistance only solves the situation temporarily, and it remains to be seen what the long-term consequences will be.

Thankfully, the pandemic has slowed in certain areas of the world, and government regulations have been loosened, allowing sporting events and spectators to take place while staying within social distance guidelines. This hasn't been simple, and reports of the virus spreading during small-scale sales events have already surfaced. This will be a burden for event organizers until the virus is eradicated globally. Even while the epidemic has receded in some nations, it continues to spread rapidly in others, preventing passengers from travelling for lengthy periods of time and harming the sports tourism business. While sport will remain an essential part of society, the pandemic is expected to have an impact on sports organization management in the future. Digitalization will become more prevalent, and adaptive, durable, and agile sports organizations will be necessary to recover from this calamity.

In the case of a global economic downturn, all aspects of risk management, including sports management, will be more important to incorporate. We may also need to rethink how we consume sports, particularly in terms of stadium utilization, participant- and spectator-based events, immersive technology, and the rise of esport. During international limits, innovative new means of organizing athletic events in conventional sports online have already emerged, and this development must continue for event organizers to preserve their financial viability. When their seasons begin, several major league baseball organizations are already worrying about viral transmission. In summary, the pandemic's lessons show that unpredictability is a typical occurrence in the sports industry.

Economic consequences of professional team sports

The COVID-19 outbreak, in its current form, poses an unparalleled threat to the sports industry. The previous global pandemic, the Spanish flu in 1918, happened in a world where the sports industry did not have the size and importance that it does now, with a market value of $471 billion USD in 2018. (Taubenberger and Morens, 2006). The goal of this paper is to look at COVID-19's economic impact on the sports industry, with a focus on professional team sports. The considerable income drop caused by the COVID-19 epidemic is the first item to investigate. Of the three key sources of revenue for professional team sports, gate receipts have probably had the most immediate detrimental impact. Events that were cancelled or held behind closed doors as a result of social distancing methods robbed event organizers of an immediate revenue stream that is unlikely to be recovered until a viable vaccine can be mass-produced on a large scale.

Cancellation of events might lead to renegotiation of broadcast contracts, which are the major source of revenue for professional team sports and the reason why all organizers have been unwilling to postpone/cancel events or desire to finish their seasons. Finally, the global economic crisis, which has impacted many firms, may lower the value of future commercial/sponsorship agreements, requiring contract renegotiations.

In the case of partially reopened stadiums, no renegotiation of broadcasting deals, and a 5%–20% drop in commercial revenue, the revenue loss for the 2019–2020 season is estimated to be between 1.31 and 2.94 billion dollars, while the loss for the 2020–2021 season is estimated to be between 0.36 and 1.30 billion dollars, or between 2.73 and 4.80 billion dollars in the case of games played behind closed doors. This effect will be even more obvious in professional leagues, where gate receipts remain the major component of the teams' revenue stream, due to declining popularity and media attention.

The second area of contention is the labour market for professional athletes, which is influenced by the financial limits faced by professional clubs. As a result of the lower cash flow, professional clubs have been obliged to renegotiate player contracts, with Juventus being the first to accept a temporary wage cut of up to four months just one month following the COVID-19 pandemic in Italy (12). Not all professional clubs have been able to reach an agreement with their athletes, even in the most competitive leagues, where a small loss of money is unlikely to impair players' well-being. As a result, it's easy to see how less successful leagues would struggle to make ends meet if their athletes were paid less than the average worker.

The third and final component is peculiar to non-American professional leagues, in which players are traded between teams for agreed-upon transfer fees. As a result, unpaid transfer fees account for 10%–30% of a club's total debts and credits (Grohmann, 2020). Professional teams may struggle to repay these loans as a result of the COVID-19 outbreak's detrimental influence on income streams, as well as owners' decreased willingness to invest stock, exacerbating the league's economic and financial situation.

As COVID-19 spreads, authorities need more information on whether, when, and how to run athletic events securely. While Olczak et al. (2020) warn against reopening outdoor stadiums, their findings are based on pre-COVID-19 fan behaviour, before social distancing, the wearing of facial coverings, and the renovation of public areas to eliminate possible pressure points where people gather. On matchdays, as well as at athletic arenas, fans have a wide range of viewpoints. These issues might be looked into further to see if there are any limitations that can be placed alongside COVID-19 that aren't as harsh as a complete shutdown.

Another study used a similar empirical technique to investigate the influence of large-audience English football matches on the spread of the pandemic (Olczak et al. 2020). Sports research has hardly scratched the surface thus far without the social pressure of a crowd. For example, the research thus far suggests that the lack of a crowd has a greater impact on referee bias than the fact that different match results are the consequence of variations in player behaviour. Future research might clarify this by examining the circumstances in which referees made their choices during games. Do referees, for example, "level things up" less when there isn't a crowd? Is it more likely that they will award a penalty or a red card to one team after they have already awarded one to the other? Do referees add less stoppage time at the end of a game when the home side is losing and there is no crowd? The first sport was football.

The impact of COVID-19 on athletic events and societal ramifications

Most major sporting events have been cancelled or postponed to safeguard the health of participants and spectators, including marathons, football tournaments, athletics championships, basketball games, handball, ice hockey, rugby, cricket, sailing, skiing, weightlifting, wrestling, and more. The Olympics and Paralympics have been postponed for the first time in modern Olympic history, and will now take place in 2021. On a global basis, the sports industry is projected to be worth US$756 billion each year. COVID-19 will affect millions of employment worldwide, not just for athletes, but also for those working in associated retail and athletic services sectors like travel, tourism, infrastructure, transportation, catering, and media broadcasting, which are all tied to leagues and tournaments.

Professional athletes are also under pressure to rearrange their training in order to stay in condition at home, and they risk losing professional sponsors who may not be able to help them. Aside from the financial implications, game cancellations have an impact on many of the social benefits of global and regional sporting events, such as strengthening social bonds, increasing fans' social and emotional excitement, and increasing their identification with athletes, all of which can lead to increased physical activity. Sport has long been seen as a valuable instrument for fostering intergenerational conversation and bridging generational divides. Sport, especially in divided cultures, may assist diverse socioeconomic groups to play a larger role in societal growth and advancement. Sport is utilized in this context to give learning opportunities and to reach out to underserved or at-risk communities.

Measures to stop the virus from spreading have been approved by major sports leagues. FIFA and the World Health Organization (WHO), for example, have launched a 13-language 'Pass the message to kick out coronavirus' campaign, urging people to follow five key steps to prevent the disease from spreading, such as hand washing, coughing etiquette, not touching one's face, physical distance, and staying at home if sick. Several global sports for development and peace organizations have linked together to demonstrate solidarity with one another during this time, conducting regular online community meetings to share concerns and issues.

Participants in such online discussions have also attempted to find novel solutions to larger social issues by identifying ways that sporting organizations can address issues faced by vulnerable people who would otherwise participate in sporting programmes in low-income communities but are unable to do so due to mobility restrictions. COVID-19 has influenced the sports education sector, which includes national ministries and local governments, public and private educational institutions, sports organizations and athletes, non-governmental organizations and the business community, teachers, scholars and coaches, parents, and, most importantly, the – primarily young – learners. Despite the fact that this group has been disproportionately affected by the current crisis, it may be able to assist in its management and resolution, as well as advocate for rights and ideals in times of social isolation.

Major problems will need to be addressed as the world recovers from COVID-19 in order to ensure the safety of sports events at all levels and the well-being of sporting organizations. These will include, among other things, event changes to preserve the safety of athletes, fans, and merchants in the near future. Given the potential of a global recession, initiatives to increase participation in athletic clubs, particularly among the young, may be vital in the long run.

Lack of access to exercise and physical activity can have negative mental health repercussions, aggravating the stress and anxiety that many individuals experience as a result of being cut off from their usual social lives. These repercussions will be amplified by the prospect of losing relatives or acquaintances as a result of the virus, as well as the illness's impact on one's economic well-being and access to food.

For many people, exercising at home without any equipment or in a small space is still a viable option. If you spend a lot of time sitting at home, there are undoubtedly some activities you may perform during the day to increase your activity level, such as stretching, cleaning, climbing stairs, or dancing to music. There is also a wealth of free information available on how to keep active throughout the epidemic, particularly for people with internet access. People of all ages may enjoy physical fitness activities, which can even be performed in tiny places. Strength training, which does not take up a lot of room but helps maintain muscular strength, is another key part of maintaining physical health. This is especially crucial for people who are old or have physical limitations. The international community reacted quickly by generating online material suited to certain persons, ranging from free social media accounts to paid social media accounts.

Many gyms provide low-cost subscriptions to apps and online video and audio sessions of varying lengths that are updated on a regular basis. There are a number of live fitness demos on social media sites. Many of these workouts require no special equipment, and others even use common household items as weights. People can utilize these online services to get access to lectures or programmes that are otherwise inaccessible. However, because not everyone has access to digital technologies, not everyone has access to such materials. Individuals in poor communities and many developing countries typically have little or no access to broadband internet. As a result, the digital divide has an impact on virtual sports, as well as remote banking, education, and communication.

Individually stimulating radio and television programmes, as well as the availability of printed material that encourages physical activity, are critical in bridging the digital divide for many low-income homes. Because sport is widely used to create collaboration and sportsmanship, encourage friendly competition, and learn to handle disagreement, young people are particularly impacted by social and physical distancing. Many young people will lose their support system if they do not participate in sports. Virtual training is already being used by a number of organizations and institutions to allow leagues, coaches, and young people to participate in sports while staying at home.

Adaptability and ingenuity

Fans were worried about how long they'd have to wait to see their favourite athletes again after the COVID-19 virus banned all athletic activities globally in early 2020. Cricket, football, rugby, basketball, athletics, badminton, and golf were all put on hold as COVID-19 caused havoc throughout the planet. The administration established a strategy for resuming sports in mid-2020. Following much deliberation, it was agreed that sports competitions would proceed with minor modifications. The most important problem is that there isn't enough crowd engagement in the arena. COVID-19 is still a major concern across the world, therefore athletes competed in empty stadiums while using technology to enhance the watching experience. Different leagues and sports employed various methods to get fans to participate. Different live updates, social media updates, food delivery pickup, more camera viewpoints, and virtual reality headsets resulted in a greater watching experience and interaction.

The sporting goods sector has progressed

COVID-19 took us all by surprise, leading the entire world, including the sports world, to come to a halt and re-calibrate. Things are gradually improving as we enter a period known as the "new normal," with live sports returning, albeit behind closed doors, and the majority of the world now "flattening the curve." Sports fans want to witness live action, even if it means watching from afar. The pleasure of simply watching from the comfort of your own home, however, will not last long. With the reintroduction of COVID-19 laws for sports, a new age of rapid invention has begun, with no apparent end in sight.

Cheerleaders from Taiwan and South Korea performed in Belarus, robots played the drums, mannequins and cardboard cutouts of generic supporters were scattered around the seats, and viewers were able to engage in the game through the internet. All of these steps were done in order to make the stadium feel more alive and to give the players on the field the sense that they were not alone. They fall short of recreating the stadium experience for at-home fans. Sports must place a greater emphasis on techniques to keep people glued to their sofas than ever before. Clubs and leagues may also benefit financially from this.

For Fan-Driven Creativity, COVID-19 was the inspiration

COVID-19 tests might take anything from two months to a year to complete. We have no way of knowing how quickly or slowly things will return to "normal," or what this "new normal" will look like right now. To innovate on an expiration date, it doesn't have to be a tough technological advancement. As we navigate through the "right now" COVID-19 age, innovative techniques may be most beneficial to teams, leagues, venues, and broadcasters.

Take Union Berlin's concept for a virtual stadium menu, for example. The team has a virtual food truck where fans may "order" items that they would normally purchase at the stadium without having to pick them up in person. The presents will help the team overcome its financial troubles. Why not team up with a delivery company or recruit personnel that were laid off due to COVID-19 to deliver these things to fans? Another option is to work with local supermarkets to provide "match day packs" that may be picked up or delivered right before the game.

These possibilities provide jobs for the unemployed, allow stadiums to profit from product sales, allow package sponsors to monetize their sponsorship, and provide a more stadium-like experience to the living room. Inventing new ways to deliver more content to devoted followers necessitates creativity and content thinking outside the box. Season ticket holders may get access to unique information, and non-roster players can use their social media presence to encourage attendance during games. Teams may make money by linking resources to new items and using QR codes to get access to unique content or rewards.

These possibilities create jobs for the jobless, allow stadiums to earn from product sales, allow package sponsors to monetize their sponsorships, and give the living room a more stadium-like experience. Inventing innovative ways to provide more content to committed fans demands creativity and content thinking outside of the box. If non-roster players take on social media identities during the money to boost involvement, season ticket holders may be entitled to money to purchase special items.

The influence on athletes

As a result of technology improvements, new and distinct kinds of athletes may emerge. The first category includes athletes who are physically fit and do not require help. They will have the same features as of today's athletes but will benefit from significantly more technological assistance in their training. In the next 20–30 years, humanoid robots are expected to compete with humans.

Athletes from both the Paralympic and able-bodied worlds compete using technology. Exoskeletons are now being employed in rehabilitation and the military, for example. Athletes from both robots and humans will compete in the future. Humans (for example, by eye movement) or artificial intelligence can control them (for example, in automobile races with autonomous vehicles). Finally, algorithm-controlled virtual athletes might be created using holograms. These can be utilized for training as well as human competition. As a result, a similar situation has arisen.

New athlete categories will complement existing ones in every way. According to sports executives and technology experts, any new notion must not only be technically viable but also meet client wants. These are just a few examples of how sports technology allows for new kinds of customer contact. The number of use instances that resulted from the epidemic might be far greater.

Conclusion

Authorities need additional information on if, when, and how to run sporting venues safely as COVID-19 continues to spread. While Olczak et al. (2020) advise against reopening outdoor stadiums, their findings are based on pre-COVID-19 fan behaviour, prior to the introduction of social distancing, the wearing of facial coverings, and the redesign of public spaces to reduce potential pressure points where people cluster. Fans' opinions on a matchday, as well as sporting venues, are quite diverse. These concerns might be investigated further to determine if there are any limits that can be implemented alongside COVID-19 that aren't as severe as a total shutdown.

Professional sports have been subjected to huge shocks as a result of COVID-19, resulting in natural experiments. These have helped to address problems including how airborne viruses propagate in crowds, how crowds react to infection risks and news, how the lack of crowds affects social pressure and decisions, and how rapidly betting markets change to new information.

The COVID-19 epidemic has wreaked havoc on the global sports sector in a variety of ways. As a result, several prominent sports throughout the world have seen significant income drops. Millions of people's careers and lives have been damaged by job losses, pay or salary cuts, rising living costs, loss of health and general well-being, and other factors. As a result, companies and governments are working to reduce the epidemic's economic impact. To reduce the outbreak's devastating effects, sports authorities will need to develop appropriate guidelines on a worldwide strategic level. Many countries must collaborate, with established or wealthy economies having the means and resources to analyse and re-evaluate the issue on a regular basis, enhancing their knowledge and skills while also disseminating it to the world's poorer nations.

COVID-19 wreaked havoc on the sports business, as well as a number of other social and economic sectors. Throughout the years, this industry has evolved to be a multibillion-dollar industry with massive revenues. Millions of people throughout the world are employed in the sports industry, and they rely on it for their livelihood. Tourists, corporations, museums, and others that supplement ticket earnings from their tours have given money to teams from all around the world. For example, the Allianz Arena made around €7 million from the sale of beers, sausages, and soft drinks during the match in 2019, as well as €10 million from visitors to the FC Bayern Munich Museum (MUIC, 2020). These figures show how much money teams are squandering by competing in closed-door competitions, which were mandated when the crisis began. It has both economic and psychological ramifications.

References

Ahammer, A., Halla, M., and Lackner, M. (2020). Mass gatherings contributed to early COVID-19 spread: Evidence from US sports. *Covid Economics*. Retrieved from https://voxeu.org/article/mass-gatherings-contributed-early-covid-19-mortality

Battistini, N. and Stoevsky, G. (2020). Alternative scenarios for the impact of the COVID-19 pandemic on economic activity in the euro area. *ECB Economic Bulletin*, Issue 3/2020.

Becker, G. S. and Rubinstein, Y. (2011). Fear and the response to terrorism: An economic analysis. CEP Discussion Paper No 1079.

Cardazzi, A., Humphreys, B. R., Ruseski, J. E., Soebbing, B., and Watanabe, N. (2020). Professional sporting events increase seasonal influenza mortality in US cities. West Virginia University Working Paper Series 6–2020.

Clarkson, B., Culvin, A., Pope, S., and Parry, K. (2020). Covid-19: Reflections on threat and uncertainty for the future of elite women's football in England. *Managing Sport and Leisure*. https://doi.org/10.1080/23750472.2020.1766377

Doherty, A., Millar, P., and Misener, K. (2020). Return to community sport: Leaning on evidence in turbulent times. *Managing Sport and Leisure*. https://doi.org/10.1080/23750 472.2020.1794940

Drewes, M., Daumann, F., and Follert, F. (2020). Sportökonomische Auswirkungen der COVID-19-Pandemie am Beispiel der Fußball-Bundesligen. *List Forum*, 46, 345–357.

Duarte Muñoz, M. and Meyer, T. (2020). Infectious diseases and football – Lessons not only from COVID-19. *Science and Medicine in Football*, 4(2), 85–86.

Flatau, J. and Emrich, E. (2016). Exzessiver passiver Sportkonsum – Ist die Sucht nach Stadionfußball rational? [Excessive passive sport consumption – Is addiction to stadium soccer rational?]. *Diskussionspapier des Europäischen Instituts für Sozioökonomie*, 18. https://doi.org/10.22028/D291-27041

Follert, F. (2018). Ökonomisierung des Fußballs. *Das Wirtschaftsstudium*, 47(6), 668–670.

Follert, F. and Daumann, F. (2021). Profifußball zwischen Sport, Ökonomie und Moral (Professional football between sport, economy and morality). Retrieved from http://wirtschaftlichefreiheit.de/wordpress/?tag=follert

Frevel, N. and Schreyer, D. (2020). Behavioral responses to terrorist attacks: Empirical evidence from professional football. *Applied Economics Letters*, 27(3), 244–247.

Grohmann, K. (2020). Olympics: Games must connect with gamers to keep Olympics relevant, Available at https://www.reuters.com/article/us-olympics-ioc-idUSKBN1Z91M2

Humphreys, K. L., LeMoult, J., Wear, J. G., Piersiak, H. A., Lee, A. and Gotlib, I. H. (2020). Child maltreatment and depression: A meta-analysis of studies using the childhood trauma questionnaire, *Child Abuse & Neglect*, 102, 104361.

Huth, C. and Kraus, P. (2021). Analyse der Akzeptanz von Geisterspielen sowie der Bereitschaft und des Verständnisses von Stadionbesuchen im Kontext der COVID-19 Pandemie am Beispiel der Fußball-Bundesliga. Sciamus – Sport und Gesellschaft.

Ludvigsen, J. A. L. and Hayton, J. W. (2020). Toward COVID-19 secure events: Considerations for organizing the safe resumption of major sporting events. *Managing Sport and Leisure*, 1–11. https://doi.org/10.1080/23750472.2020.1782252

Maglovska, C. R. (2020). Sports event tourism: An evolving business opportunity for the hostel industry. *Activities in Physical Education and Sport*, 10(1–2), 6–9.

Memish, Z. A., Steffen, R., White, P., Dar, O., Azhar, E. I., Sharma, A., & Zumla, A. (2019). Mass gatherings medicine: Public health issues arising from mass gathering religious and sporting events. *The Lancet*, 393(10185), 2073–2084.

Mohr, M., Nassis, G. P., Brito, J., Randers, M. B., Castagna, C., Parnell, D., et al. (2020). Return to elite football after the COVID-19 lockdown. *Managing Sport and Leisure*, 1–9. https://doi.org/10.1080/23750472.2020.1768635

MUIC. (2020). Jan-Christian Dreesen: A remarkable achievement. Retrieved from https://fcbayern.com/en/news/2021/11/2020-21-revenue-and-profit-strongly-influenced-by-covid-19

Olczak, M., Reade, J., and Yeo, M. (2020). Mass outdoow events and the spread of an airborne virus: English Football and COVID-19. *Covid Economics*. Retrieved from https://voxeu.org/article/spread-covid-19-and-attending-football-matches-england

Parnell, D., Widdop, P., Bond, A., and Wilson, R. (2020). COVID-19, networks and sport. *Managing Sport and Leisure*, 27(1–2), 1–7.

Reade, J. J., Schreyer, D., and Singleton, C. (2021). Stadium attendance demand during the COVID-19 crisis: Early empirical evidence from Belarus. *Applied Economics Letters*, 28(18), 1542–1547.

Reade, J. J. and Singleton, C. (2020). Demand for Public Events in the COVID-19 Pandemic: A Case Study of European Football. European Sport Management Quarterly, em-dp2020–09, Department of Economics, University of Reading.

Stoecker, C., Sanders, N. J., and Barreca, A. (2016). Success is something to sneeze at influenza mortality in cities that participate in the Super Bowl. *American Journal of Health Economics*, 2(1), 125–143.

Taubenberger, J. K. and Morens, D. M. (2006). 1918 Influenza: The mother of all pandemics. *Emerging Infectious Diseases*, 12(1), 15–22.

Toresdahl, B. and Asif, I. (2020). Coronavirus Disease 2019 (COVID-19): Considerations for the competitive athlete. *Sports Health*, 12(3), 221–224.

Tovar, J. (2020). Soccer, World War II and coronavirus: A comparative analysis of how the sport shut down. *Soccer & Society*, 22(1–2), 66–74.

Webb, T. (2020). The future of officiating: Analysing the impact of COVID-19 on referees in world football. *Soccer & Society*, 22(1–2), 12–18.

Weed, M. (2020). The role of the interface of sport and tourism in the response to the COVID-19 pandemic. *Journal of Sport & Tourism*, 24(2), 79–92. https://doi.org/10.1080/14775085.2020.1794351

World Health Organization. (2020). Coronavirus disease 2019 (COVID-19). Situation report. https://www.who.int/docs/default-source/coronaviruse/situation-reports/20200303-sitrep-43-covid-19.pdf?sfvrsn=2c21c09c_2. Accessed September 13, 2020.

Zülch, H., Ottenstein, P., and Manz, E. (2020). *The German Bundesliga Clubs and their future: An outlook on the robustness of the clubs in times of Covid -19*. Odgers Berndtson: Germany.

Chapter 3

Sports Communication in the COVID-19 Period

Selcuk Bora Cavusoglu and Merve Uskuplu

Sports Communication in the COVID-19 Period

Today communication, which is shaped through five basic terms, namely a source, a receiver, a message, the channel on which the message runs, and feedback, is the subject of every field that contains human factors (Aytekin, 2014). One of these areas is sports. Media is a very effective tool for the communication of sports. However, today, a new type of media has emerged with social media. Mass media content producers and audiences have become consumers and producers of social media. In this way, the roles of media content producers and consumers have changed, and there is no clear blue water between those definitions.

With the COVID-19 pandemic, both mass media and social media consumptions have increased. However, the cancellation and postponement of live sports competitions, which are the most fundamental sports media content, pushed people to search for new media. While the traditional media was looking for new ways to reach the audience, the audience also sought a new media concept and became a producer there at the same time. The sports media audience has turned to social media platforms where it can directly reach the athlete. Therefore, a change that started before has been fueled by the COVID-19 pandemic.

In this study, based on the concepts of communication and communication in sports, it is addressed how the current COVID-19 pandemic plays a role in sports communication. First of all, concepts such as communication and sports communication were examined. Afterward, the COVID-19 pandemic was introduced, and then how sports communication progressed in this period was explained with examples.

Communication in Sports

Communication enables the transfer of information, feelings, thoughts, and experiences to society or individuals. This transfer may be indirect or direct (Aytekin, 2014). Communication which is old as humanity, can occur verbally, nonverbally, written, or visually (Çavuşoğlu, 2019). Although communication is difficult to clearly define due to its complex process (Dumangöz, 2021), it is a phenomenon that deals with the transmission of information rather than the knowledge of the

DOI: 10.4324/9781003253891-3

person who initiates the communication (Çavuşoğlu, 2019). Because to speak of the communication, there must be actors, a message, and a channel (Aytekin, 2014). Communication used by humanity can be divided into two parts, verbal and written (Çavuşoğlu & Dumangöz, 2019). To successfully communicate, two essential points are to learn the elements of communication and to apply what is learned (Çavuşoğlu, 2019).

Communication, which provides a multidisciplinary field of study, is closely related to sports. Sports communication emerges with the interaction of people in the sports environment as a result of the need for a common understanding (Dumangöz, 2021). This form of communication is that clubs and athletes establish with the masses and includes concepts such as advertising and sponsorship. Sponsorship is generally at the point of organizational communication (Danış & Yengin, 2020). The two oldest significant events in sports communication are the Ancient Roman gladiator fights and the Ancient Greek Olympics. In Ancient Rome, communication used to take control of the people by making them watch these fights. Communication was also used to instill a combative spirit in the people watching the Olympics in ancient Greece. It is vital to use intelligence in sports communication (Çavuşoğlu, 2019).

Another essential point in sports communication is which tools are used while communicating (Danış & Yengin, 2020). Communication tools also affect the number of spectators (Çavuşoğlu, 2019). These tools of communication, namely mass media, transfer information to the determined target audience in written, visual, and electronic forms (Şahan & Çınar, 2004). The tools of mass communication, which in its singular form is medium and in its plural form is media, are developed for communication with other people and the masses (Aytekin, 2014). Information is transferred to the audience interested in sports through the same tools of communication. The relationship between sports and mass media has developed as such and has turned into a symbiotic process. Therefore, the phenomenon that we can also call sports media has emerged. In addition to its informing and entertaining function, this phenomenon is also a stimulant and affects the popularity of sports branches in general (Şahan & Çınar, 2004).

The first sports news emerged in newspapers in the early 1900s and continued as radio and television news (Şahan & Çınar, 2004). In mass communication, the broadcaster will always have the final say. In this process, fans or viewers cannot have the last word (Majumdar & Naha, 2020). In today's digital world, the importance of these tools has decreased, especially clubs have started to adapt to new communication tools (Danış & Yengin, 2020). Sports activities worldwide have become watchable uniformly (Çavuşoğlu, 2019), and as McLuhan said, the world has turned into a global village. Time and place have lost their meaning. Sports competitions are accessible not only from where they actualize but also from whatever they are streaming (Danış & Yengin, 2020). Even if the spectators cannot attend the sportive event to watch at the venue, they can watch the competition with the digital equipment they own (Vardı, 2021). Social media is an essential tool for sports organizations to communicate with sports audiences.

Therefore, fandom has also changed shape, and the passive audience has left its place to the active supporter. At that point, success depends on the sports audience and its understanding of the created language and the initiation of the interaction process (Danış & Yengin, 2020).

The media also use sports to create the concept of the citizen regarding culture. Concepts such as digitalization and globalization challenge this situation. However, we see that mass communication adapts social media opportunities to itself (Ramon & Rojas-Torrijos, 2021).

Really, What Is This COVID-19 Pandemic?

COVID-19, a type of coronavirus, causes diseases in the respiratory system and affects a scale ranging from the common cold to multiple organ failure and death (Türkmen & Özsarı, 2020). Today, this epidemic has an enormous impact that is greater than the wars (Sharpe et. al., 2020). On March 11, 2020, governments started to take some measures at the global level when WHO (World Health Organization) announced the virus called COVID-19 as a pandemic. In Turkey, precautions have been taken regarding environments where people will be in groups with a high risk of contamination. Solutions such as flexible working hours, alternating working hours, or working from home have been introduced for workplaces. Education has been transformed into distance learning. At the same time, sports, artistic and scientific activities have been canceled or postponed indefinitely (TÜBA, 2020).

COVID-19 Pandemic and Sports

For the first time in its history, the COVID-19 pandemic stopped sports without a war or a similar event (Horky, 2021). Sportive activities, especially the organized ones, have been subjected to strict measures because they are held with too many spectators in large areas and increase the risk of contamination (TÜBA, 2020; Türkmen & Özsarı, 2020). On March 19, 2020, football, basketball, handball, and volleyball leagues were postponed indefinitely. (TÜBA, 2020). The remarkable point is that the competitions took place until these postponements, which were called "biological bombs" (Koçak & Özer Kaya, 2020).

The League season finally started. However, both the delays and the fact that the spectators were not allowed to enter the stadium caused financial losses (Üçüncüoğlu et al., 2021). This restriction lasted until June 1 for individual sports. Sports facilities were opened (Türk Tabipleri Birliği COVID-19 İzleme Kurulu, 2020). Within the scope of organized sports, the fact that sports are performed in a social environment becomes restricted in this way. Today, spectators are allowed to get in the competitions. However, a HES code is required to watch sports competitions on location (TRT Haber, 2021). This process started with a limited audience intake. Today, there are examples that there is no spectator restriction in stadiums. The most recent example is the match between Galatasaray and Fenerbahçe on November 21, 2021 (Ntvspor, 2021).

Some of the canceled or postponed sporting events are as follows:

European Football League matches, EURO 2020, Formula 1 Grand Prix (China, Vietnam Grand Prix 2020), Six Nations Rugby Championship, Grand National 2020, France cycling tour, national and world championships (Goldman & Hedlund, 2020). The Tokyo 2020 Olympic Games and Paralympic Games were postponed to the summer of 2021 on March 4, 2020 (Toresdhl & Asif, 2020). This is the first in history (Üçüncüoğlu et al., 2021). The postponed EURO 2020 indicated a loss of approximately 700 million euros (Türkmen & Özsarı, 2020). In Turkey, all lower and upper leagues and sports activities have been postponed or canceled (Türkmen & Özsarı, 2020). In addition to the suspension of domestic and international sports organizations, national athletes were brought to Turkey urgently from other countries (Yurtsızoğlu, 2021). Studies show that, in March, when the pandemic was declared, approximately 33% of all sporting events took place (Goldman & Hedlund, 2020). In this case, 2020 is defined as a lost year for the sports world (Türkmen & Özsarı, 2020).

In the sports world, the COVID-19 pandemic has caused training programs and competition times to change. In addition, athletes who did not suffer from the disease were also affected by this situation (Koçak & Özer Kaya, 2020). Sports physicians informed the athletes about hand hygiene, social distancing, travel regulations, and the need to wear masks and suggested that they take precautions on these issues (Toresdhl & Asif, 2020). In Turkey, on the other hand, TMOK (Turkish National Olympic Committee) gathered the topics and took the initiative to publish them as a guide. These are the division of sports branches according to risk groups, the size of the sports organization, area, opportunities, and measures. In addition, local governments also made publications on sports and physical activity in this period (Aygün, 2021).

As the measures taken differ from country to country, unequal practices among athletes also come to the fore. In addition, at the end of the process, it is foreseen that the athletes will experience injuries in the musculoskeletal system during their sports journeys. The positive aspect of the process is that the athletes will recover during social distancing and isolation (Koçak & Özer Kaya, 2020).

The results of postponement or cancelation of sports leagues, international sports organizations, and mega-events in the world are felt not only in sports but also in economic and sociological dimensions. Especially when we look economically, sponsorship, (live-re) broadcasting revenues, matchday revenues, stock market shares, compensations, and advertisements have been lost. Sports resources were used to fight against the epidemic. In this case, the sports media received one of the greatest setbacks (Türkmen & Özsarı, 2020). FIFA has provided 10 million dollars of support to WHO (Türkmen & Özsarı, 2020). One of the ways of spending these resources to fight against the epidemic was by providing accommodation for COVID-19 patients. For example, Chelsea Football Club offered National Health Service (NHS) employees to stay at the Millennium Hotel (Sharpe et al., 2020). In addition, one of Europe's largest skate parks in Deeside, Wales, has been demolished, remodeled, and turned into a dormitory for COVID 19 patients (Smith, 2020).

COVID-19 Pandemic and Sports Communication

The primary sources of income in sports leagues are broadcasting, commercial, and matchday revenue. There are media rights in broadcasting, sponsorship, advertising in commercials, and tickets in matchday revenue (Salman & Giray, 2020; Türkmen & Özsarı, 2020). Sponsorship is a widely used communication tool and is effective in reaching the target audience. On the other hand, sports is the sponsorship area with the highest revenue (Varlı, 2021). Due to canceled or post-poned sports competitions because of the COVID-19, the sports media was gravely affected (Salman & Giray, 2020), and approximately 2 million dollars was lost in the field of advertising and sponsorship, the effects of which will be felt worldwide (Türkmen & Özsarı, 2020). Bein Sports, the owner of the sports broadcasting rights in Turkey, has announced that it has stopped paying 600 million TL and will resume payments only after the leagues start post-pandemic (Varlı, 2021). It is claimed that the loss of Super League clubs reaches 1.5 billion TL, which corresponds to approximately 35% of Turkey's football income (Yurtsızoğlu, 2021).

Although the cessation of sports communication and sports media brought massive financial problems, life continued (Horky, 2021). Although the effects of COVID-19 on sports media has had a great financial impact, it has made sports media broadcast and content production to explore innovative ways (Coche & Lynn, 2020). The great difficulties experienced in media, broadcasts, broadcasting rights, and sponsorship have turned into a search for new ways to reach the audience (Vardı, 2021). However, studies show that approximately 56% of the fans participating in a study are willing to watch sports competitions with crowds (Salman & Giray, 2020). That is a constructive situation. Because of the fanless competitions, the media could not capture emotional moments. The fans are essential for spiriting up the field where the competition takes place. According to a study, this can be solved by fans, who become digital citizens and can shoot videos with their smartphones, sending emotional moments to the channels while watching the match (Majumdar & Naha, 2020). We see that it is inevitable for organizations to keep up with the digital world. And those new ways include digital fields and phenomena such as social media (Salman & Giray, 2020).

An example of one of the new ways is the NASCAR broadcast that was actualized in South Carolina on May 17, 2020. Instead of a crowded shooting crew and spectators, this broadcast was conveyed without an audience and with only the camera operators, technical director, and director in the field. The producers and presenters were in the studio in North Carolina, while the graphics and mixers were involved from Los Angeles. In this way, the risk of contracting the virus, especially in the shooting containers or minibusses where the shooting crew used to work, was prevented, and social distancing, in general, was ensured (Coche & Lynn, 2020). This is the REMI model and looks like the future of sports broadcasting.

Traditional sports broadcasts, in which the entire shooting crew would be on the field, have been trying to move on to a new dimension for at least 20 years from now. The primary purpose of this attempt to change is to make a profit. One of the models that will make a profit is REMI. In this model, the technical team has to be in the shooting area. However, the production team can be involved from anywhere else where virtual production equipment is installed. In today's pandemic conditions, this model provides an opportunity for the vast majority, if not all, of the team to work from home. That minimizes the risk of contracting the virus which would be the result of working in crowded environments. In addition, this model does not require any changes in the workflow. It also does not change the number of people who are involved in this work. There may be changes in the number of people who may have to go to the shooting field. However, this model isn't fully adopted yet, because of insufficient technical facilities related to communication systems, delays in frames, the construction of equipment and hubs which are relatively expensive and time-consuming to set up, and the inability of industries to adapt to large-scale changes. The applicability of REMI has been accelerated in the pandemic process (Coche & Lynn, 2020).

Another way tried in sports communication is sports media broadcast versions of old competitions shots with old technology and new but amateur footage. This situation was criticized by the audience (Coche & Lynn, 2020). From a gender equality perspective, the male-dominated sports media, which usually transmits live broadcasts or other sports organizations to the masses, had to interrupt these broadcasts due to the COVID-19 pandemic. However, sports broadcasts continued, albeit in different ways. Even though the gap is tried to be filled with different methods, women have not been treated differently in the sports media. Digital media, on the other hand, can give us the desired democratic broadcasting (Symons et al., 2021).

In addition to the replays of the matches played, significant moments, and interviews in the history of sports, we also come across live esports events in broadcasts (Üçüncüoğlu et al., 2021). Despite there being a few roughnesses of the REMI model, that model and a live stream broadcast with that model are preferred by the audience (Coche & Lynn, 2020). The effect of the pandemic on sports media has caused sports media to enter an innovation process. However, due to this method, students and employees who have just entered the sports media sector will not have the chance to gain the insight and experience they will gain in a stadium.

Social media, which transforms its users into content producers, enabled people and fans to interact with their favorite athletes, teams, sports brands, and other fans in this period (Sharpe et al., 2020). The absence of social environments and their search for new ways to maintain their relationship with the fans push the athletes to use social media. On the other hand, social media allows the athletes and their supporters to meet without any hindrance. Fans and the audience do not only watch but also interact with the athlete. The picture of the athlete presented on this platform is undisrupted, natural, and a slice of life. However, social media platforms differ according to the purpose of usage. Athletes produce content on well-established social media platforms such as Twitter, Facebook, and Instagram, on newly popular social media platforms such as TikTok. Twitter, Facebook, and Instagram are used for more professional purposes. More about the athlete than about sports content TikTok provides a new opportunity for athletes to create their brands. Especially, challenges related to sports have been popular (Su et al., 2020).

Athletes also found the opportunity to meet their fans economically, especially for sports organizations, with social media. Athletes not only came together with their fans, but they also collected donations for the social "sports" media and the National Health Service (NHS), supported them with messages about hygiene practices, health, social distance, and produced content about their exercise routines. For example, Cristiano Ronaldo shared a visual image about cleaning hands with his children. Likewise, football players Lionel Messi and Marcus Rashford respected the "stay at home" warnings and made relevant posts on social media. They also participated in the super popular toilet paper challenges. In this way, the activities on social media increased the traffic related to sports. Even though social media usage is a brownie point for sports and brands marketing, that usage during the pandemic was not selfish and not for advertising purposes (Sharpe et al., 2020).

Social/new media is changing the relationship between sports and their fans today. New media includes not only social media platforms but also the concept of "esports" (Goldman & Hedlund, 2020). During the COVID-19 pandemic period, interaction with esports and digital games has increased. Esports ensures that the interest in sports remains active, a new type of content in the field, a new investment area (Üçüncüoğlu et al., 2021). Esports is a kind of sport in which the primary principles of the sport are provided through electronic systems. While playing alone or against the computer/medium in a video game, in esports, through technology, the person plays with a person/persons or against the person/ persons (Goldman & Hedlund, 2020). Esports gives birth to the concept of "playing together separately from each other." That is the exact condition for a sports event that is doable during the pandemic process. In this way, esports fills a void created in the sports (mass) media (Ke & Wagner, 2020). Esports has been the helper of organizations that have difficulties reaching their masses in the sports world. Organizations use esport tools to differentiate their content and reach their audience use esport as a tool (Üçüncüoğlu et al., 2021).

Some sports organizations allow professional athletes to take part in "esports" events. For example, during the pandemic, NASCAR positions its pilots in a simulator called eNASCAR IRacing Pro Invitational Series Race on IRacing, an online e-racing platform. That has been the most seen broadcast in esports broadcast history. However, branded clubs/organizations' use of their names in different areas can also be perceived as a spark that can go out after the pandemic. However, even before the pandemic, we see the names of branded clubs/organizations on the esports platform. For example, Paris St. Germain's esports team has a different board, and another target audience and it hardly interacts with the original team (Ke & Wagner, 2020).

Investment in the esports field has also increased in Turkey. The Turkish E-Sports Federation was established in 2018. The federation organized various tournaments to increase participation. One of them is the Stay Home Cup. On the other hand, The Turkish Super League organized the Turkey E-Football Tournament on May 9–10, 2020 over the FIFA 2020 game. This tournament is the first official esports event of the Association of Clubs Foundation. Players from the Super League teams participated in the game (Üçüncüoğlu et al., 2021). Although esports gained popularity during this period, there are opinions that this situation will increase in the future (Üçüncüoğlu et al., 2021). Another study defends that this rise will not continue after the COVID-19 pandemic. That may be because esports derives from video games and includes a different concept of competition. Also, there is no physical activity in this area. At these points, esports and sports are separated from each other. The new media of esports may require a new definition in the field of traditional sports broadcasting (Ke & Wagner, 2020).

Conclusion

The media, whose origin is communication, has evolved specific to sports and sports communication has begun to be made through the sports media with the increasing interest of the masses. Sports media has become a financial, male-dominated power in the sports industry with the usage of concepts such as marketing and sponsorship. It creates an essential economic resource that provides a symbiotic relationship for sports organizations and media organizations since that includes many details such as live sports competitions, ticket revenues, and broadcasting rights.

Today, the COVID-19 pandemic, which has emerged worldwide and has affected all areas of life, made us question all our practices and re-form them, continues. At the beginning of the pandemic, sports competitions, which carry the highest risk of contamination because of their crowded and social environment, were stopped, postponed, or canceled. This situation has caused a great economic loss in sports media as well as in every field. The media, which broadcasts past competitions and footage, has sought new ways to reach the audience. Parallelly, the audience has chosen social media to be both a viewer and a content producer. The use of social media, which has already attracted attention from both mass media and the audience, increased in this period. However, when we consider the frequency of use of social media today, the questions come to mind whether this increase will already occur and whether this transformation experienced by sports media will already occur. Undoubtedly, this change will happen someday. The pandemic has played an accelerating role in this transformation process. It is essential to interpret this wind of change in the sports world correctly and create a plan for the future. For example, the preparation process of the last Olympics should be re-evaluated and a new Olympic model should be created (Türkmen & Özsarı, 2020). It is thought that the media industry will experience a very rapid recovery after the pandemic (Varlı, 2021).

The pandemic shows that sports media should develop a visionary and different content approach to adapt to such situations. The most important measures to be taken in the competitions are hygiene-related and fanless competitions. In this way, the virus transmission risk can be reduced. It is thought that sponsorship revenues will decrease in the future, and fanless competitions will not be able to cover the damage. When there were live chants of fans at the packed stadium, the income was higher, but with fanless competitions, the organizers faced heavy losses. Some studies refer to this year as the "lost year." It is predicted that the damages in the sports fields cannot be compensated for many years and many people will lose their jobs (Türkmen & Özsarı, 2020). In this process, many sports media workers lost their jobs due to canceled sports events and broadcasts (Coche & Lynn, 2020).

It seems inevitable that the actions to be taken will be online-driven in today's conditions. The process could begin with the simulative training of sports events. Semi-live semi-virtual broadcasts could be aired. For example, the use of innovative solutions such as esports can be increased. Today, it is a fact that the esports economy is at its peak and almost 32 million people play esport (Türkmen & Özsarı, 2020).

References

Aygün, M. (2021). Spor Organizasyonlarında Covid-19 Etkisi. *Gençlik Araştırmaları Dergisi*, 9(23), 43–48.

Aytekin, M. (2014). Sadece İletişim. Editör Aytekin, M. Yeni(lenen) Medya. Kocav Yayınları. 15–24.

Çavuşoğlu, S. B. (2019). Sporda İletişim Stratejileri. Editör Hergüner, G., Her Yönüyle Spor. Güven Plus Grup A.Ş Yayınları. 487–511.

Çavuşoğlu, S. B., & Dumangöz, P. D. (2019). Examining the viewpoints of the sports journalists in turkey on traditional and internet journalism. *European Journal of Physical Education and Sport Science*, 5(5), 19–34.

Coche, R., & Lynn, B. J. (2020). Behind the scenes: COVID-19 consequences on broadcast sports production. *International Journal of Sport Communication*, 1(aop), 1–10.

Danış, E., & Yengin, D. (2020). Türkiye'de Spor İletişiminin Futbol Kulüpleri Üzerinden İncelenmesi: Fenerbahçe, Beşiktaş ve Galatasaray Örneği. *Yeni Medya Elektronik Dergi*, 4(2), 89–105.

Dumangöz, P. D. (2021). Spor Bilimleri Alanında Yapılan İletişim Araştırmalarına İlişkin bir Değerlendirme. *İletişim Çalışmaları Dergisi*, 7(3), 425–452.

Goldman, M. M., & Hedlund, D. P. (2020). Rebooting content: Broadcasting sport and esports to homes during COVID-19. *International Journal of Sport Communication*, 13(3), 370–380.

Horky, T. (2021). No sports, no spectators – No media, no money? The importance of spectators and broadcasting for professional sports during COVID-19. *Soccer & Society*, 22(1–2), 96–102.

Ke, X., & Wagner, C. (2020). Global pandemic compels sport to move to esports: Understanding from brand extension perspective. *Managing Sport and Leisure*, 27, 1–6.

Koçak, U. Z., & ve Özer Kaya, D. (2020). COVID-19 Pandemisi, Spor, Sporcu Üçgeni: Etkilenimler ve Öneriler. *İzmir Kâtip Çelebi Üniversitesi Sağlık Bilimleri Fakültesi Dergisi,* 5(2), 129–133.

Majumdar, B., & Naha, S. (2020). Live sport during the COVID-19 crisis: Fans as creative broadcasters. *Cultures, Commerce, Media, Politics,* 23(7), 1091–1099.

Ntvspor. (2021). Süper Lig'de derbi heyecanı: Galatasaray-Fenerbahçe Erişim tarihi; 22 Kasım 2021; https://www.ntv.com.tr/amp/spor/super-ligde-derbi-heyecani-galatasaray-fenerbahce, Rp7HSR4td0-WE2saCuukvw

Ramon, X., & Rojas-Torrijos, J. L. (2021). Public service media, sports and cultural citizenship in the age of social media: An analysis of BBC Sport agenda diversity on Twitter. *International Review for the Sociology of Sport,* 0(0), 1–22.

Şahan, H., & Çınar, V. (2004). Kitle İletişim Araçlarının Spor Kamuoyu Üzerine Etkisi. *Selçuk Üniversitesi Sosyal Bilimler Enstitüsü Dergisi,* 12, 313–321.

Salman, G. G., & Giray, C. (2020). Artan Dijital Çözümlerin Sporda Kullanımı ve Pandemi Sonrası Spor Dijital Dönüşüm Gerekliliği. Editörler Öz, S., Celayir, D., Onursal, F., S. Pandemi Sonrası Yeni Dünya Düzeninde Teknoloji Yönetimi ve İnsani Dijitalizasyon, 553–587.

Sharpe, S., Mountifield, C., & Filo, K. (2020). The social media response from athletes and sport organizations to COVID-19: An altruistic tone. *International Journal of Sport Communication,* 13(3), 474–483.

Smith, W. R. (2020). A post-COVID-19 lifestyle sport research agenda: Communication, risk, and organizational challenges. *International Journal of Sport Communication,* 13(3), 352–360.

Su, Y., Baker, B. J., Doyle, J. P., & Yan, M. (2020). Fan engagement in 15 seconds: Athletes' relationship marketing during a pandemic via TikTok. *International Journal of Sport Communication,* 13(3), 436–446.

Symons, K., Breitbarth, T., Zubcevic-Basic, N., Wilson, K., Sherry, E., & Karg, A. (2021). The (un)level playing field: Sport media during COVID-19. *European Sport Management Quarterly,* 22, 1–17.

Toresdhl, B. G., & ve Asif, I. M. (2020). Coronavirus Disease 2019 (COVID-19): Considerations for the competitive athlete. *Sports Health,* 12(3), 221–224.

TRT Haber. (2021). Stadyumlara giriş şartları: Aşı, PCR, HES. Erişim tarihi 22 Kasım 2021; https://www.trthaber.com/haber/spor/stadyumlara-giris-sartlari-asi-pcr-hes-598362.html

TÜBA. (Nisan, 2020). COVID-19 Pandemi Değerlendirme Raporu. Türkiye Bilimler Akademisi Yayınları. Ankara.

Türk Tabipleri Birliği Covid-19 İzleme Kurulu. (Eylül, 2020). Covid-19 Pandemisi Altıncı Ay Değerlendirme Raporu.

Türkmen, M., & Özsarı, A. (2020). Covid-19 Salgını ve Spor Sektörüne Etkileri. *International Journal of Sport Culture and Science,* 8(2), 55–67.

Üçüncüoğlu, M., Özdemir, H., & Çakır, V. O. (2021). Covid-19 Pandemisi Sırasında Sporda Kriz Yönetiminin Bir Parçası Olarak Espor Kullanımı. *Gençlik Araştırmaları Dergisi,* 9(Özel Sayı), 81–95.

Varlı, A. (2021). Spor Endüstrisinde Sponsorluk ve Yayın Hakları Ekseninde Covid-19 Depremi. *Sosyal Bilimler Dergisi,* 6(1), 41–57.

Yurtsızoğlu, Z. (2021). Spor Endüstrisinde Bir Krizin Öyküsü (Covid-19). *Sivas Cumhuriyet Üniversitesi Spor Bilimleri Dergisi,* 2(1), 45–50.

Chapter 4

Live Sports Consumption

New Horizons

Aylin Seçkın

Introduction

The sudden and unexpected outbreak of coronavirus pandemic in the world caused a serious crisis in the sports industry since March 2020. Global sports activities almost ceased and sports activities were launched at home using the Internet and virtual networks. Sports competitions were stopped and clubs were closed. Matches and competitions were being cancelled or postponed, disrupting governing bodies, organizers, teams, and athletes – as well as the non-stop live sports content we have come to expect. Owners, broadcasters, and sponsors are trying to navigate the impacts and implications of event cancellations and modifications. Sports production was in total crisis. In the meantime, sports media programmes were in a state of uncertainty. Hence, all these events led to financial losses and economic problems for industry owners, producers, athletes, coaches, and in short, those involved in the sports industry. Many professional leagues across the globe suspended their seasons and hundreds of thousands of jobs were put at risk as public sporting events across the world were cancelled. Many analysts suggest that revenue in the sports industry will be under 74 billion US dollars in 2020 as a result of the crisis, almost half that of the pre-COVID-19 estimates.

COVID-19 has changed the products and process of managing sports and leisure industry, and it seems that the effect of these changes will last long even after the disease is controlled. Predicting and forecasting the sports industry in the post-corona era will play an important role in future planning and helping the industry grow in the future.

This chapter aims to provide extensive discussions related to the impact of the ongoing coronavirus disease (COVID-19) pandemic on global live sports consumption. For decades, TV programmes were as "appointment television." In today's digital landscape, streaming services, on-demand content, and recording technology have largely rendered appointment television obsolete – with one exception, sports. Broadcasters and programming providers try to guess what consumers want from their viewing experience and closely monitor emerging trends to keep fans engaged. With this pandemic, mobile devices now serve as the primary screen for sports leagues. With the isolation reinforcing further the interactive

DOI: 10.4324/9781003253891-4

importance of social platforms, fans engage even more with each other on an entirely new scale while watching live. With channels like Facebook, Twitter, Instagram, TikTok, Clubhouse, and WEchat, fans can share their reactions and commentary with a much wider audience, an atmosphere in a sports bar.

That customization begins with a deep understanding of the viewer (fan) as an individual consumer and puts them in charge of their live sports package. Through the new applications and devices at the viewers' disposal, fans could have the ability to curate their own content – putting them in the seat of the broadcaster. They will continue to watch games played live, in real time. Beyond the real-time nature, live attendance to sports events provides a shared experience to fans bringing them together under team bonding. What are the new technologies promoting newer viewer experiences for live sports events? How can broadcasters deliver these interactive customized experiences? While it is still being perfected, virtual reality is creating an entirely new form of storytelling. It adds an active element to sports consumption. How could broadcasters change, through the right use of technology, the viewer expectations, and sports games watching and sharing experiences? How would spectator sports dynamics change the way fans watch, follow and support their teams?

This chapter aims to present a brief review of the impact of the COVID-19 pandemic on the sports business and on the behaviour of sports fans' habits and preferences. A series of recent papers and research documents published on this issue have been presented to represent the climate of the post-pandemic sports sector. This brief note gauges the ability of the sports business to adapt and adjust to the new normal using social networks and technologies. With the sustained live engagement of sports fans being at the heart of the action, creative tools and contents are continuously innovated to entertain sports fans. Sports startups and applications are now more than ever demanded by sports consumers under the hard times of the pandemic.

This chapter is organized as follows. "The Economics of Professional Team Sports" section discusses the economics of professional team sports and the impact of the pandemic on club finances. The "Live Sports Consumption during the Coronavirus Pandemic" section presents live sports consumption during the coronavirus pandemic. The "Experience Design" section discusses the importance of experience design to engage fans. The "Cryptocurrency/Fan Tokens" section presents briefly the fan tokens and clubs' cryptocurrency projects. The "Conclusion" section concludes the chapter.

The Economics of Professional Team Sports

The commercialization of team sports and rising broadcasting revenues of major European leagues have already widened the gap between the top five European leagues and the periphery. Furthermore, The UEFA Financial Fair Play Regulations (FFP) were established to prevent professional football clubs from spending more than they earn in the pursuit of success, and in doing so not getting into financial problems which might threaten their long-term survival. Some have argued that they were instituted to prevent financial "doping" from outside sources injecting money into smaller clubs[1]. Lacking Sportif success at the European level, many European leagues have been under financial strain for some period. When the COVID-19 outbreak hit the global economy, the vulnerable small and heavily indebted football leagues suffered the most.

Given the size of the global sports sector measured as 471 US billion dollars for the year 2018 Statista, the slowdown meant huge revenue loss for already financially stressed clubs. Many professional leagues across the globe suspended their seasons and hundreds of thousands of jobs were put at risk as public sporting events across the world were cancelled. Analysis suggests that revenue in the sports industry dropped by 74 billion US dollars in 2020 as a result of the crisis, almost half that of the pre-COVID-19 estimates.

Broadcasting revenues, match-day revenues, and sponsorship revenues are the three main sources of revenue of professional team sports. Match-day revenues have certainly suffered the most immediate negative effect. The social distancing measures leading to events getting cancelled or staged behind closed doors have deprived the event organizers of an instant cash flow. Following Caruso, Addesa, and Di Domizio (2019), broadcasting deals represent the main source of revenue for professional team sports. Cancellation of many of those deals meant a great deal of revenue loss for many clubs. Consequently, many teams' financial problems have worsened.

Finally, the global economic crisis slowed down all the other industries and has diminished the value of the future commercial/sponsorship deals and the probability of the renegotiation of the current deals. Considering only the 20 richest European football clubs, Economico has estimated their revenue loss as between 1.31 and 2.94 billion US dollars for the 2019/20 season. The 2020–2021 season starts loss is estimated to be between 0.36 and 1.30 US billion dollars in case of stadiums partly reopened, with no renegotiation of broadcasting deals and a 5%–20% drop in commercial revenue, or 2) between 2.73 and 4.80 US billion dollars in case of games played behind the closed doors, with the renegotiation of broadcasting deals and a 30%–60% drop in commercial revenue.

The financial burden of the professional clubs hurts also athletes' labour market. The reduced revenue stream has forced professional clubs to renegotiate players' contracts. As it has been mentioned by Galardini in his Forbes article, Juventus was the first club – just one month after the COVID-19 outbreak in Italy – to reach an agreement for a temporary pay cut to their salaries for up to four months. However, many professional clubs have had difficulties finding an agreement with their athletes. According to Szymanski, between 10% and 30% of a club's debts and credits reflect unpaid transfer fees. Professional clubs may struggle to pay off these debts, which would further deteriorate the economic and Sportif success of the league itself.

Szymanski (2020) argued that a consolidation fund, financed by future broadcasting deals, may help support clubs' finances. The rationale would be to use the money that professional leagues would be able to generate in the future to save the leagues themselves today. This cross-subsidization scheme may hardly receive players' consent, could help the lower leagues in professional sports, and encourage amateur and grassroots sports.

Another possible solution specific to the European leagues consists of an adoption of the salary cap proposed by Fritz Keller, president of the German Football Association, or a luxury tax proposed by the president of the Union of European Football Associations (UEFA), Aleksander Ceferin. Dietl and Lang (2009) show that a luxury tax increases aggregate salary payments in the league and produces a more balanced league. Moreover, a higher tax rate increases the profits of large-market clubs, whereas the profits of small-market clubs only increase if the tax rate is not set inordinately high.

Eventually, it may be possible to expect a convergence of the win-maximization European leagues to the profit-maximization model of the American Leagues as well as more frequent use of players' trade rather than fees payment in the transfer market. Finally, some argue that the reduced financial resources may lead especially small clubs in the non-American leagues to adopt more autarchic policies to nurture and develop local talent. This would benefit professional clubs in terms of reduction of short-run development expenses of successful youth academies with stronger links with the local communities. However, "the autarky model of sports" for football is not an optimal model within the framework of the global open economy. Although smaller leagues suffer from the lack of financial resources when competing with larger and richer leagues clubs, a complete rejection foreign players cannot be a viable option for their sustainability. Famous foreign players always attract a strong audience and continuous support from the team's fans in smaller leagues in Europe.

Live Sports Consumption during the Coronavirus Pandemic

With the pandemic looking likely to be with us for some time, the entire sports ecosystem will need new ways to deal with threats to financial and business continuity arising from disrupted cash flows, legal and insurance challenges, and possible impacts on longer-term attendances and engagement. Then several questions are needed to be answered. How clubs simultaneously manage fan expectations and minimize operational and financial strain should be viewed as major issues that can be tackled only by specialized crisis management teams and effective public relations campaigns.

On the other hand, how new technologies and communication channels help engage fans during suspended or modified league operations should be thought of and implemented within a clear scheme of marketing operations.

The Tokyo Olympic Games, originally scheduled for July and August 2020, were postponed for the first time in modern sports history. Across the globe, sports of every kind, from grassroots community sports to the professional levels, have been cancelled or rescheduled. This has not, however, deterred sports organizations, teams, and athletes from connecting with fans. Much of this engagement has been through social media, which has had a significant influence on the connection between sports brands, high-profile athletes, and their fans.

A survey has been carried out by FSA (Football Supporters in England and Wales) in the UK during August 3–10, 2020 with 948 football fans by gender. This survey presents the distribution of the anticipated change in football spending after COVID-19 containment measures are eased and sports return in the United Kingdom (UK). When thinking about the amount of money football fans spend on watching the event, once the COVID-19 lockdown has been lifted and sports return, 32% of respondents anticipate that they will spend more money on football compared to before the pandemic.

The desire for live sports attendance throughout the disruption appears to be sustaining as fans adjust to watching their favourite teams play in empty stadiums. According to the Euromonitor study, COVID-19 is expected to have a short-to-medium term effect on consumer choices, preferences, and willingness to spend on non-essentials (Smith, 2020). As a result, sports will be affected not just by restrictions imposed within the industry (cancellations, postponements, social distancing within venues, etc.), but by external factors such as wider changes in consumer spending habits. According to the Euromonitor study, to better understand where sports properties might be more sensitive to reductions in spending, average ticket prices for both team and non-team sports events in key sports markets need to be considered. It is costly to attend sports with respect to monthly disposable income. The desire to spend a larger proportion of their income on tickets by individuals is the result of their willingness to reconsider their decisions to attend a sports event.

As in any crisis, sports industry leaders have to deal with crisis management by responding, recovering, and thriving. Fans and teams should get connected through various individual-based experiences using social media and digital platforms. How might you deliver, and monetize, one-on-one digital engagement between fans and athletes, or fans and clubs? On the other hand, relationships with partners such as broadcasters, sponsors, and vendors must be developed and strengthened. The corona crisis has also led clubs to develop and bring up alternative sporting content and activities to keep fans engaged.

The "new" working model of the remote economy is about the change in consumer habits with regard to consumption and leisure with a no point of return. Several articles published since the beginning of the pandemic reveal to a great extent, how serious the sports sector was hit by this unexpected and sudden shock and how traditional sport is dependent upon participation and fan attendance.

The COVID-19-enforced closure of local venues and facilities combined with imposed social distancing rules forced fans' participation to live sports events to come to a halt. Mastromartino et al. (2020) present the COVID-19-affected fans' participation and new social norms under the pandemic. Professional sport and its competitive leagues, already constrained in cash, suffered further from a lack of financial resources based on match-day revenues and sponsorship deals. Few sports organizations had either the reserves or state support to offset the losses. The UK government provided 300 million pounds in an emergency government bailout programme for some professional sports such as rugby and horse racing, excluding football and cricket (Evans et al., 2020; Horky, 2020; Parnell et al., 2020; Ratten, 2020), which provides evidence of the negative impact of the pandemic on attendance and league revenues.

On the other hand, some events enjoyed unprecedented growth by being "pivoted" to compensate for the need to exclude live fans. For example, the X-Games Aspen, invested heavily in a broadcast-only model with spectacular success, as viewers shifted their attention to social media and digital platforms in record numbers. As it has been mentioned in Skinner and Smith (2021), even double-digit television viewership increases were eclipsed by the triple-digit growth across social and digital media platforms, with 105 million video views across TikTok, Instagram, YouTube, Facebook, Twitter, and Snapchat (+483% year-over-year). According to Kevin Westcott, Deloitte's US Tech, Media, and Telecom leader, since spring 2020, the COVID-19 pandemic has been accelerating structural challenges and trends that have long faced the media and entertainment industry (Deloitte report, 2021). Esports and the online gaming industry are the biggest winners of the new era. The sports broadcasters were severely challenged by the pandemic since their significant long-term and largely fixed rights payments obligations with major leagues created a deep financial loss. In many leagues, the payment schemes have been re-negotiated with adjusted exchange rates. Hutchins et al. (2019) discuss extensively the broadcasting deals of major leagues. It was time to create more digital content with alternative programming to keep fans' excitement alive as Rust (2020) suggests. Furthermore, digital sporting communities have been developed and new social media platforms such as Clubhouse helped fan communities to get in touch on a regular basis and exchange views and ideas about the teams and Sportif performances of various players (Smith, 2020). Dašić et al. (2020) discuss the problems experienced by sponsors and give Adidas as an example of successful companies carefully designed digital promotion of its products on social media platforms to reach a record 90% increase in e-commerce sales.

Experience Design

Actually COVID-19 has just accelerated the structural change in the media and the entertainment industry while creating a convergence in luxury brands, fashion, movie, mobile games, and social media sectors. In the US, the deal of the National Hockey League (NHL) with Amazon Web Services is based to create and design digital-based individual fan experiences. Similarly, we observe the cooperation between the National Basketball Association with Microsoft, the National Football League with Cisco, and Major League Baseball with Google. Player tracking, bespoke insights, super-connectivity, mobile enhancement, platform interaction, social media, at-home experiences, AI and learning algorithms, and immersive technology have become keywords shaping life and leisure in the metaverse era. Sharpe et al. (2020) present how social media proved an ideal fit for a job such as sports and how athletes made brands out of tweets and posts, encouraging personal responses, media co-creation, daily following, and influenced engagement and content monetization. Sato et al.'s (2022) study of Tokyo's divided residents vis-à-vis the pandemic on how polarized are the sports consumers regarding the health risk exposure. Furthermore, the paper concludes that the unafraid followers of the event valued it highly, especially because it offered entertainment at a time when other social activities were curtailed. In their place, fans cooped up at home have been looking for their fix from something other than live sports. Many people turned to esports or other video games and streaming services, as social bakers' data showed big increases in Instagram influencer mentions for Netflix's documentary series "Tiger King" and the game "Animal Crossing: New Horizons" on the Nintendo Switch, compared to similar releases the previous year.

In the sports world, one streaming option reigned supreme: "The Last Dance", a 10-part documentary produced by ESPN and Netflix about Michael Jordan and the Chicago Bulls dynasty. The debut episode on April 19 averaged 6.3 million viewers, making it easily the most-watched documentary in ESPN history and the highest-rated non-live event on the network since 2004.

Cryptocurrency/Fan Tokens

A new digital asset for fans has been developed by Socios.com. Fan tokens or sports currencies are digital assets enabling sports teams, leagues, clubs, associations and players to strengthen fan engagement. It is especially helpful for teams to stay closer to fans who live in a different geography and provide them the opportunities to connect directly with their club. Fan tokens give the supporters of the teams the power to influence decisions of their favourite teams, unlock VIP rewards and access to exclusive promotions, games, and chat and provide them a superfan recognition. Fan tokens are also considered a new revenue opportunity for the teams. This new asset form has been also designed to compensate for the losses associated with the absence of content for which fans and others pay, sport properties turned to novel engagement strategies, often through partnerships emphasizing new forms of content monetization and the commercial exploitation of sports brands. For example, English Premier League club Southampton followed the trend set by a series of other European football clubs, including AC Milan, Swansea City, FC Barcelona, Real Madrid, and Paris Saint-Germain, in entering an agreement with a cryptocurrency firm. Such agreements transcend the traditional composition of sponsorship, incorporating match-day rights deals to engage fans with cryptocurrency opportunities as well as Bitcoin value for VIP fans. It might well have been the pandemic's impact on revenues that encouraged a cadre of big brand European football clubs to precipitously announce their formation of a European Super League, without accounting for the response from fans.

Conclusion

As Rowe (2020) observed, COVID-19 has forced various segments of the sport industry to find ways to adapt and prosper, in some cases abandoning the screams as sweats of live fans. The result has been a proliferation of creative action by the sports organizations, media and broadcasters, towards new ways to engage fans, solicit user-generated interaction, integrate digital content, expand social media, and re-package content as the paper of Majumdar and Naha (2020) emphasizes. Hence, these developments have accelerated and amplified the importance of sports' technological and media axis. Sports delivery might have shifted radically, but whether this shift has embedded into permanency has yet to be seen.

There would be some mid-term challenges in the industry regarding the digital shift. A new form of fan engagement through social media has become a true necessity, requiring a full-fledged comprehensive digital strategy for clubs. Building and leveraging online fanbases will deliver value for sponsors who are focused on maximizing brand exposure and for fans eager to connect with their favourite athletes and teams.

Furthermore, the sponsorship landscape has been disrupted, including the ability to leverage rights, getting the expected rate of investment, and activating partnerships beyond sports. Hence brands need to use creative digital tools vehicles to drive a different degree of engagement from now onwards.

The future of live sports spectatorship has been transformed. Delivering a unique and custom-tailored experience for fans attending live events has now become the best tool to keep the interest in attendance strong across sports.

Of course, the economic impact of the pandemic on financially hit fans will be felt stronger in the ticket sales once the pandemic is over. It is important to estimate sports fans' ticket price elasticity and the preferences' changes towards live attendance of sports games. Increased unemployment and global economic uncertainty have cast doubt on whether the demand for sports will return to previous heights, or whether it will be undermined by fractured confidence and high-ticket prices. Resilience and flexibility are key words to understand and interpret the new world of live sports events and to sustain a financially viable "new normal" sports market equilibrium.

Note

1 They were agreed to in principle in September 2009 by the Financial Control Panel of football's governing body in Europe (Union of European Football Associations – UEFA). The regulations provide for sanctions to be taken against clubs who exceed spending, over several seasons, within a set budgetary framework. Implementation of the regulations took place at the outset of the 2011–12 football season. The severest penalty is disqualification from the European competitions. Other penalties included fines, the withholding of prize money, and player transfer bans.

References

Black, J. (2021). Football is "the most important of the least important things": The Illusion of Sport and COVID-19. *Leisure Sciences, 43*(1–2): 97–103.

Caruso, R.; Addesa, F.; and Di Domizio, M. (2019). The determinants of the TV demand for soccer: Empirical evidence on Italian Serie A for the period 2008–2015. *Journal of Sports Economics, 20*(1): 25–49.

Dašić, D. R.; Tošić, M. Z.; and Deletić, V. (2020). The impact of the COVID-19 pandemic on the advertising and sponsorship industry in sport. *Bizinfo (Blace), 11*(2): 105–116.

Dietl, H., and Lang, M. (2009). The effect of luxury taxes on competitive balance, club profits and social welfare in sports leagues. *International Journal of Sport Finance, 5*(1): 41–51.

Economico. (2020). European football giants will lose up to 30% of the estimated revenue for this season. Retrieved from https://jornaleconomico.sapo.pt/en/news/European-football-giants-will-lose-up-to-30%25-of-theestimated-revenue-for-this-season-591383

Euromonitor. (2020). Coronavirus and sports: Effects on fans and sponsorships. Retrieved from https://go.euromonitor.com/white-paper-sports-2020-coronavirus-and-sports.html

Evans, A. B.; Blackwell, J.; Dolan, P.; Fahlén, J.; Hoekman, R.; Lenneis, V.; McNarry, G.; Smith, M.; and Wilcock, L. (2020). Sport in the face of the COVID-19 pandemic: Towards an agenda for research in the sociology of sport. *European Journal for Sport and Society, 17*(2), 85–95.

Fest, S. (2020). UEFA's Aleksander Ceferin: 'Football with fans will come back very soon'. Retrieved from https://www.theguardian.com/football/2020/may/19/uefas-aleksander-ceferin-football-with-fans-will-come-backvery-soon

Fort, R. (2000). European and North American sports differences. *Scottish Journal of Political Economy, 47*(4): 431–455.

FSA. (2021). Survey: three quarters of fans will be straight back into grounds in August. Retrieved from https://thefsa.org.uk/news/survey-three-quarters-of-fans-will-be-straight-back-into-grounds-in-august/

Galardini, G. (2020). Juventus players agree to salary cuts as soccer clubs face 'existential threat'. Retrieved from https://www.forbes.com/sites/giacomogalardini/2020/03/29/juventus-players-agree-to-salary-cuts-as-soccerclubs-face-existential-threat/#703aba565ab5

Grohmann, K. (2020). German FA chief calls for salary cap to help win over fans after coronavirus pandemic. Retrieved from https://www.independent.co.uk/sport/football/european/bundesliga-salary-capcoronaviruspandemic-a9531456.html

Horky, T. (2020). No sports, no spectators – No media, no money? The importance of spectators and broadcasting for professional sports during COVID-19. *Soccer & Society, 22*(1–2): 96–102.

Hutchins, B.; Li, B.; and Rowe, D. (2019). Over-the-top sport: Live streaming services, changing coverage rights markets and the growth of media sport portals. *Media, Culture & Society, 41*(7): 975–994.

Majumdar, B., and Naha, S. (2020). Live sport during the COVID-19 crisis: Fans as creative broadcasters. *Sport in Society, 23*(7): 1091–1099.

Mastromartino, B.; Ross, W. J.; Wear, H.; and Naraine, M. L. (2020). Thinking outside the 'box': A discussion of sports fans, teams, and the environment in the context of COVID-19. *Sport in Society, 23*(11): 1707–1723.

Parnell, D.; Widdop, P.; Bond, A.; and Wilson, R. (2020). COVID-19, networks and sport. *Managing Sport and Leisure, 27*(1–2), ISSN 2375–0472.

Ratten, V. (2020). Coronavirus disease (COVID-19) and sport entrepreneurship. *International Journal of Entrepreneurial Behavior & Research, 26*(6), 1379–1388.

Rowe, D. (2020). Subjecting pandemic sport to a sociological procedure. *Journal of Sociology, 56*(4): 704–713. https://doi.org/10.1177/1440783320941284

Rust, R. (2020). The future of marketing. *International Journal of Research in Marketing, 37*(1): 15–26. https://doi.org/10.1016/j.ijresmar.2019.08.002

Sato, S.; Oshimi, D.; Bizen, Y.; and Saito, R. (2022). The COVID-19 outbreak and public perceptions of sport events in Japan. *Managing Sport and Leisure, 27*(1–2): 1–6.

Sharpe, S.; Mountifield, C.; and Filo, K. (2020). The social media response from athletes and sport organizations to COVID-19: An altruistic tone. *International Journal of Sport Communication, 13*(3): 474–483. https://doi.org/10.1123/ijsc.2020-0220

Skinner, J., and Smith, A. C. T. (2021). Introduction: sport and COVID-19: Impacts and challenges for the future (Volume 1), *European Sport Management Quarterly, 21*(3): 323–332.

Smith, R. W. (2020). A post-COVID-19 lifestyle sport research agenda: Communication, risk, and organizational challenges, *International Journal of Sport Communication, 13*(3): 352–360. https://journals.humankinetics.com/view/journals/ijsc/13/3/article-p352.xml

Statista. (2020). Sports & Fitness. Statistics and Market Data on Sports & Fitness. Retrieved from https://www.statista.com/markets/409/topic/442/sports-fitness

Szymanski, S. (2020). Covid-19 and football club insolvency, paper presented at Reading Online Sport Economics Seminars (ROSES), April 17th, 2020. Retrieved from https://www.soccernomics-agency.com/?p=1670

Westcott, K. (2021). 2021 media and entertainment industry outlook. Retrieved from https://www2.deloitte.com/us/en/pages/technology-media-and-telecommunications/articles/media-and-entertainment-industry-outlook-trends.html

Chapter 5

COVID-19 and Youth Sports

Psychological, Developmental and Economic Impacts

Pero Duygu Dumangöz

Introduction

Coronavirus is a large family of viruses with phenotypic and genotypic diversity that cause many diseases from the common cold to more dangerous diseases such as Middle East Respiratory Syndrome (MERS) and Severe Acute Respiratory Syndrome (SARS) (T.R. Ministry of Health, 2020). The new type of coronavirus, encoded as COVID-19, usually causes diseases in the respiratory and gastrointestinal systems in humans. The clinical picture in adults can range from the common cold to bronchitis, pneumonia, severe acute respiratory distress syndrome (ARDS), and multi-organ failure resulting in death (Türkmen & Özsarı, 2020).

Tyrell and Bynoe first identified the coronavirus in 1966 when they studied the viruses that cause flu symptoms. They were called the coronavirus because of their appearance. Its name comes from the Latin word "corona" meaning crown. Coronaviruses are divided into alpha, beta, gamma, and delta subgroups. Alpha and beta coronaviruses are derived from mammals, while beta, gamma, and delta are derived from pigs and birds. There are seven subtypes of the coronavirus that can infect humans. Beta coronavirus can cause various diseases and death, while alpha coronavirus causes infection with an asymptomatic infection and mild symptoms. SARSCov2 belongs to the beta coronavirus of lineage B and is similar to the SARS-Cov virus (Danilović, 2020; Velavan, 2020).

When a person infected with COVID-19 coughs or sneezes, it can easily be transmitted to other people with droplets suspended in the air, as well as by contact with contaminated objects or surfaces. The disease spreads faster at close range. In order to prevent this, measures to follow social distancing were at the forefront of the implemented public health protection policies (Kara, 2020).

COVID-19, which spread to countries around the world, posed a global threat, and as a result, the World Health Organization (WHO) declared it a pandemic on March 11, 2020 (Australian Institute of Sport, 2020).

The World Health Organization has recommended maintaining interpersonal social distancing and reducing interaction as much as possible in order to minimize the risk of transmission of the disease. With these measures, the epidemic has emerged as an important obstacle especially for youth sports. In line with

DOI: 10.4324/9781003253891-5

the measures taken, sportpersons could not participate in training sessions, and almost all of the individual and team competitions were canceled. The Tokyo Olympic Games, which is supposed to be the biggest sports event, and which was planned to take place on March 24, 2020, was postponed to July 23, 2021, thus leaving the sports world in a situation it never knew before. Wimbledon Tennis Tournament, one of the four Grand Slam Tournaments, was canceled for the first time in its history. When allowed again, the games were in most cases described as "ghost games", as the stands were empty and the enthusiastic, encouraging pulse of the fans faded. For the first time since the Second World War, all competitions in which professional athletes would participate were either suspended or canceled.

Due to the policies designed by states to take preventive measures for public health, there have been sudden pauses and changes in youth sports activities all over the world. In particular, the cancelation or restriction of schools and sports activities has affected young people, whose development processes continue, in physical, mental, and psychosocial dimensions. For this reason, while designing policies to protect public health, it has become an important necessity to design sports policies that will significantly increase participation in sports during the COVID-19 process.

Considering the spread rate and course of the epidemic worldwide, there are significant uncertainties about the future of youth sports. If we accept this period as a stagnation period in this respect, we will consider programs that can be developed to increase participation and access to physical activity and decrease participation costs, by making important studies on factors such as the cost of participation and access to participation, which were obstacles for the participants of youth sports before the COVID-19 epidemic period or opportunities to invest in organizations arise. This allows us to consider the economic dimensions of youth sports.

The revenues of the youth sports industry, which is an important sector for countries in economic terms, show a significant decrease, and youth sports tourism takes its share of this situation. Loss of sponsorship, tournaments played without spectators, important organizations that have been invested but canceled, and canceled seasons are just some of the problems the youth sports industry has faced during the COVID-19 process.

As it is known, participation in youth sports provides multi-faceted developmental and psychological benefits to young people. However, the situation we are in due to the COVID-19 epidemic has led to an increase in negative situations such as anxiety, stress, depression, and health problems due to inactivity among the participants of youth sports. However, we can say that the consequences of inactivity are another pandemic that has negative effects on human life. In addition, it has been demonstrated by scientific data that wearing a mask within the framework of the precautions taken during sports activities increases the physiological load on athletes. When it is considered in the economic dimension, studies have shown that the children of families with low income are more affected by these negative situations. In line with these outputs, the importance of innovation studies in the way of building healthy societies, increasing performance in youth sports and contributing to them, and also in sports tourism has been understood once again.

COVID-19, which we define as a global health crisis, has affected almost all sectors around the world. According to the statistics recorded to date (July 11, 2021), this crisis, which resulted in 186.240.393 cases and 4.027.861 deaths, continues to expand and develop with different variants (Kelly et al., 2020; World Health Organization, 2021). These variants were seen as alpha variants in 178 countries, Beta variants in 123 countries, Gamma variants in 75 countries, and delta variants in 111 countries (World Health Organization, 2021).

As part of the fight against COVID-19, all countries have taken various protective measures nationally and regionally. Social distancing and self-isolation practices that lead individuals to limit their social interactions are at the forefront of these measures. All these measures and government policies developed against the COVID-19 pandemic have put youth sports, as well as international sports activities, into an impromptu pause (Kelly et al., 2020). Humanity has come face to face with COVID-19, which has a significant impact on all aspects of life all over the world (Watson & Koontz, 2020).

Youth Sports

If we need to define the concept of youth from a sociological perspective, it is a definition constructed in status or social dimension. It has three different uses. The first of these covers the stage between infancy and adulthood, the second is a preferred concept against adolescence, and the third is the concept used to understand the emotional and social problems allegedly brought about by growing up in an industrial society. The third definition is not used much today (Marshall, 2009). The terms adolescence and youth are often used interchangeably. However, adolescence is a special developmental period in which the individual experiences physiological and psychological changes; youth refers to a period with a wider upper age limit, including adolescence (Koç, 2004).

Sports enable individuals to socialize, mediate to prove themselves and gain a place in peer groups, give self-confidence, inhibit stress and violent tendencies by creating psychological relief in the individual, reinforce the feelings of feeling physically beautiful, healthy and fit, strengthen friendship ties, and act together. It is a versatile therapy resource that contributes positively to the feelings of being able to share and being able to share (Türker, 2020).

It is known that participation in sports has many positive effects on young people. These are, in summary, as follows:

- It uncovers and develops motor and sport-specific skills.
- It improves health, provides well-being, and promotes physical well-being.
- It increases the sense of self-confidence, self-esteem, and positive self-image.

- It develops teamwork and team spirit.
- It provides a sense of responsibility and disciplined work (Coakley, 2020).

It is very difficult for young people to reach social and professional skills during the periods when schools are closed, child and youth work is prohibited, meeting with peer groups is prohibited and they are removed from public spaces. Youth, which is a shorter stage than other stages of life, is a very important stage for personal development (Voigts, 2021).

Regular participation in sports will make an important contribution to the desired development of character formation in young people. Young people participate in a wide variety of social activities. These activities are extracurricular activities such as various hobby programs, dance groups, instrument lessons, and sports. Among them, sport is the most popular activity for young people in most countries.

Dynamic Elements for Sports Development in Youth

Studies in the field of sports psychology and development talk about three basic dynamics in the provision of sports development. What are these? Who? Where? Responding to their questions are individual participation, quality social interactions, and appropriate organizational structures.

Individual Participation: Youth sports have a meaning and content beyond organized sports activities. Its content includes a wide variety of activities beyond fully planned workouts or competitions. During the COVID-19 pandemic, young people were interrupted from participating in organized sports activities or training, as well as in participating in various activities when evaluated in the context of youth sports. Disruption of such activities has the potential to affect developmentally, especially young people. Offering a model for the sports development of young people, the Sports Participation Development Model (DMPS) makes seven recommendations for promoting continuous participation and personal development in sports as well as performance development for children and youth (Côté & Vierimaa, 2014). In addition, this model offers two alternatives that will affect professionalization in sports for children. The first of these is early diversification. It refers to the participation of children in multi-sport activities. For example, in line with the main purposes of summer sports schools, children's participation in more than one sporting activity within a program has important consequences for their sports development. The second is early specialization. It refers to participation in trainings and competitions specific to any sports branch (Zibung & Conzelmann, 2013). Therefore, long-term interruption of existing sports activities will adversely affect youth sports development and performance.

Although still in its infancy, virtual teaching platforms in sports applications have been the most effective and widespread application used in the COVID-19 process. Thanks to the virtual tools that emerged as an alternative due to the limited access to traditional training, young people were encouraged to participate in sports in different environments (garden of their house, bedroom, living room, etc.) (Kelly et al., 2020).

Quality Social Interactions: Sport is a social phenomenon. This social phenomenon requires the interaction of all the components it contains with each other. With people isolating themselves in their homes and distance measures to stay safe, COVID-19 seems to have targeted this interaction. Coaches, parents, and athletes are the most important components of this interaction.

During the COVID-19 process, there have been families who have been constantly with them physically, who directed and followed the physical activities of young people and were worried about not being affected by the process. Therefore, in this process, a lot of information can be obtained from the studies on the parent-child relationship. In most geographies, parents represent not only consumers of youth sports but also the volunteer workforce, such as coaching, refereeing, and making the activity fun (Trussel, 2016). Therefore, the participation of parents in youth sports is also an important element.

One of the important components of sports environments is trainers. They had to adapt quickly to all the changes brought about by the COVID-19 pandemic (Kelly et al., 2020). The coaches, whose sports branch was available to a certain extent, continued to work with their athletes in online sessions. However, the coaches of branches such as tennis, basketball, and volleyball that require physical unity and a suitable environment for sports have not been able to provide quality social interaction with their athletes. They were only able to train part of the training (such as fitness) online.

Another type of interaction affected by the pandemic process is between the athlete and their peers. Interaction with peers, which is an important motivational support for participation in sports, has been seriously damaged. The quality of peer interaction was affected by the interruption of sports activities (Kelly et al., 2020).

Supporting all kinds of innovative studies in order to continue or increase the quality of all these interactions in the same way in the COVID-19 pandemic is an important issue for the existence of youth sports.

Appropriate Organizational Structures: Sports environments can have an impact on the sports development of individuals. The environments where youth sports were organized before COVID-19 were moved to more micro-environments (home areas, garden of the house, etc.) after the pandemic. This change caused many dynamics to change in youth sports. Participation in sports activities during the pandemic seems to have increased due to the online presence of sports environments. Of course, one of the important conditions of online access is the socio-economic level and/or geographical location of the families. This process can create inequalities among consumers of youth sports (Kelly et al., 2020).

It has been determined that elite, semi-elite, or recreational athletes are affected both physically and mentally due to the uncertainty of the pandemic, cancelation of leagues, economic concerns, change/decrease in training routines (Andreato et al., 2020; Håkansson et al., 2021; Mehrsafar et al., 2020; Yüksel, 2021). It has been reported that taking a break from the leagues for a while and then restarting them in an accelerated manner puts pressure on the athletes and slows down their physical and mental recovery (Håkansson et al., 2020).

During the youth period, which is known as the most active and most important period of human life, the existence of a global epidemic struggle and how and at what level the youth and youth sports were affected by the epidemic, as a result of the measures taken within the scope of this struggle, has been an important research topic.

The negative effects of the pandemic have been so far-reaching that many youth associations and sports organizations have closed their doors, the psychosocial effects of COVID-19 caused by immediate and long-term factors have affected the mental health and socialization abilities of young people, as well as the absence of leisure activities and social restrictions. It has been shown to have a disproportionate effect on children and young people.

Various studies show that social distancing measures created in the face of the COVID-19 pandemic have significant effects on young people. These studies highlight challenges related to mental health, less physical activity, and a sedentary lifestyle. We can basically consider the effects of the COVID-19 crisis in the context of youth sports in three different dimensions. These are psychological, developmental, and economic effects. Let us now explain these effects in turn.

Psychological Effects of COVID-19

It would be appropriate to evaluate the psychological effects of COVID-19 on youth sports from the perspective of parents and athletes. For most families, sport is an important activity. Moreover, families who accept sports as a way of life show both economic and social sacrifices in this regard. Sports is an important parent investment for their children in line with a plan that centers on sports. All kinds of activities in family planning (such as vacations, travel plans, meetings, and other social events) are created according to the sports calendar (Sanderson & Brown, 2020).

With the increase and spread of youth sports, a child from almost every family participates in these activities and spends his/her time with sports after school. Maybe this is a sacrifice they show voluntarily for a family that comes together only in the evenings, no matter how hard it is.

During the COVID-19 process, this order was suddenly interrupted. Sports activities were suspended for a long time. Postponing or canceling sports seasons has created grief, stress, frustration, and panic in young athletes. Within the framework of public health protection measures, athletes and their parents found themselves in an unfamiliar situation. It hasn't been easy for families. This created a significant gap for everyone involved in youth sports. After a certain period of time, it became imperative to find ways out in the sports sector, as in all sectors. The importance of the situation for young people is clear given that sport fulfills important social functions and promotes values such as social inclusion, integration, harmony and mutual respect and understanding, solidarity, diversity, equality, and gender equality, among others (European Parliament, 2021).

Limitation of physical space, being away from school, friends and social environments, not being able to travel outside and uncertainties in many subjects cause feelings such as anger, loneliness, doubt, loss of social confidence, sadness, frustration, anxiety, hopelessness, and stress in the houses we have closed (Cao et al., 2020). In addition, some parents' loss of work and related income may increase the problems experienced at home and make the process of staying at home difficult for all family members (Günay, 2020).

In the compulsion to stay at home, especially children can act impulsively and egocentrically, not fully comprehending the danger of the epidemic and wanting to meet their needs for play and entertainment. This situation can force their parents physically and mentally (Günay, 2020).

Particularly, parents whose work lives have been affected by the pandemic are struggling to keep the family economy alive, while the inability to allocate a budget for their children's sports activities may push them to a sense of guilt. The same is true for children. Expecting financial support from their parents for sports activities while their parents are in an economic struggle may cause their children to feel guilty (Sanderson & Brown, 2020). This is an important psychological struggle for both athletes and their families. In order to get through the process more easily, it will be beneficial to get support from a sports psychologist.

The reactions of young people, who are in a sensitive period in terms of development, to the epidemic process can be more realistic than children. The deadly results and many unknown features of the newly emerging and rapidly spreading COVID-19 have created a sense of fear, curiosity, and anxiety in young people. In a study conducted on university students living in Hubei Province, China, it was revealed that 24.9% of young people were worried about the COVID-19 outbreak (Cao et al., 2020).

For children aged 6–17 years, 60 minutes of physical activity per day is recommended by the World Health Organization (WHO). The implementation of a regular and continuous exercise program during the pandemic process can reduce the negative physiological and psychological effects of staying at home (Günay, 2020). So what is physical activity? The World Health Organization defines physical activity as any movement of the body that uses the musculoskeletal system and requires energy expenditure. Physical activity also includes activities done while at work, playing games, doing chores, traveling, and performing leisure activities. The terms physical activity and exercise have different meanings. Exercise belongs to a subgroup of physical activities and refers to planned, structured, repetitive training aimed at improving or maintaining one or more components of fitness (World Health Organization). Why is it necessary to participate in physical activity for young people during the pandemic period? Physical activity strengthens the immune system and reduces inflammation and infection. It reduces the risk of chronic diseases such as cardiovascular disease and diabetes, which increases the chances of developing COVID-19. It has also been stated that physical activity is a good way to reduce symptoms of stress, anxiety, and depression (Danilović, 2020).

For young people who put sports at the center of their lives, make significant sacrifices for their athlete identity, and hope to receive an athletic scholarship from the university, stress and other mental and psychological health problems often arise with the suspension of sports activities and sports organizations (Jewett et al., 2019).

The closure of sports centers and the long-term confinement to home mean such a sudden change in the life routines of children and young people, and the changes in their emotional states (fear of contagion, death of loved ones, decrease in the purchasing power of the family) in the process.

The results of Guan et al.'s (2020) studies, which refer to 15 different countries, show that children are less physically active, sit more, and sleep worse at school and club closures than before the pandemic. In principle, the findings and trends suggest that major restrictions on the range of sports and exercise offered will have a lasting negative impact on children, adolescents, and their activity behaviors.

During lockdown, many working parents have had to work from their homes. Carrying out academic duties from home, trying to run and manage chores with phone traffic, as well as meeting the needs of children, taking care of them (without the help of a caregiver), and taking care of household chores create a situation that most parents find it difficult to cope with. The difficulty of living together in small or crowded houses is increasing (Castillo & Velasco, 2020). Panic feelings of parents can negatively affect the psychology of young people (Türker, 2020).

Eliminating the negative aspects of staying at home during the pandemic process and turning the process into an opportunity is one of the things that needs to be done. So what can be done?

- Young people can discover and develop their talents.
- You can spend quality time with family members, participate in online exercise programs, play home-based games, cook meals or engage in activities such as reading a book or watching a movie.
- Various home activities can be planned to strengthen family ties.
- Young people can take on some responsibilities at home.

In this process, it is seen that some children share with their parents and chat, do sports and various activities together. The sharing of family members and the increase in effective communication can increase the child's and young people's sense of trust and increase their loyalty to family members (Günay, 2020).

Developmental Impacts of COVID-19

Children participating in sports usually participate once or twice a week in structured training and games at different levels, which will support their full development. Children who take part in high school or club teams train more frequently. These children, who usually plan a professional sports career for themselves, focus on developing their sports-specific skills with intense effort. Monitoring the development of athletes and preparing training programs suitable for their development is an important issue for coaches (Sanderson & Brown, 2020).

It has been very difficult to monitor the development of children who are locked in their homes due to the cancelation of competitions, the postponement of large organizations, and the closure of most sports environments for training due to COVID-19. Of course, the children were able to manage, albeit partially, on their own or under the supervision of their parents. However, families facing economic difficulties during the pandemic may have difficulties in providing this opportunity to their children (Sanderson & Brown, 2020).

In addition, young people who could not participate in sports activities regularly experienced the negative effects of this in the developmental dimension when the process of participation in sports began. This long break in sports activities has caused some young people to quit sports altogether.

The obligation to stay home during the pandemic period threatens the health of young people and children. We can explain these threat elements as follows; This period of confinement, especially in confined and narrow spaces, can lead to a higher risk of vitamin D deficiency, mental health problems, and myopia. Although children may appear less susceptible to COVID-19, maintaining or increasing their level of physical activity can reduce the risk of respiratory infections. Benefits that help children cope with life-changing conditions, such as the role of physical activity in building resilience, may be compromised. The interactive effects of each movement behavior may be more pronounced – for example, children who are less active and spend more screen time are likely to have worse sleep. If negative behavioral adaptations, such as less activity, become the new normal, there may be potential longer-term health and economic consequences (Guan et al., 2021). In addition to all these, negative effects such as slowing down of daily life, lack of physical activity, and living under constant stress have also led to the formation of nutritional disorders. The nutritional habits of young people, who are the consumers of youth sports, are very important for their development and performance.

The use of digital methods has increased in many areas during the pandemic process. In order to ensure the continuity of the physical condition and skill development of their athletes, most coaches have posted their videos on online platforms. There were coaches who gave live lessons privately. Especially in the early stages of the pandemic, local governments have published videos to ensure that individuals stay healthy during their stay at home using digital methods including sports and physical activity (Atalı et al., 2020). However, due to economic reasons or technological deprivation, not every athlete could benefit from these digital opportunities. In all these unequal conditions, the developmental gap between athletes began to widen.

Especially young people who are actively involved in sports have experienced a serious decrease in their physical activities with the cancelation of education and sports activities and they have faced some mental health problems (Watson & Koontz, 2020). This sudden decrease in physical activity can lead to decreased blood circulation and subsequent coronary perfusion (Thompson, 2007). National organizations, in order to prevent individuals from experiencing cardiovascular problems, walking, individual sports, etc., within the rules. emphasized the importance of doing activities (Lippi et al., 2020).

Within the scope of public health measures, the long-term vacation from educational institutions and home isolation can cause problems such as excessive spending time on the internet, boredom, watching TV for a long time, overeating, and an increase in weight gain. The lack of activity caused by the epidemic process can negatively affect young people and all individuals mentally and physically. The results of the researches indicate that physical activity is important in the protection and development of health (Günay, 2020).

Regular exercises during childhood and youth affect a person's whole life. It is important to increase the time that children will provide exercise and physical mobility and stay active by adjusting them well. Planning the exercises and finding risk-free areas to do or transforming the existing areas and encouraging the child to physical activity are important in terms of health, but it imposes a great responsibility on the parents first and then on the coaches, teachers, sports scientists, and doctors (Çelik & Yenal, 2020).

Involving young people who stay at home in exercise programs that they can do on their own or through online platforms will help them overcome the pandemic process both physically and psychologically. However, it would be more beneficial if these programs contain more than one component. Just moving is not enough. Balance exercises, coordination development, resistance, and aerobic exercises can be included in the program (Türker, 2020).

Aerobic exercises are especially recommended during the pandemic process. Aerobic exercises are defined as exercise that elicits low, moderate, or high cardiovascular tension. In-home exercise programs can be planned and bodyweight exercise, dance-based exercise, and game activities can be applied, including aerobic exercise using stationary bikes or treadmills (Bingöl et al., 2020). It will be beneficial for young people in the developmental age to have check-ups during the quarantine period by getting support from sports doctors.

Due to all the developmental effects listed above, if an appropriate regeneration program specific to the sports branch cannot be provided after returning to sports, the performance of the athlete will decrease and the risk of injury (ligament tear, muscle injury) will probably increase.

Economic Impacts of COVID-19

Sports organizations attract visitors from all over the country and are an income potential for facilities, accommodation sector, and retailers. Athletes, parents, spectators, and sportspeople contribute to the development of the local economy as they spend money to meet their needs in the region where the sports organization is held. Countries or regions that have invested in and hosted sports events canceled due to COVID-19 have suffered from economic difficulties (Sanderson & Brown, 2020).

Sports organizations postponed to a later date or canceled caused the closure of sports facilities and the change of training programs, competitions, and exercise courses. With the rapid spread of the epidemic, as of April 2020, many professional sports branches and sports clubs have declared that they need support to get rid of bankruptcy (Aygün, 2021). In the research conducted by Sports Value, it has been stated that the 1-year movement of the sports market globally is 756 billion dollars. Due to the COVID -19 pandemic, not just professional sports; travel, tourism, transfer service, media, food, and accommodation service sectors, as well as many occupational groups in marketing and sports services related to sports events (Sports Value, 2020).

The removal of restrictions on sports has not completely eliminated this economic problem experienced by the sports industry. An example of this is the Olympic Games held in Tokyo. The Olympic Games started on July 23, but spectator participation was not allowed. Considering that serious investments have been made in such a large and important organization, the absence of an audience has been a significant economic loss for the region.

Due to COVID-19, sponsors experienced some difficulties. Small or big brands have withdrawn from sponsorship due to the crisis, which has increased the participation fees of athletes. The children of the families who could not afford these increased wages had to withdraw from the stage.

Families who have mobilized all their resources for their athletes' children and planned their lives according to their children's sports career are perhaps the most affected by this situation. Considering the families who left small settlements and reorganized in big cities so that their children could train with better opportunities, the economic dimension of this situation will be better understood. For example, today, while the world-famous tennis player Maria Yuryevna Sharapova was living in Russia, in a coastal town of Suci, she went to America at the age of 7, complying with the decision of her father. Here, many sources write that under difficult conditions, her father enrolled his daughter in Nick Bollettieri Tennis Academy with all the money he earned and drew a sports career for his daughter. What if COVID-19 had emerged around the time Sharapova's career began? Will all of his father's financial and moral sacrifices be rewarded? Would we know Sharapova today?

This sudden pause in sports activities during the pandemic period provides an important opportunity to evaluate and invest in all kinds of programs and organizations that will be developed not only to ensure the return of young people to youth sports but also to increase access to physical activity and sports that all children need. (Watson & Koontz, 2020).

The economic contraction of sports due to the COVID-19 pandemic has led sports institutions and organizations to seek new ones. As a result of this search, innovative solutions were sought in areas such as sports media, sports tourism, sports marketing, and sports consumption. The shrinking economic situation allows the resumption of sports activities within the scope of protective measures of national/international federations and clubs under the leadership of sports institutions and organizations. The resumption of sports activities will be effective in planning new regulations by considering the spread rate and characteristics of the epidemic by health and sports organizations (Aygün, 2021). In addition, the measures to be taken during the COVID-19 process, which affects many sectors, were decided as follows as a result of the Council of the European Union and the council numbered 8926/20 held with the representatives of the European Union member states;

- Considering that people who are interested in indoor, contact, and team sports cannot continue playing sports due to social distancing, focus should be placed on their ability to continue activities.
- Sports sector should be supported.
- Motivation should be provided for individuals to act.
- Inter-sectoral cooperation should be ensured.
- Erasmus+, etc., where projects and student exchanges are carried out at the national and international levels. programs and supports for the sports sector should be encouraged.
- National sports organizations should be updated according to the international sports calendar.
- It should be ensured that individuals are active through digital methods (Council of the European Union, 2020).

Also, the impact of the pandemic on semi-professional, grassroots, and leisure activities has been disastrous and as a result, many sports clubs face the problem of existence and continuity as they operate non-profit. The work of these clubs is mostly voluntary and therefore operates without reserve funding (European Parliament, 2021). Also, some sports, minor clubs, lower leagues, and grassroots activities are highly volatile, particularly due to their financial dependence on minor sponsors or athlete quotas. This development is very worrying because amateur sports are experiencing financial difficulties in continuing their activities. Amateur sports are a springboard and bridge to professional sports, as small sports clubs contribute significantly to the development of young athletes working mainly on a voluntary basis (European Parliament, 2021).

Because of all these effects expressed in this section, it has become very important to encourage the participation of young people in physical activity and sports.

The constraints that we are not accustomed to were brought in by the COVID-19 epidemic have caused us to better understand the ongoing situation of disadvantaged individuals, especially those with disabilities or chronic diseases. There are more than 1 billion people with disabilities worldwide. Among them, almost 200 million disabled people face serious difficulties while living their lives (World Health Organization, 2011b).

Many studies focus on the importance of exercise and physical practices for disadvantaged individuals. Participation in exercise, sports and physical activities, and youth sports are very effective especially for the health, socialization, and integration of disabled youth (Driscoll et al., 2019). Restrictions can mean extra difficulty for people with disabilities who have a habit of doing all this on a regular basis. In this process, they need the attention of their parents and more physical support for exercises that can be done at home. The cooperation to be established between parents and sports experts during the pandemic period will prevent disabled individuals from being inactive, even if it is online (Bingöl et al., 2020).

It may be difficult for people with disabilities to comply with some personal care measures or some other protective measures that must be followed for everyone during the COVID-19 period (World Health Organization, 2020). Personal cleanliness and cleanliness of the place of residence; may not be possible due to physical impairments or interrupted services. Disabled people, who can survive with the support of other people in many issues, cannot apply the social distance rule and it is difficult to isolate themselves from others comprehensively (Kara, 2020).

Digitalization Era in Sports during the COVID-19

During the COVID-19 process, digitalization has gained speed in the sports sector, as it is in almost every sector. For example, technology-based online solutions have started to be produced in the fitness sector and performance sports.

Some sports seem to be benefiting from the COVID-19 crisis, especially all forms of esports that are growing in popularity almost everywhere. There is also a lot of interest in converting live sports into digital versions. An interesting example could be related to sailing, a sport that reacted very quickly to COVID-19 and turned the sailing championship into a digital competition with a large number of users (Horky, 2021). In any case, the entire sports system will need new ways to deal with emerging threats to financial and business continuity, for example.

Esports, which has just begun to develop in many countries, has attracted more attention among young people during the pandemic process. Esports is the name given to video games played professionally in a competitive environment (Akgöl, 2019). When we look today, we see that the International Esports Federation (IeSF) has a national federation in 61 countries. With millions of athletes and billions of viewers, esports has a large community. Games played with technological devices such as desks and laptops, smartphones, and game consoles create a safe sports environment for the pandemic process since they do not require physical contact. The reason why it spread so quickly during the epidemic period may be due to this situation (Türkmen & Özsarı, 2020).

While moving toward digitalization in sports, some problems related to access are emerging. Young people who cannot access e-learning technologies and distance learning opportunities, which are rapidly spreading during the pandemic period, and who study in schools in disadvantaged and rural areas, are adversely affected by this situation. According to the results of a study, 89% of young people in Africa do not have a computer that they can access at home, and 82% of them do not have internet access (Chauke & Chinyakata, 2020).

It is possible to foresee that humanity will become more digital both personally and socially in this period when humanity is starting to open the door to a digital world. Therefore, supporting and developing virtual environments, software, and innovation projects will benefit humanity in the future.

Back to Sports and Physical Activity Recommendations for Youth

There is no sport left unaffected by the COVID-19 pandemic. It is possible to say that youth sports have taken a hard and deep blow. A concerted effort is needed to get everything back on track within the context of youth sports. Considering the risk of transmission of COVID-19, a strategy should be developed that will allow athletes to train in a controlled environment with the sports movement globally (Begović, 2020). In these moments of quarantine, one of the biggest concerns for many parents, coaches, and professionals associated with athletes, especially young athletes, is that they are not motivated to continue training. In order to increase the motivation of young athletes, we can list the important points to be avoided as follows (Carrasquillo, 2020):

Do not think that the quarantine process is a factor that reduces performance! For young people, there can be positive and negative moments in sports as well as in all areas of life. Quarantine is on the non-positive side. Many athletes have had to change their training routines and adapt to the new situation. But the important thing is that their coaches and parents continue to support them in all circumstances. During the quarantine period, any expression, gesture or action that may discourage young people and make them feel that their sports training is hindered should be avoided.

Don't let him compare his/her athletic performance with his/her latest performance! The measurement of the values of the athletes by their performance is unfortunately an existing perception situation. If successful, it can be considered as "good", otherwise as "bad". We must support young people to gain self-esteem and convince them that the results they achieve are independent of their egos.

Set personal goals! For young people, realistic goals should be set. There may be limitations, fears, and new stressors in the quarantine process, but the important thing here is to determine the right methods. In order to maintain or increase the motivation of young people, it is very important that the goals set seem achievable to them and that they believe in it. It is necessary to ensure that the athlete is always aware of his abilities and capacity. They should know that their abilities are as important as the environmental factors that can affect them in achieving the set goals.

Do not give negative feedback! Young athletes who are psychologically sensitive during quarantine place more value on positive and encouraging comments. Of course, the coach should correct the mistake, but it will be useful to focus more on the truth of the athletes during this period and encourage them.

Stop the exercises from being monotonous! It is important that each of the trainings is planned very well and that measurable data is obtained. Improvements should be tracked and recorded. Monotonous training will wear out the athletes and cause a significant decrease in motivation.

Make them believe they can succeed! The quarantine period is a great opportunity for young people to do self-assessment. It would be wrong to associate sporting success with a victory that can only be achieved from competition. Small steps are needed for success and young people must be made to understand this.

Remind them often that they are a team! In team sports, there are individuals who fight together for the same goal. This diversity within the team reveals different needs. It is important that the coach recognizes, respects, and meets the needs of young people. Group harmony should be ensured and team spirit should be developed. Trying to develop the common aspects of each young person in the team and not focusing on differences will help increase group motivation.

Do not be overly insistent on participating in sports! The quarantine period should not be seen pessimistically as an obstacle to the holistic development of new sports generations. It should be the duty of parents and coaches to increase their courage during the quarantine period, which is a very difficult struggle for young people. Within the scope of public health protection measures, young people who continue their academic education online at home may have difficulty participating in sports activities. Moreover, if they are not fully devoted to sports, this is inevitable. In order to prevent the feeling of burnout in young people, it is necessary not to insist on their participation in sports activities.

Physical activity for children and youth aged 5–17 includes games, sports, outings, recreational activities, physical education or planned exercise as part of family, school, or community activities. The WHO makes the following recommendations to improve cardiorespiratory and muscle function and bone health and reduce the risk of Chronic Non-Communicable Diseases:

- Children and adolescents aged 5–17 years should do at least 60 minutes of moderate to vigorous-intensity physical activity per day.
- More than 60 minutes of physical activity per day will provide even greater health benefits.
- Daily physical activity should be mostly aerobic. It is recommended to include strength exercises that strengthen muscles and bones at least three times a week.

These recommendations apply to all healthy children between the ages of 5 and 17 unless there are other health problems that recommend otherwise in this age group (World Health Organization, 2011a).

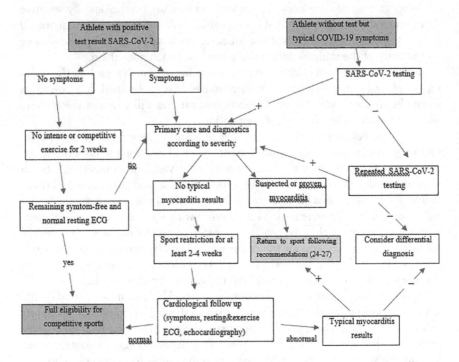

Figure 5.1 Suggested algorithm for returning to sports of an athlete with a positive SARS-CoV-2 test result or typical COVID-19 symptoms.
Source: Schellhorn et al., 2020.

Athletes who have been confirmed to have COVID-19 can resume training once their symptoms have completely disappeared and their energy levels have returned to normal. The 72 hours after the disappearance of the disease symptoms are important. This period should be spent in isolation at home. Athletes in this process can do low-intensity indoor training at home. For these trainings, a fitness trainer or exercise physiologist can be provided to guide the athlete remotely. They can gradually return to training after the process is complete (Brett & İrfan, 2020).

It is known that viral replication can be increased during vigorous activity, which may lead to greater structural damage to heart tissue. Therefore, as suggested in Figure 5.1, it is recommended that an athlete diagnosed with COVID-19 but without any symptoms should avoid intense training or competition-like exercise for at least two weeks. After this period, if there are no symptoms and abnormalities in the resting ECG (electrocardiogram), returning to sports may be recommended (Schellhorn et al., 2020).

In any case of myocarditis, it is recommended that sport be strictly prohibited for a period of at least 3–6 months, based on animal data suggesting a virulence-enhancing effect of exercise (Maron et al., 2015; Pelliccia, 2005). Return to training and competition is appropriate if left ventricular function and cardiac dimensions have returned to normal, Holter ECG (electrocardiogram) monitoring and exercise testing do not have clinically significant arrhythmias, and serum markers of inflammation and heart failure are present. In symptomatic COVID-19 positive athletes without evidence of diagnostic myocarditis, a comprehensive medical examination (physical examination, rest and exercise EKG, and echocardiography) should be performed before resuming sports activities, following at least 2–4 weeks of sports restriction. In the absence of abnormal results, it will be possible to return to sports (Schellhorn et al., 2020).

References

Akgöl, O. (2019). Spor endüstrisi ve dijitalleşme: Türkiye' de espor yapılanması üzerine bir inceleme. *TRTakademi, 4*(8), 206–225.

Andreato, L. V., Coimbra, D. R., & Andrade, A. (2020). Challenges to athletes during the home confinement caused by the COVID-19 pandemic. *Strength and Conditioning Journal, 42*(3), 1–5. Doi: 10.1519/SSC.0000000000000563

Atalı, L., Altuntaş, T., & Tarım, T. (2020). Koronavirüs (COVID-19) salgını sürecinde büyükşehir belediyelerinin spor ve fiziksel aktiviteye yönelik hizmetlerinin incelenmesi. *Focuss Spor Yönetimi Araştırmaları Dergisi, 1*(1), 46–64. Retrieved from https://dergipark. org.tr/tr/pub/focuss/issue/55523/760357

Australian Institute of Sport (2020). Covid-19. Retrieved from https://ais.gov.au/ healthwellbeing/covid-19

Aygün, M. (2021). Spor organizasyonlarında covid-19 etkisi. *Gençlik Araştırmaları Dergisi, 9*(23), 43–48.

Begović, M. (2020). Effects of COVID-19 on society and sport a national response. *Managing Sport and Leisure*, 1–6. Doi: 10.1080/23750472.2020.1779115.

Bingöl, H., Canpolat, B., Demiralp, İ., & Öncü, H. (2020). COVID-19 Sürecinde Egzersiz Uygulamaları ve Fiziksel Etkinlik. Rukiye Aylaz ve Erman Yıldız (Ed.). Yeni Koronavirüs Hastalığının Toplum Üzerine Etkileri ve Hemşirelik Yaklaşımları İçinde (ss.97–102). ISBN:978-605-7853-43-1 İnönü Üniversitesi Yayınevi: Malatya.

Brett, G. T., & İrfan, M. A. (2020). Coronavirus disease 2019 (COVID-19): Considerations for the competitive athlete. *Sports Health, 12*(3), 221–224. Doi: 10.1177/1941738120918876

Cao, W., Fang, Z., Hou, G., Han, M., Xu, X., Dong, J., & Zheng, J. (2020). The psychological impact of the COVID-19 epidemic on college students in China. *Psychiatry Research, 287*. Doi: 10.1016/j.psychres.2020.112934

Carrasquillo, C. B. (2020). Como no caer en desmotivación deportiva en tiempos de cuarentena? Retrieved on July 20, 2021 from http://hdl.handle.net/11722/2561

Castillo, R. P., & Velasco, M. F. P. (2020). Child mental health and covid-19 pandemic: Questions and challenges. *Revista De Psiquiatría Infanto-Juvenil, 37*(2), 30–44. Doi: 10.31766/revpsij.v37n2a4

Çelik, F., & Yenal, T. H. (2020). Covid-19 ve Hareketsiz Yaşam. *Mediterranean Journal of Sport Science, 3*(2), 249–259. Doi: 10.38021/asbid.804705

Chauke, T. A., & Chinyakata, R. (2020). The effects of the Covid-19 outbreak on the positive development of young people. *The Thinker, Special Edition: COVID-19, 84*(2), 70–75.

Coakley, J. (2020). Youth sports: What counts a "positive development?". *Journal of Sport and Social Issues*, 35(3), 306–324. Doi: 10.1177/0193723511417311

Côté, J., & Vierimaa, M. (2014). The developmental model of sport participation: 15 years after its first conceptualization. *Science & Sports*, 29, 63–69. Doi: 10.1016/j.scispo.2014.08.133

Council of the European Union. (2020). Erişim tarihi: 18.07.2021. Erişim adresi: https://www.consilium.europa.eu/media/44622/ st08926-en20.pdf

Danilović, L. (2020). Fızıčka aktıvnost kod kuće za vrıjeme pandemıje COVID-19 (Diplomski rad). University of Rijeka, Faculty of Health Studies, Sveučilište u Rijeci Fakultet zdravstvenih studija u Rijeci, Rijeka. Retrieved from https://urn.nsk.hr/urn:nbn:hr:184:138960

Driscoll, W. S., Conlee, M. E., Brandenburg, E. J., Landry, W. B., Rabatin, E. A., Prideaux, C. C., & Laskowski, E. R. (2019). Exercise in children with disabilities. *Current Physical Medicine and Rehabilitation Reports*, 7, 46–55. Doi: 10.1007/s40141-019-02135

European Parliament. (2021). Texts Adopted. P9_TA(2021)0045. The impact of Covid-19 on youth and on sport. European Parliament resolution of 10 February 2021 on the impact of COVID-19 on youth and on sport (2020/2864(RSP)). European Parliament. Retrieved on July 22, 2021 from https://www.europarl.europa.eu/doceo/ document/TA-9-2021-790045_EN.pdf.

Guan, I., Kirwan, N., Beder, M., Levy, M. and Law, S. (2021). Adapations and innovations to minimize service disruptions for patients with severe mental illness during COVID-19: Perspectives and reflections from an assertive community psychiatry program. *Community Mental Health Journal*, 57(1), 10–17.

Guan, H., Okely, A. D., Aguilar-Farias, N., del Pozo, C. B., Draper, C. E., El Hamdouchi, A., Florindo, A. A., Jáuregui, A., Katzmarzyk, P. T., Kontsevaya, A., Löf, M., Park, W., Reilly, J. J., Sharma, D., Tremblay, M. S., & Veldman, S. L. C. (2020). Promoting healthy movement behaviours among children during the COVID-19 pandemic. *The Lancet Child & Adolescent Health*, 4(6), 416–418. Doi: 10.1016/s2352-4642(20)30131-0.

Günay, U. (2020). Salgın Döneminde Gençler. Rukiye Aylaz ve Erman Yıldız (Ed.). Yeni Koronavirüs Hastalığının Toplum Üzerine Etkileri ve Hemşirelik Yaklaşımları İçinde (ss.83–88). ISBN:978-605-7853-43-1 İnönü Üniversitesi Yayınevi: Malatya.

Håkansson, A., Jönsson, C., & Kenttä, G. (2020). Psychological distress and problem gambling in elite athletes during COVID-19 restrictions – A web survey in top leagues of three sports during the pandemic. *International Journal of Environmental Research and Public Health*, 17(18), 1–17. Doi: 10.3390/ijerph17186693

Håkansson, A., Moesch, K., Jönsson, C., & Kenttä, G. (2021). Potentially prolonged psychological distress from postponed olympic and paralympic games during COVID-19 – Career uncertainty in elite athletes. *International Journal of Environmental Research and Public Health*, 18(1), 2. Doi: 10.3390/ijerph18010002.

Horky, T. (2021). No sports, no spectators–no media, no money? The importance of spectators and broadcasting for professional sports during COVID-19. *Soccer & Society*, 22(1–2), 96–102. Doi: 10.1080/14660970.2020.1790358

Jewett, R., Kerr, G., & Tamminen, K. (2019). University sport retirement and athlete mental health: A narrative analysis. *Qualitative Research in Sport, Exercise, and Health*, 11(3), 416–433. Doi: 10.1080/2159676X.2018.1506497

Kara, E. (2020). The function of the social service workforce during the COVID-19 pandemic in disadvantaged groups. *Türkiye Sosyal Hizmet Araştırmaları Dergisi*, 4(1), 28–34. Retrieved from https://dergipark.org.tr/tr/pub/tushad/issue/54680/726487

Kelly, A. L., Erickson, K., & Turnnidge, J. (2020). Youth sport in the time of COVID-19: Considerations for researchers and practitioners. *Managing Sport and Leisure*, 1–11. Doi: 10.1080/23750472.2020.1788975

Koç, M. (2004). Gelişim psikolojisi açısından ergenlik dönemi ve genel özellikleri. Erciyes Üniversitesi *Sosyal Bilimler Enstitüsü Dergisi*, 1(17), 231–256.

Lippi, G., Henry, B. M., & Sanchis-Gomar, F. (2020). Physical inactivity and cardiovascular disease at the time of coronavirus disease 2019 (COVID-19). *European Journal of Preventive Cardiology*, 27(9), 906–908. Doi: 10.1177/2047487320916823

Maron, B. J., Udelson, J. E., Bonow, R. O., Nishimura, R. A., Ackerman, M. J., Estes, N. A. III, Cooper, L. T. Jr, Link, M. S., & Maron, M. S. (2015). Eligibility and disqualification recommendations for competitive athletes with cardiovascular abnormalities: Task Force 3: Hypertrophic cardiomyopathy, arrhythmogenic right ventricular cardiomyopathy and other cardiomyopathies, and myocarditis: A Scientific Statement from the American Heart Association and American College of Cardiology. *Journal of the American College of Cardiology*, 66(21), 2362–2371. Doi: 10.1161/CIR.0000000000000239

Marshall, G. (2009). *Sosyoloji Sözlüğü*. Akınhay, O. ve Kömürcü, D. (çev.). Ankara: Bilim ve Sanat Yayınları.

Mehrsafar, A. H., Gazerani, P., Zadeh, A. M., & Sánchez, J. C. J. (2020). Addressing potential impact of COVID-19 pandemic on physical and mental health of elite athletes. *Brain, Behavior, and Immunity*, 87, 147–148. Doi: 10.1016/j.bbi.2020.05.011

Pelliccia, A., Fagard, R., Bjornstad, H. H., Anastassakis, A., Arbustini, E., Assanelli, D., Biffi, A., Borjesson, M., Carrè, F., Corrado, D., Delise, P., Dorwarth, U., Hirth, A., Heidbuchel, H., Hoffmann, E., Mellwig, K. P., Panhuyzen-Goedkoop, N., Pisani, A., Solberg, E. E., van-Buuren, F., Vanhees, L., Blomstrom-Lundqvist, C., Deligiannis, A., Dugmore, D., Glikson, M., Hoff, P. I., Hoffmann, A., Hoffmann, E., Horstkotte, D., Nordrehaug, J. E., Oudhof, J., McKenna, W. J., Penco, M., Priori, S., Reybrouck, T., Senden, J., Spataro, A., & Thiene, G. (2005). Recommendations for competitive sports participation in athletes with cardiovascular disease: A consensus document from the study group of sports cardiology of the working group of cardiac rehabilitation and exercise physiology and the working group of myocardial and pericardial diseases of the European society of cardiology. *European Heart Journal*, 26(14), 1422–1445. Doi: 10.1093/eurheartj/ehi325

Sanderson, J., & Brown, K. (2020). COVID-19 and youth sports: Psychological, development, and economic impacts. *International Journal of Sport Communication*, 13, 313–323. Doi: 10.1123/ijsc.2020-0236

Sarto, F., Impellizzeri, F. M., Spörri, J., Porcelli, S., Olmo, J., Requena, B., Suarez-Arrones, L., Arundale, A., Bilsborough, J., Buchheit, M., Clubb, J., Coutts, A., Nabhan, D., Torres-Ronda, L., Mendez-Villanueva, A., Mujika, I., Maffiuletti, N. A., & Franchi, M. V. (2020). Impact of potential physiological changes due to COVID-19 home confinement on athlete health protection in elite sports: A call for awareness in sports programming. *Sports Medicine*, 50, 1417–1419. Doi: 10.1007/s40279-020-01297-6

Schellhorn, P., Klingel, K., & Burgstahler, C. (2020). Return to sports after COVID-19 infection. *European Heart Journal*, 0, 1–3. Doi: 10.1093/eurheartj/ehaa448

Sports Value. (2020). Coronavirus' economic impact on the sports industry. Erişim tarihi: July 18, 2021. Erişim adresi: https://sportsvenuebusiness.com/index.php/2020/03/19/coronavirus-economic-impact-on-the-sports-industry/

T.C. Sağlık Bakanlığı (2020). Covid-19 Nedir? Erişim adresi: https://covid19.saglik.gov.tr/TR-66300/covid-19-nedir-.html

Thompson, P. D., Franklin, B. A., & Balady, G. J. (2007). Exercise and acute cardiovascular events placing the risks into perspective: A scientific statement from the

American Heart Association Council on nutrition, physical activity, and metabolism and the Council on clinical cardiology. *Circulation, 115*(17), 2358–2368. Doi: 10.1161/ CIRCULATIONAHA.107.181485

Trussel, D. E. (2016). Young people's perspectives of parent volunteerism in community youth sport. *Sport Management Review, 19*(3), 332–342. Doi: 10.1016/j.smr.2015.09.001

Türker, A. (2020). Pandemide (Covid-19) Egzersiz ve Beslenme. İhsan Kuyulu ve Davut Atılgan (Ed.). Spor Bilimlerinde Yeni Fikirler-2 içinde (ss. 195–211). Ankara: Akademisyen Kitabevi.

Türkmen, M., & Özsarı, A. (2020). Covid-19 salgını ve spor sektörüne etkileri. *International Journal of Sport Culture and Science,* 8(2), 55–67. Doi: 10.14486/IntJSCS.2020.596

Velavan, T. P., & Meyer, C. G. (2020). The COVID-19 epidemic. *Tropical Medicine and International Health, 25*(3), 278–280. Doi: 10.1111/tmi.13383.

Voigts, G. (2021). Young people and child and youth welfare in Corona times. *Standpunkt-Sozial,* 2021/1. Doi: 10.48441/4427.22

Watson, A., & Koontz, J. S. (2020). Youth sports in the wake of COVID-19: A call for change. *British Journal of Sports Medicine, 0,* 1–2. Doi: 10.1136/bjsports-2020-103288

World Health Organization (WHO). (2011a). Global Recommendations on Physical Activity for Health. Retrieved on July 20, 2021 from http://www.who.int/dietphysicalactivity/pa/en/index.html

World Health Organization (WHO). (2011b). World Report on Disability. Retrieved on July 19, 2021 from https://apps.who.int/iris/bitstream/handle/10665/70670/WHO_NMH_VIP_11.01_eng.pdf;jsessionid=5A5665BFC2 7ABAA3975E9C512EC9DDA8?sequence=1

World Health Organization (WHO). (2020). *Disability Considerations During The COVID-19 Outbreak.* Retrieved on July 20, 2021 from https://www.who.int/publications-detail/disability-considerations-during-the-covid-19-outbreak

World Health Organization (WHO). (2021). COVID-19 Weekly Epidemiological Update. Edition 48. https://www.who.int/publications/m/item/weekly-epidemiological-update-on-covid-19---13-july-2021

World Health Organization (WHO). Physical activity – Data and statistics. Retrieved on July 21, 2021 from https://www.euro.who.int/en/health-topics/diseaseprevention/physical-activity/data-and-statistics

Yüksel, A. (2021). COVID-19 pandemi döneminde elit sporcuların uyku kalitesi ile beslenme durumunun değerlendirilmesi. *OPUS–Uluslararası Toplum Araştırmaları Dergisi, 17*(Pandemi Özel Sayısı), 3918–3942. Doi: 10.26466/opus.909434

Zibung, M., & Conzelmann, A. (2013). The role of specialisation in the promotion of young football talents: A person-oriented study. *European Journal of Sport Science, 13*(5), 452–460. Doi: 10.1080/17461391.2012.749947

Chapter 6

Crisis Management in Sports Events

Solutions from the Perspective of COVID-19

Murat Yalçın Beşiktaş

Introduction

The continuous and rapid change experienced in today's competitive environ-ment, where sports have become an industry, can render existing goals and strat-egies invalid and inadequate. In crisis situations, organizations can be dragged into uncertainty (Toffler, 1996). In such cases, the ability of sports organizations to preserve their existence depends on how well they adapt to external environ-mental conditions. Crisis literally means "suddenly emerging developments in the direction of deterioration and a dangerous moment, a mixed phase in which an event goes through, a difficult situation to get out of" (Edwin, Johnson, 1988). It is very difficult to make a generally accepted definition of a crisis in terms of the management of sports organizations. A crisis is a state of tension encountered as a result of inadequate solutions to problems that arise unplanned and that cause malfunctions in the organizational and managerial processes of sports organiza-tions and the organizational order to be shaken to a large extent in the face of the factors that cause the crisis (Akgemci, 2008). Crises affecting sports organiza-tions are inevitable situations that create imbalance and destroy the routine ac-tivities of the organization. It is a process that threatens the long- and short-term goals of the organization, requires immediate response, shortens the decision-making time for response, and leads to indecision. The most basic feature of a crisis is that it happens unexpectedly and is unpredictable in nature, which af-fects an organization. Even if some symptoms related to the crisis have emerged, these symptoms may not have been perceived correctly and in a timely manner by the organization's management. During the COVID-19 pandemic, this situa-tion has been observed very often in sports organizations. The uncertainty at the beginning of the pandemic has caused each sports organization to take different decisions. After the situation has turned into a global crisis, countries started to take similar measures in terms of sports organizations. Since its onset, the COVID-19 pandemic has spread to almost all countries of the world. Social and physical distancing measures, lockdowns of businesses, schools, and overall social life, which have become commonplace to curtail the spread of the disease, have also disrupted many regular aspects of life, including sports and physical

DOI: 10.4324/9781003253891-6

activities. This policy brief highlights the challenges COVID-19 has posed to both the sporting world and to physical activity and well-being, including marginalized or vulnerable groups. It further provides recommendations for Governments and other stakeholders, as well as for the UN system, to support the safe reopening of sporting events, as well as support physical activity during the pandemic and beyond (United Nations, 2020). On December 13, 2020, *The New York Times* ran a detailed piece entitled "2020: The Year in Sports When Everybody Lost". The article lamented the economic impact of the COVID-19 pandemic across the world's sporting organizations, describing losses of US$13b in the US sporting leagues, US$28.6b in wages and earnings, and nearly 1.5 million jobs in the US alone, while revenue losses exceeded 1 billion euros among some of Europe's biggest football clubs. Similarly, dire outcomes careered through all sub-sectors of sports when major events and competitions were canceled, postponed, and shortened, including Wimbledon and the Olympic Games, the latter polarizing the residents of Tokyo. Participation in sports ground to a halt or a series of stop-starts, and leisure, recreation, and exercise continued only outdoors and in homes (Skinner, Smith, 2021). During the Spring of 2020, the COVID-19 pandemic wreaked havoc on everyday life for over 7.5 billion people around the globe. While the initial declaration of the outbreak was announced in January, it was not until March that regulations on social distancing, group gatherings, business operations, and various facility closures (including sports training facilities) were put into place. Within the sports sector, the closing of facilities, events, businesses, tournaments, and previously normal operations lead to a freeze on a multibillion-dollar global industry (Dixon et al., 2020). In addition, the limited time to solve the problems that caused the crisis, the uncertainty of the information that caused the crisis to be unreliable, and the threat posed by the crisis to the existing financial and human resources are the most important features of the crisis. Especially in the global epidemic crisis, being able to predict where the situation will evolve can be a great advantage for organizations. Predicting the course of diseases in such cases is a difficult task. For this reason, especially sports organizations can take various measures in order to continue organizations in the safest way, according to the external environmental conditions they are in. This way, the organization can continue to exist throughout the pandemic. These measures can be implemented by using the opportunities brought by technology in direct proportion to the seriousness of the situation. If the crisis situation is managed with the right strategic management, taking into account the adaptation to the external environmental conditions, some elements that seem disadvantageous in a crisis can be turned into an advantage. This situation has emerged quite clearly in the COVID-19 pandemic. Most of the sports events, educational activities, scientific congresses, fairs, and shopping activities, which we did not think were possible on online platforms before the pandemic, were carried out on online platforms. The uncertainty and change in the environment constantly expose unexpected dangers or opportunities to sports organizations. The survival of sports organizations depends on their protection from these dangers or taking advantage of opportunities. Whether it is a danger or an opportunity, unexpected and unpredictable events force to change unplanned and even lead to a crisis in sports organizations. A crisis is first of all related to changes that the sports organization has not anticipated. This situation forces the system of sports organizations to respond quickly and hastily to change and therefore to go beyond the existing experience, knowledge, and functioning. However, a crisis develops and grows because of unsuccessful management. An effective management mentality can anticipate some of the signs of a crisis. It can determine the applications to be made within this framework. Crisis literally means a difficult situation to get out of the complex phase in which a job or an event is going through, the developments in the direction of the sudden deterioration and the dangerous moment. A crisis also refers to the discomfort that emerges for improvement or disappearance when there is a significant change or development. In terms of sports management, a crisis is, above all, an unexpected and unpredictable situation by the sports organization. There may be some symptoms related to the crisis. However, what is important at this point is that sports organizations have not sensed these symptoms. The most important feature that distinguishes a crisis from routine situations is the obligation to respond urgently. It is imperative to both respond and act quickly. In this respect, a crisis needs to be countered that requires quick and hasty adaptation. In a crisis, the situation that creates the most gap, and even pushes the management of sports organizations into tension, is the uncertainty of the events that are or may happen and the need to do something before it is too late. The crisis intensifies in direct proportion to the uncertainty. On the other hand, management is insufficient to follow rapid developments with little time and limited inputs. Therefore, adapting to the changes and developments that take place becomes more urgent and vital for the sports organization. Another feature of the crisis is that the management of the organization is insufficient in determining the goals to be achieved and the activities to be carried out with limited resources. Since the changing situation cannot be predicted and it is necessary to act quickly, the goals are diversified. The activities that previously led to success or failure are subject to change in the new situation. Usually, there is no one generally accepted activity to follow. It is necessary to make decisions in a wide area full of problems caused by a lack of information both economically and strategically. In addition, crisis situations may cause a forced change for sports organizations. The crisis threatens the former values of sports organizations, their established basic goals, and business. However, if such positive or negative conditions require a change in the basic philosophy, purpose, approach, and values of the sports organization, it may cause another crisis when the risk of winning or losing will be very high. The changes and developments that occur will make the sports organization's crisis prevention mechanisms inadequate, as it requires the change of the basic goals and values of the sports organization, whether it is positive or negative. Crisis arises when the sports organization fails to detect, prevent or respond appropriately to changes. According to this situation, the crisis in sports organizations is an unexpected and unpredictable state of tension that needs to be answered quickly and urgently, and there is a dire need to make the prevention and adaptation mechanisms of the sports organization quite adequate despite its current values, goals, and assumptions being threatened. From this point of view, crisis management can be defined as special measures taken to solve the problems caused by a crisis. The Crisis Management Plan is a documented plan for the sports organization detailing the actions that managers want to take when a crisis comes up. It is designed to streamline complexity. After the crisis emerges, the managers selected to serve in the crisis management team work to control the crisis to minimize the effects of the crisis. When a crisis reaches the acute stage, the team must quickly take control, determine the facts, prepare in a planned way, and seek ways to fix the problem. Adhering to these steps will enable the organization to take control of the crisis. One of the key elements of successfully managing a crisis is preparedness. During the COVID-19 period, the sports industry and sports organizations were adversely affected and unprepared like many sectors. It has been a difficult period to manage both for sports organizations and sports businesses. Especially for sports organizations, the COVID-19 process is an experience they have never experienced before. For this reason, almost all sports organizations have been caught unprepared for this process. But the continuation of the COVID-19 process has forced sports organizations to seek new solutions. For sports organizations, especially the decrease in audience income has been one of the worst effects of the COVID-19 process. In direct proportion to the absence of the audience to sports competitions, many different sectors other than sports have also been negatively affected by this, a butterfly effect has been experienced. In addition, the cancelation of many large sports organizations has created different crises on many different issues (economic, political, sociological, psychological, sports performance management, etc.). The life of such a pandemic period has forced the sports sector to seek different solutions, as in many other sectors. One of the most accepted of these solutions is to serve all organizations in the world on online platforms. The rapid spread of the COVID-19 virus has made it necessary for sports organizations to meet with the audience online. Online broadcasting methods that were not used so often before will reshape the strategies of sports organizations in the future. The new lifestyle that took shape in the COVID-19 period led to innovation studies in the management of sports organizations, as in many areas. It is based on analyzing the needs using rational and collective working models and technology. In times of global crisis, where the daily routine is broken, it creates a basis for innovation. This new period which has emerged creates a basis for the emergence of innovative solutions in times of crisis by straining the working efficiency for a limited period and increasing the amount of investment. For this reason, in terms of crisis management in sports organizations in the COVID-19 period, innovations that use health measures increasingly with technology support, bringing many organizations online, and making participation of the audience in an organization by using image technologies have seen the emergence of online recreational organizations.

The Causes of the Crisis

Due to the nature of sports organizations, they cannot be isolated from their environment, but they are constantly under the influence of external environmental conditions. There are many factors that are very diverse and interrelated or that can develop completely independently, both from outside the organization and within the organization, in the emergence, spread, termination, or chronicity of crises. In the COVID-19 pandemic, many factors that people can and cannot control have emerged, and these factors have affected life. Factors that will cause crises for organizations can be divided into three groups.

Environmental Factors: External environmental factors, which are effective in the emergence of the crisis, are the factors that develop without the knowledge of the organizations and are difficult to control. There are constant changes in the external environmental conditions of organizations. These changes can affect the organization positively or negatively. Strategic planning activities of organizations are one of the main factors determining success. Ineffective strategic management can lead to various problems in the preparation, as well as in the implementation of the strategy. In addition to the constant change in the external environment, the unsuccessful strategic plan of the organization management can leave sports organizations in a difficult situation, especially in times of crisis. However, the majority of external crises are caused by factors that organizations cannot directly control. The fact that the external environment of the organization becomes more and more uncertain and complex in the face of constant changes, makes it impossible to predict events and prepares the ground for the crisis to grow even more in terms of the organization (Karaman, 1999).

Managerial Factors: Crises arise in an unexpected and unpreventable way, except for natural disasters and events that are completely beyond the control of organizations. If the behavior of organizational management takes place effectively and strategically after the crisis occurs, organizations will not be affected by the crisis or will be affected very little. An effective and successful management approach can ensure that the organization is minimally affected by a crisis that may arise. The crisis can affect the organization badly due to the managers' lack of vision, lack of foresight, lack of plans to be made in possible crisis situations, and managers who are resistant to change. When organizations are evaluated as a system and organizational management is accepted as teamwork, it can be said that the role of the manager in the success of the organization is as important as the role of the incompetent manager in crisis situations that arise as a result of unsuccessful management. Therefore, the inexperience and inadequacy of the top managers of the organization in monitoring environmental changes, collecting, interpreting, and evaluating data about changes are also factors that cause the crisis to negatively affect the organization (Peterson, Hronek, 1992).

At the beginning of the COVID-19 pandemic process, all sports organizations stopped their activities because the epidemic occurred very quickly and the structure of the virus could not be fully defined. Afterward, as a result of the studies of scientists, the virus was identified and the public began to be warned about how to minimize the risk of infection. In this process, sports organizations could not practically be held. Even if the managers of the organization strategically evaluate the external environmental conditions, they did not have many solutions.

In this period, measures such as holding sports organizations without spectators were taken. With the innovation studies carried out in this period, sports organizations were enabled to meet with the audience on digital platforms. In the later stages of the pandemic, with the development of vaccines for the COVID-19 virus and its variants, sports organizations have also started to require participation in the organizations depending on whether they are vaccinated or not. As can be seen, many controllable and uncontrollable factors created by external environmental conditions have determined the behavior of sports organizations in this process.

Structural Factors: Although the external environmental factors, which are unpredictable and very difficult to control, have an important role in the drift of organizations into a crisis environment, the weaknesses of the structural factors of the organizations such as not being able to predict and manage the crisis are the internal problems of the organizations. As organizations grow structurally, the hierarchical structure of management strengthens, and the distance between organizational managers and employees increases. Therefore, problems arise in the implementation of the general policies and strategies of the organization. Since organizational structures that resist change affect the interaction between employees negatively by reducing sensitivity to change, disruptions may occur in the execution of organizational activities. In addition, since communication barriers will arise in multi-level structures, managers are aware of the problems very late. Therefore, such negative activities put organizations in a more difficult situation in crisis environments. The COVID-19 pandemic has affected structurally unprepared organizations much more negatively. Especially in sports organizations with structural problems, management gets centralized and control increases in the case of crisis, there is an increase in risky and quick decisions in efforts to solve the problems, and in conflicts, the quality of decisions taken under stress and time pressure deteriorates, authoritarian and conservative tendencies increase, employees become defensive or hesitant, the feeling of trust decreases, anxiety increases, motivation decreases, job satisfaction decreases.

Interaction of Internal and External Environmental Factors in the Emergence of Crises

The interaction of internal and external environmental factors plays an important role in the emergence and severity of crises. This interaction has three basic dimensions. These dimensions are as follows: Control – the degree to which the organization controls the external environment (low or high); Perception – perception of crisis situations as positive (creating opportunities to achieve goals) or negative (reducing the chances of achieving goals); and Sensitivity – the sensitivity of the organization to changes (low or high). If the organization does not have a structural preparation for the crisis, its sensitivity to the crisis will be high and the degree of response to the crisis will prove insufficient. Some of the main characteristics of organizations with high crisis sensitivity are: Strategic decision-making activities are not compatible with the organization, passive approach, low self-esteem, high-concern decision makers. Lack of flexibility, adaptability and stability. Senior executives who won't give up on their old views. Management structure that does not take into account changes. These three criteria that we have mentioned above are the criteria that determine the severity of the crisis and how the organization can respond effectively to the crisis. A better fit between the goals and needs of the organizations and the conditions offered by the external environment reduces the likelihood of it encountering a crisis (Huang et al., 2020). The high control and low sensitivity of sports organizations to the external environment reduce the need for harmony between the environment and the organization. The more indecisive the organization is in responding to a crisis situation, the more severe the crisis. Success in resolving the crisis continues to the extent that the organization maintains its integrity in diversity, flexibility, and decision-making structure (Milburn et al., 1984). In this context, sports organizations, which also use innovation opportunities in the COVID-19 process, have tried to find solutions for the continuity of the organization by overcoming the unknown and fear situations in the first period of the pandemic. Tokyo 2020 Olympic Games is the most important example of these organizations. The uncertainty experienced at the beginning of the pandemic, rapidly spreading death rates, collapsing health systems, and the unpredictability of the scientific spread of the virus necessitated the postponement of the Olympic Games. Afterward, it was decided that the Olympic Games would be held with a one-year delay, with vaccines developed against the virus, the change of countries in a more organized way, and the development of various control methods. Similar processes were experienced in many large and medium-sized sports organizations during this period.

Stages of Crisis

A crisis occurs in four different stages. The four stages of the crisis include: prodromal crisis stage, acute crisis stage, chronic crisis stage, and crisis resolution stage. In the first phase of the crisis, important clues about a potential crisis begin to emerge. When these warning messages are noticed, organizations offer repeated messages and continuous clues that can prevent or help reduce the potential effects of the crisis.

Organizations that remain sensitive to the trends and developments in their environment may be more fortunate in detecting a crisis and preventing its emergence. The second stage is "the emergence of a crisis or acute crisis". At this stage, some factors cause the crisis to turn into a damaging reality. In this period, the physical, financial, and moral shocks incurred by the organizations can be very high. At this stage, the top management of the organization will give the most serious test, and wrong practices that can be made may cause the organization to disappear. The continuation of the crisis constitutes the third stage. This stage is also called the "chronic crisis stage". The effects of this stage can last many years. The corrosive aspects of the crisis can prolong the effects of the crisis. The final stage is the stage of resolving the crisis. At this stage, the crisis is no longer a threat to the organization and its environment (Tüz et al., 2013).

Crisis Response Methods

The way organizations respond to a crisis can be examined in the most general way in three groups, namely an active method, passive method, and interactive method.

Active Response Process to Crisis (Proactive Method)

With an active approach, different alternatives can be developed before the occurrence of a crisis, and the crisis can be prevented from harming the business. This method will not only prevent organizations from getting caught in a crisis but will also provide significant advantages in overcoming crises that may arise from the external environment that the business cannot control. Active crisis response creates the opportunity for the transition from the industrial age to the information age. The application steps of the active method are as follows (Ren, 2000). Immediate detection and identification of the crisis, taking advantage of preventive actions if available, limiting the impact of the crisis, neutralizing the crisis if possible, initiating the appropriate recovery plan immediately when the crisis is neutralized or ends on its own. Organizations that aim to develop an active approach to crisis management can use the following elements:

Ensuring Continuity of Information Flow

Necessary information that enters the decision process creates an effective information flow in organizations and prevents overloads in the system. This way, the confusion in communication channels is reduced. This ensures that the right information reaches the right person at the right time and prevents risk factors from turning into a crisis due to lack of information or misunderstandings.

Determining the Risk Ratio

According to the resources they have, there is a risk that organizations must take to achieve their goals. Therefore, it is important to determine the amount of risk to be taken. Because, exceeding this amount may prepare the ground for the risky situation to turn into a crisis at any time (Peterson, Hronek, 1992). Sports organizations can make innovative plans, especially for crisis situations that may be related to health. Thus, the continuity of the organization is ensured.

Creating Emergency Systems

Thanks to emergency systems, the presence, severity, and intensity of the crisis can be determined. This way, the possibility of maintaining the existence of the organization with stability arises. The emergency system is the set of plans to be implemented in possible crisis situations. These plans can be changed, stretched, and differentiated according to the extent to which the emerging crisis affects the organization. Such emergency systems require organizations to have a learning organizational structure (Robinson, 2010).

Preventive Planning Against the Crisis

Managers do not tend to direct their attention by predicting the external environment that may occur in the future for future crises. The important point in crisis management is the existence of action plans that must be fulfilled when the organization encounters a crisis (Tüz et al., 2013). The preparation of the plans applied for crisis management is generally similar for all crises. Plan implementation strategies do not differ significantly for different types of crises. Basically, the plans developed to prevent crisis are prepared as a result of similar stages.

Registering The Plans

It is very important that the plans prepared for crisis prevention are put into writing. It is very often seen that the plans expressed in words do not pass the implementation phase or do not appear in the thoughts of a few people. Plans should not be too long and rigid. Plans should provide structure and flexibility to recognize the unpredictable aspects of the crisis situation and give managers plenty of room to act comfortably using common senses. By putting the plans into writing, it is possible to avoid entering into wrong decision processes that occur in times of crisis by determining who will do what and in what way in crisis situations. In this way, the destructive effect of the crisis can be prevented.

Creation of Crisis Prevention Teams

Teams are formulated in accordance with organizational policies for potential crisis risks in organizations. In order for the policies determined by the team to be implemented, they must be supported by financial and other resources. It should also be given authority and responsibility for the implementation of policies. In order to lighten the work of the prevention team, it is needed to create audits to control practices. In this case, the principle of authority-responsibility equivalence should not be forgotten. Especially in crisis situations, who will act with which body of authority should be determined in advance. This type of action can prevent the chaos that may occur, especially for crises that come at unexpected moments. The COVID-19 pandemic process is one of the best examples of such chaotic environments.

Passive Response Process to Crisis (Reactive Method)

The passive method includes actions such as supporting structures against natural disasters, providing adequate hospital beds and supplies, and locating population centers in areas away from potential hazards. The main purpose of the passive method is to minimize the severity of the crisis when it comes up (Ren, 2000). In the period when the COVID-19 pandemic crisis started, all countries firstly had a passive response process to the crisis. The process that includes the stages of limiting the damage and healing when a crisis occurs is called the Passive Crisis Management Model. The passive model focused on the activities to be done after the crisis occurred. The purpose of this method is to minimize the damage of the crisis. These activities are carried out after the crisis and are focused on the rapid recovery of the effects of the crisis as much as possible. A crisis is generally defined as a situation that occurs unexpectedly and causes significant losses in businesses. In fact, this is not the case. Most of the time, when the arrival signals of the crisis are obvious, the managers disregard them and they find themselves in the crisis. In this respect, the techniques developed to prevent the crisis are important for the continuation of the organization's life. Starting from the establishment process, organizations are constantly faced with risks and crises that arise as a result of not evaluating these risks correctly. Proactive techniques and strategies developed for crisis prevention before entering the crisis period can prevent entering the crisis process, as well as allowing to come out of a possible crisis by gaining strength. In fact, we can see all the plans that organizations develop with the idea of continuing their life and implementing, even though there are no signs of crisis, as strategies developed against crisis prevention. Because even if there is a threat outside the organization, it is possible to turn this into an advantage with the right management, thanks to the right decisions being taken and implemented. In this respect, although some techniques and strategies have been specified, the successful practices of organizations starting from the establishment stage to the growth periods can be seen as activities aimed at preventing the crisis. Whether these activities are consciously put forward as studies aimed at preventing the crisis, or whether they are applications carried out without ever bringing the concept of crisis to the agenda, they can be considered a crisis prevention study. All the aspects such as the right choice of the place where the organizations will carry out their activities, the right choice of the technology to be used, and the selection of personnel with the appropriate skills are actually potential efforts to prevent the crisis. Because, apart from natural disasters such as earthquakes, floods, and diseases, it can be said that almost all the crises are caused by management errors. The fact that the risks that have the potential to turn into a crisis are not seen by the management and that their precautions are not taken is the result of the bad management of the organizations. In this context, organizations can be prevented from entering a crisis. However, the necessary infrastructure for this is that the administration continues its activities by scientific means. It is clear that in today's world, it is not possible to survive only with Passive Crisis Management Models. Active crisis management, which would be ahead of the crises and includes continuous preparation and prevention activities, and the Interactive Model, which is based on learning and learning from the crisis, will be important fighting tools in the hands of the organizations of the 21st century.

Interactive Response Process to the Crisis

Effective crisis management includes five different stages that all crises go through: recognizing signs, preparing and preventing, controlling harm, healing, and learning management (Gottschalk, 2002). The most important difference of the interactive crisis process is that it has a process based on learning and improvement during the crisis resolution phase.

The stages of the interactive crisis management process and the main features of these stages are as follows: The first stage; Recognizing the signs includes perceiving the first warning signs that indicate the possibility of a crisis. The second stage; preparedness and prevention includes activities aimed at both preventing and being prepared for crises. The third stage; contain the crisis; It aims to mitigate the effects of the crisis and prevent the spread of the crisis to unaffected parts of the organization. In the fourth stage; improvement; organizations develop and implement short- and long-term programs that have been tested and designed to restart their routine activities. The fifth stage; learning; focuses on the continuous examination and questioning of important lessons learned from the experiences of the organization themselves and others, which they have done for improvement in the past (Tüz et al., 2013).

Crisis Response and Strategic Priorities

The crisis plan needs to be integrated with the strategic management process of the organization, and especially the use of scenario planning in this process as a crisis plan reveals the importance of crisis management on the basis of strategic management. Strategic planning, crisis response, and strategic management processes can be divided into three main areas of action. These are strategic arrangement, strategic implementation, and strategic evaluation.

Strategic Arrangement

It consists of the analysis of the external environment that affects the organization through the establishment of missions, goals, and objectives for the organization and the selection of internal resources and strategic alternatives.

Evaluating the power of stakeholders and the impact of organizational culture on strategic decision-making are important areas in this analysis. Strategic choice is the organization's goal, its resources, and its prospects for success with available competence. It also depends on factors such as how attractive the possible strategies might be. Various techniques have been developed to address strategic regulation more broadly. The environment outside the organization is prone to high levels of change. Therefore, it is possible to estimate the crisis impact of these factors by using the scenario planning method. A good crisis scenario is the type of crisis that includes cases that the organization did not anticipate and prepare for. It is the best example and worst case scenario that can be constructed about how a crisis can affect. The implementation of scenario planning requires attention to a number of factors. These include team building and organizational culture. At the same time, the responsibility of leadership and management is vital. Scenario planning is a long-term planning by its nature. It provides the emergence of new options with various methods and management tools. Each scenario describes how various elements interact under certain conditions (Masterman, 2009).

Strategic Execution

It is the implementation of the directly selected organizational strategy through scenario analysis at the strategic regulation level or bypassing this level. Strategic implementation often means a transition from the current structure of the organization into a different formation. In this sense, it requires a certain level of change. The effective management of change is significantly effective in the successful implementation of the desired strategy. After the understanding that the process would take a long time during the COVID-19 pandemic period, the new normal period for sports organizations brought about change (Elliott et al., 2021). Although measures were taken in order to organize sports organizations without spectators in the early stages of the pandemic, most of the organizations were canceled in order not to endanger the health of their athletes. Evaluation of the success level of the chosen strategy in implementation is also of vital importance. Strategy is not a cross-section of a simple event, it is a process that must be followed continuously. Strategy is not just related to performance and metrics because it requires constant adjustment with experience and rapidly changing environmental conditions. It also helps detect crisis signals.

Consolidation Strategy, Crisis Management

A crisis can change the strategic orientation of an organization by imposing certain limitations on its operations, reducing costs, or increasing profitability. Similarly, the crisis can force the organization to take new directions. There are similarities between crisis management and strategy, such as the evaluation of environmental conditions. Stakeholder assessment and senior management's role, responsibility and commitment are important elements of strategic planning and crisis management. Crisis management and strategy are separated from each other in the design and implementation stages of the planning process. Both assess the impact of the chosen strategy and shape the process of updating routines and organizational learning. Evaluating the organization's resources as strengths and weaknesses also creates a risk assessment in achieving the determined goals. Beech, Chadwick, 2004). The implementation phase bears importance for both crisis management and strategy. The establishment of crisis teams and the provision of their work are also important in terms of the success of the implementation phase. In organizations that prioritize classical stakeholder analysis strategically, the impact of crises is primarily handled. In this strategy, it is thought that if the management has information about the cause of the crisis, strategies can be developed to combat the crisis. In the strategy process, potential barriers to the success of strategic choices can be assessed simultaneously as strategic options are reviewed and evaluated, especially when scenario planning or other environmental analysis techniques are applied. Likewise, evaluating strategic achievements should include evaluating the success of crisis plans. On the other hand, it is known that strategy, organizational structure, culture, and human resources have simultaneous effects in determining the organization's preparedness or tendency to crisis. For this reason, human resources management is seen as an important part of crisis management (Masteralexis et al., 2019).

It is not possible to talk about a single most suitable structure for an organization at all times and everywhere. The best organizational structure changes depending on the conditions of the organization. Businesses operating in an open system are exposed to many internal and external factors. The COVID-19 pandemic period is one of the best examples of organizations being affected by external environmental conditions. During this period, all sports organizations had to take a break from their activities due to unexpected pandemic conditions from the outside environment. Establishing an organizational structure that will adapt to internal and external environmental changes and developments, taking into account environmental factors, plays an important role in preventing the crisis. For this reason, one of the ways to prevent the crisis is a flexible organizational structure that will adapt to environmental conditions (Pedersen, Thibault, 2019). The mechanical organizational structure is suitable for situations where the environmental conditions are balanced and stagnant and the rate of change is very low. But today, environmental conditions are changing rapidly. For this reason, rigid and mechanical organizational structures prevent the timely identification of crises as they make it difficult to adapt to the environment. The organizational structure that can adapt more easily to the very dynamic and variable environment is a more flexible and organic structure. In an environment where change takes place rapidly and where confusion and uncertainty are intense, businesses can detect environmental changes faster with their flexible and organic organizational structures and can see the developments that may cause the crisis in time and take precautions.

Creation and Training of the Crisis Team

Crisis Team

The crisis team was established by the top management of the organizations in order to prevent the crisis and minimize the effects of the crisis. For this reason, crisis teams should consist of people who can manage and control the crisis. The primary role of this team is to prevent a crisis from occurring. With the occurrence of the crisis, firstly, to minimize the possible damage of the crisis, secondly to prevent and reduce the damage that the crisis will cause to the organization, and finally to succeed in changing the culture of the organization in a positive way (Tüz, 2008). The crisis team should consist of people with skills, knowledge, and experience in different specialties. The crisis team consists of a team leader and members. The team leader should be a top-level executive with sufficient knowledge and expertise in crisis management and group problem-solving techniques. The crisis team should perform the following tasks in an organization: Anticipating crisis situations that may affect the organization. Playing an active role in the preparation of crisis management plans. Checking whether the plans and programs to be prepared for the crisis are implemented. Continually discussing the plans prepared according to the crisis possibilities and adapting them to the conditions of the day. To carry out all the work related to the crisis in a time of crisis. To ensure faster recovery of the business by preventing mistakes that can be made immediately after the crisis. In order for the crisis team to fulfill these tasks successfully, it should be equipped with full authority in its own areas of responsibility. The crisis team should not be constrained in making their decisions. Organizations may feel the effects of crises more deeply if the crisis team is not equipped with the necessary powers within their field of duty.

Decision-Making in Times of Crisis

Decision-making is a process of making choices. It refers to the solution of the problem among the alternatives or the selection of the most appropriate solution method to achieve the goal. In this context, the decision-making process includes the stages of determining goals or defining problems, examining goals and problems, determining priorities, determining alternatives, examining and evaluating alternatives, determining selection criteria, and making choices. In times of crisis, it becomes difficult for this process to function effectively. Because it is seen that the crisis has negative effects on organizations such as the necessity of making quick decisions, the tendency of management decisions to centralize and the deterioration of the quality of the decisions taken. In the period when the COVID-19 process first started, sports organizations decided to take a break from their organizations due to the uncertain nature of the process. The most important example of this situation is the Tokyo 2020 Olympic Games. Afterward, as the process was brought under control, sports organizations continued their activities in a controlled manner. For this reason, the importance of taking an effective decision in times of crisis increases even more. Decision support systems that will support effective and correct decision-making by providing rapid information flow and necessary information in making urgent decisions in times of crisis can be used. Group decision support systems have been developed in order to increase the effectiveness of decisions and ensure participation in times of crisis. Group Support Systems is an information processing process carried out to contribute to the decision-making process. It is a decision support system that helps the crisis team to perform their duties more effectively (Pedersen, Thibault, 2019). In order for the decision support system to provide the desired support in the decisions to be taken, it should have the following features (Tüz, 2013): It provides support in making semi- or fully structured or semi- or fully programmable decisions, helps managers at all levels, primarily the upper levels, in their decisions, especially in a crisis, enables the crisis management team to be formed during the periods to benefit significantly from the group decision support systems and provides support at all stages of decision-making based on concrete data. There are many factors that managers should consider when making a good decision. Because there are qualities that a good decision has. In times of crisis, it is even more important whether the decision is good or not. Any ineffective decision may put a business in a worse position. For this reason, the qualities sought in a good decision can be grouped into five groups as follows (Eren, 2010).

A good decision, especially in times of crisis, should first consider the goals of the organization and be designed in such a way as to help achieve these goals. A good decision, especially in times of crisis, should first consider the goals of the organization and be formed in such a way as to achieve these goals. Therefore, the best decisions are those made on time. A good decision is one that is appropriate to the possibilities of the organization and departments; in other words, it is realistic. Otherwise, it cannot be implemented and becomes a figment of the imagination. A good decision is one that is put into practice without wasting time and results are obtained. Speed is very important in this century of the information age. For this reason, the one who takes action quickly evaluates the opportunities earlier (Fullerton, 2007). In this context, taking innovation-based decisions, especially in times of crisis, may reveal results that will affect the organization the least from the effects of the crisis.

In an organization, managers are faced with the situation of making their decisions according to the conditions they encounter in an environment of certainty, risk environment, and uncertainty. In a certainty environment, the decision-maker makes a decision under familiar conditions. All alternatives are obvious to the decision-maker, and he knows the outcome of each alternative. The environment of certainty refers to an environment in which the decision-maker easily predicts the outcome of the decisions to be made. It is easy to take a decision in this environment. In risky environments, the decision-maker cannot know all the alternatives and their consequences with certainty. But they know their possibilities. In other words, risky environments are situations where decision makers can predict the results of their decisions with certain probabilities. Although there is uncertainty in risky environments, since certainty is limited, this uncertainty is measurable. In an environment of uncertainty, the alternatives are not fully known, and the probability of their realization is also unknown. An environment of uncertainty is an environment in which the decision-maker cannot predict the consequences of his decisions. Decision makers lack the necessary information in this environment. Crises are risky and create an environment of uncertainty for managers according to their types and severity. The decisions taken by the managers in times of crisis may cause their organizations to return to their former state, as well as lead to worse situations. Because there are many constraints that affect managers' decision-making in crisis conditions. The most important of these constraints is the time constraint. Decision makers must make a quick decision in a very short time. The tendency of management decisions to become centralized is also among the results of this period. Because crises are extraordinary situations and the circumstances caused by them are unusual. For this reason, decisions cannot be expected to be taken as in usual circumstances. In this period, it can be recommended to use various decision-making techniques used in teamwork while determining the basic strategies in times of crisis, since it will not be enough for one person to make a decision, especially in terms of creativity (Tüz, 2008). Since the expert knowledge, experience, and abilities of more than one person are used in decision-making in the form of teamwork, there is an opportunity to make more effective and consistent decisions than individual decisions. Everyone tries to come up with the best solution by putting forward their own ideas and thoughts, that is, solution methods. This situation may trigger individuals' creativity to come to the forefront in times of crisis. Such creative solutions have also emerged during the COVID-19 pandemic period, especially by using technology on the basis of innovation. One of the most important examples of this is the use of digital platforms more than ever to bring sports organizations together with their audiences.

In addition, since the decision is made together, the responsibility of the result will belong to everyone. Therefore, the individuals will be more careful. It will also motivate the employees as they will participate in the crisis management process in the efforts of the team. They will work together to get out of the crisis. Such a situation will also be beneficial in preventing gossip, rumors, and conflicts within the organization (Ren, 2000; Gottschalk, 2002; Tüz, 2008).

Communication Dynamics in Times of Crisis

While organizations continue their lives, they are in contact with many people and institutions inside and outside of the organization. Internal stakeholders with whom the organizations are in relationship; employees, shareholders and directors, suppliers, customers, government, competitors, investors, nongovernmental organizations and the media, while external stakeholders. Since these stakeholders are in a direct or indirect relationship with the organization, they need more information about the organization not only in normal periods but especially in crisis periods. When organizations are drawn into crises, these stakeholders want to have reliable, accurate, honest, fast, clear, and clear information about the crisis-related situation of the business. This is because these stakeholders will make decisions based on this information while making their decisions about the future in their relations with the organization. If organizations cannot provide reliable, accurate, honest and immediate information to their stakeholders and cannot do this systematically during the crisis, gossip, rumor, which is information obtained from unreliable sources, will damage the image and reputation of the organization before the stakeholders. In order to prevent this, organizations can systematically provide crisis communication and establish an effective crisis communication plan. Since the crisis communication plan will deliver information to the stakeholders at the right time, in the right place, and in the right way, it will also prevent the deterioration of the relationship between the stakeholders and the organization. It is also very important that the messages sent by the organization to all these stakeholders are compatible and consistent with each other. Otherwise, the fact that one stakeholder has less information than the other and the disclosure of it will affect the not very good relationship between the organization and some stakeholders, and perhaps cause the crisis to deepen. In the crisis communication plan that organizations will prepare to provide relevant stakeholders with the necessary information at the time of crisis, they should first determine who will be responsible for conveying relevant information to employees, people who will be affected by the crisis, and the media in a crisis. Second, it should be determined where a crisis control center can be established, where all communication activities can be carried out within the organization in the event of a crisis, and who will be assigned to the established center. After these stages, answers to questions such as how and where press conferences can be held, with which media organizations and how should be contacted (Haşit, 2000). In times of crisis, the public relations department has great responsibilities in tasks such as creating communication plans, ensuring information flow, and protecting the image of the organization and corporate reputation. Public relations studies can be handled in two stages in three crisis periods such as pre-crisis, crisis period and post-crisis. In the first stage, the existence of the crisis is accepted, the information about the crisis is collected and the crisis management team formed during the preparation for the crisis is activated. In the second stage, informing the organizational environment about the crisis, informing the employees, informing the target audience, and informing the media (Akdağ, 2005). In fact, public relations is an effective communication element for organizations before, during, and after the crisis period. For this purpose, organizations should carefully review and plan their public relations programs. In this way, it will be able to have a plan that can be made during the crisis, to avoid being unprepared for the sudden crisis and to suffer the least damage from a possible loss of image and negative effects during and after the crisis, and even turn this crisis into an opportunity.

Conclusion

The COVID-19 pandemic process has had many negative effects on sports organizations as well as affecting all areas of life. These effects still continue, albeit partially. The economic damage of the crisis to the world has also manifested itself in many sports organizations, regardless of sports branch. Although it turned into a controlled structure after the general panic situation at the beginning of the pandemic, this process took longer than expected in terms of sports organizations. While some countries in the world did not take precautions at the beginning of the pandemic, some others postponed or canceled all sports organizations. The state of unpredictability, which is one of the main elements of the crisis, has manifested itself in the COVID-19 pandemic period. In this period, factors such as match-day revenues, TV rights, sponsorships, and player transfer, which are the main income source of professional sports, came to a standstill. In this process, the economic damage caused by the decisions taken by the sports organizations was tried to be minimized. Especially within the first six months of the beginning of the pandemic, innovation studies were given weight. Thus, sports organizations were tried to be brought together with the audience on various platforms. The new lifestyle that has emerged in all areas of life has brought on various innovations in sports organizations. This period has led to the invention of technology-supported ways to make organizations without an audience. Spectators started to participate in the events as remote access. After the pandemic was taken under control to some extent with the end of the vaccine studies, although sports organizations have returned to the systemic structure they used to apply, situations such as the COVID-19 pandemic have now become the normal reality of humanity. For this reason, sports organizations should continue their innovation-based research and development studies during such periods. Organizations with strategic plans of crisis management have been the organizations that have emerged out of the COVID-19 pandemic with the least losses in this process. This global crisis, which the world has faced for the first time, has also revealed that collective efforts for the solution are needed especially in organizational structures.

References

Akdağ, M. (2005). Halkla ilişkiler ve kriz yönetimi, *Selçuk Üniversitesi Sosyal Bilimler Enstitüsü Dergisi*, 14, 1–20.

Akgemci, T. (2008). *Stratejik Yönetim*, Gazi Kitabevi.

Beech, J., Chadwick, S. (2004). *The Business of Sport Management*, Pearson Education Limited.

Dixon, M. A., Hardie, A., Warner, S., M., Owiro, E., A., Orek, D. (2020, December 23). Sport for development and covid-19: Responding to change and participant needs. *Frontiers*. https://www.frontiersin.org/articles/10.3389/fspor.2020.590151/full#B16

Edwin, R. A. S., Johnson, A. (1988). *Crises*, Encyclopaedia of Social Science.

Elliott, S., Drummond, M. J., Prichard, I., Eime, R., Drummond, C., Mason, R. (2021). Understanding the impact of COVID-19 on youth sport in Australia and consequences for future participation and retention. BMC *Public Health*, 21, 448.

Eren, E. (2010). *Stratejik Yönetim ve İşletme Politikası*, Beta Basım Yayın.

Fullerton, S. (2007). *Sports Marketing*, McGraw Hill.

Gottschalk, J. (2002). *Crisis Management*, Capstone Publishing.

Haşit, G. (2000). İşletmelerde Kriz Yönetimi ve Türkiye'nin Büyük Sanayi İşletmelerinde Yapılan Araştırma, Eskişehir: Anadolu Üniversitesi Yayınları, No: 1177.

Huang, A., Makridis, C., Bakera, M., Medeiros, M., Guo, Z. (2020). Understanding the impact of COVID-19 intervention policies on the hospitality labour market. *International Journal of Hospitality Management*, 91, 102660.

Karaman, A. (1999). *Profesyonel Yöneticilerde Güç Yönetimi*, Türkmen Kitabevi.

Masteralexis, L. P., Barr, C. A., Hums, M. A. (2019). *Principles and Practice of Sport Management*, Jones & Bartlett Learning.

Masterman, G. (2009). *Strategic Sports Event Management*, Elsevier.

Milburn, T., Schuler, R., Watman, K. (1984). Organizational crisis part ı: Definition and conceptualization. *Human Relations*, 36(12), 1140–1160.

Pedersen, P. M., Thibault, L. (2019). *Contemporary Sport Management*, Human Kinetics.

Peterson, J. A., Hronek, B., B. (1992). *Risk Management*, Sagamore Publishing.

Ren, C. H. (2000). Understanding and managing the dynamics of linked crisis events. *Disaster Prevention and Management*, C. 9(S. 1), 12–17.

Robinson, M. J. (2010). *Sport Club Management*, Human Kinetics.

Skinner, J., Smith, A. C. T. (2021). Introduction: Sport and Covid-19: Impacts and challenges for the future (Volume 1), *European Sport Management Quarterly*, 21(3), 323–332.

Toffler, A. (1996). *Gelecek Korkusu Şok*, Çev: Selami Sargut, Altın Kitaplar Yayınevi.

Tüz, M. (2008). *Kriz Yönetimi*, Şah-Mat.

Tüz, M., Haşit, G., İplikçioğlu, İ., Suher, K. İ. (2013). *Kriz İletişimi ve Yönetimi*, Anadolu Üniversitesi Yayını.

United Nations. (2020, May). The impact of Covid-19 on sport, physical activity and well-being and its effects on social development. https://www.un.org/development/desa/dspd/wp-content/uploads/sites/22/2020/05/PB_73.pdf

Chapter 7

Digitalization of Recreation and Sports in the COVID-19 Pandemic Period and Social Identity of Exergamers and ePlayers

Electronic Sports as Autochthonous Worlds in Metaverse

Tuna Uslu

Introduction

Despite the impact of the pandemic on the industry, esports has become one of the fastest-growing technologies in the entertainment and commerce sectors in the world with its participant numbers and growing revenues. It is seen that many countries have started to make very serious investments, especially after the countries that pioneered in the field of esports in terms of establishment and event organization before the pandemic period. Spor Istanbul, a subsidiary of Istanbul Metropolitan Municipality, is preparing to give theoretical and practical lessons to children in the field of esports according to protect their physical and mental health through online training. Participation of children in esports training also receives theoretical healthy nutrition, sports psychology and physiotherapy lessons from experts in their fields. The modular education program for the 13–15 age group aims to develop children's cognitive and creative thinking abilities, motivation and leadership skills, empathy and individual control, computer and social media usage knowledge, and in-game communication. The courses are given by esports coaches, managers, and field experts (Spor İstanbul, 2021). Since esports players peak at an early age and in childhood compared to other elite sports, the health and well-being of these athletes should also be carefully evaluated in terms of child psychology and child protection.

In the literature, game is a concept that has no output as a result of a production process, that participation is voluntary, works regularly, can be repeated within its own time-space limit, that interactions is self-structured in the process, the results are variable, and the act of playing should be serious in its own universe. Game is defined as a break to get rid of the demands of daily life, which is considered essential and serious in the individual's uniqiue time (Calliois, 2001). Society expresses its interpretation of life and the world through play. It is not meant here that the game has turned into culture, but rather that the culture has a game character in its early stages, that it progresses and develops in the shape and mood of the game (Huizinga, 1949/2003). The act of playing together is a

DOI: 10.4324/9781003253891-7

feature of the social nature of digital games and electronic sports, as in traditional games (Zabet, 2012).Around 30 million people play video games in Turkey, and it can be estimated that around 12 million of them are the younger generation interested in esports. It was stated that the tickets for the final match, which will be played in the 15,000-seat arena in Istanbul, one of the largest sport complexes in Europe, were sold out within four hours (Esen, 2019). One of the largest banks in the country is holding esports tournaments open to all its staff. Similarly, human resources departments give importance to esports and organize various activities to improve discipline, motivation, and team spirit among employees. It is obvious that these physical investments and live events with large participation in the field of esports will be moved to online environments with the pandemic. Virtual video games and esports events host an environment that will create diverse social communities powered by the connections of their consumers.

Technologies developed through modernity and digitalization are shaping the way people communicate, socialize, play, and manage their lives. New technologies have changed the nature of work and leisure. The hyper-reality of cyberspace has created new forms of entertainment, including virtual realities and new forms of information and entertainment. Capital has produced a new technoculture, a new form of entertainment and information society, and everything from business to everyday life is changing dramatically. This process has transformed the concept of leisure and recreational activities first into packaged products that are subject to trade and then into commodities.

As a result of the industrialization process and paradigm shift, individual creativity gave way to mass adaptations, and even if the brands and packaging of products and services changed, they became similar to each other. Personal intuition and power have been replaced by automatic processes. This transformation has affected every sector industrialized in the past centuries (Esen et al., 2019). In the 20th century, people began to lead a sedentary and monotonous life due to the change in lifestyle and the convenience of technology. This situation has led to problems such as loneliness, inactivity, weakness and fatigue, obesity, mental hesitation and chronic depression in the individual, and psychological deterioration in the society. These moods and problems can leave individuals dissatisfied or even fed up with life, alone and helpless in crowds. Despite increasing opportunities and alternatives, the overall quality of life is not improving (Korkmaz & Uslu, 2020: 1–2).

The sports industry started to be an industrialized sector in the 20th century. However, with the innovation approach at the beginning of the 21st century and the COVID-19 pandemic process, the importance of individual creativity in sports has gained importance again. It is believed that every destructive process and crisis such as the epidemic in today's world brings along innovative efforts and agile approaches in order to survive in the Schumpeterian sense if progress toward the future is continued (Uslu, 2017). With the increase of crises, social chaos, and confusion in the past 50 years, future projections have played an increasingly central role in reproducing the current economic and social life. The efforts by technocratic policy makers and social order-makers to predict and manipulate the dynamics of social fragmentation they cause have increased (Nelson, 2020). The third wave civilization that came with the technoculture brings with it a prosumer practice that combines the roles of producer and consumer, similar to the lifestyle of the farm population working from home at the beginning of the industrial revolution (Toffler, 1980). Developments in information and communication technologies, the storage of big data and the timely calculation of consumer demands, the need for agile techniques, the determination of individual needs without intermediaries, and the development of continuous innovation as the tools of digital transformation. In addition, with digitalization, the concept of leisure time has turned into processes that follow new forms of social interaction and interconnected lives, coordinated with daily and business life.

Leisure Recreation and Sports Ecosystem in the COVID-19 Pandemic

The emergence of motion sensor models of video game consoles at the beginning of the 2000s, by absorbing the characteristics of male adolescents sitting and playing at home with new technologies, made electronic games an active playground that also serves learning and health, including the entire household (Maddison et al., 2013). In addition, in recent years, well-designed digital games are thought to offer rich, fun and interactive experiences that can encourage children's learning from an early age, cognitive and skill development, social interactions, self-management, physical activity and healthy behavior. On the other hand, unhealthy fictionalized violent digital games lead to depersonalization and detachment from reality and/or hostility, fear, aggressive attitudes and behaviors, ultimately consuming leisure time that can be better spent on physical activity and social interaction (Lieberman et al., 2009).

Although leisure time and working hours seem to be intertwined in recent years through digitalization, electronic communication tools, and new media, especially during the pandemic period, remote working practices reinforce this process and expand the areas where business and entertainment such as esports will work together. Agile digitalization is based on evidence that successful digital transformations are changing radically over time and as resources permit, with continuous innovation, measured steps in sports industry business models and capabilities. This innovative perspective allows organizations to start, learn and re-launch digital initiatives and become a mechanism that quickly responds to changing market conditions and players' needs. Even giant companies that fail to grasp this perspective and the psychology of the players fail. This section focuses on the acceleration of the digitalization process of sports and recreational activities in the COVID-19 pandemic, the growth of the video game and electronic sports industry, and the reflection of this situation on the psychology of gamers, as a result of individuals spending their lives more intensively through the internet and multi-user virtual worlds during the COVID-19 epidemic process.

With the pandemic, many questions have arisen about how to digitally manage the expectations of players, fans, and followers, how to minimize operational disruptions and how to upgrade the streaming and flow experience, how to plan for a future different from the past, both in the short and long term. The pandemic will likely be around for a while, so new ways to deal with threats to financial and business continuity, cash flow disruption, insurance challenges, and potential declines in long-term participation and engagement from the entire sports ecosystem will be required (Deloitte, 2020). At the same time, for some organizations and companies, this process will be either an opportunity or a necessity for transitioning to new business models that they have thought of before. Others will have to adapt to this new paradigm, whether they plan or not. This devastating process will ensure that this period is commemorated as a breaking point during and after the epidemy period and in the long run.

During pandemic period, the number of people affected by mental health issues may be higher than the number of people affected by the infection at the physical level (Reardon, 2015). In addition, it is thought that the psychosocial and economic effects of pandemic on mental health are higher than expected (Reardon, 2015; Shigemura et al., 2020). It is seen that the pandemic causes problems such as anxiety, panic disorder, and depression in young people (Lau et al., 2008; Cao et al. 2020). On the other hand, it is known from the studies in the literature that regular physical activity and doing sports are effective in stress management, reduce depression and increase life satisfaction (Sabiston et al., 2019). Today's electronic sports activities do not include sufficient support for a fit life and physical health, since they do not include sufficient physical activity. However, it would not be right to seek the reasons for this only in terms of esports and the features of electronic entertainment. This phenomenon is also a result of industrialization and modernization of the leisure time concept, exercise, and sports activities.

Modern Society and the Paradigm Shift of Sports and Leisure Time

In the last century, under the influence of liberal thought, the capitalist system and the mass media, sports have turned into a commodity that is traded, a service industry where millions of people work, and an applied science field. Although Bourdieu (1978) states that the history of sports has a relatively independent and unique chronology with its own pace and crises, he does not deny that it has been affected by economic and social transformations.

The changes experienced in the transition from a pre-industrial society to industrial society and then to a post-industrial society have also significantly changed the characteristics of leisure time. Recreation, which was previously in the perspective of a certain habitus, a small minority, or a certain segment, has spread to wider sections of the society as a result of the shortening of working hours, the expansion of the middle class, and the increase in economic capital with industrialization. In the past century, the economy, social systems, and technology have likely transformed the spiritual and creative essence of leisure, making recreation an aspect of life driven by consumption and productivity (Honoré, 2005). The leisure time concept is no longer a philosophical ideal but a socially constructed set of behaviors, meanings, structures, and ideologies (Kelly, 2000), indicating that the traditional definition of leisure time associated with natural human needs, state of mind, free will, and choice can no longer be supported.

With the idea of linear time coming to the fore in the Western influence, the concept of cyclical time has been dragged out of human perception. The future was no longer perceived as a cyclical repetition of what had once happened but as an object of temporal planning and desire from which the promises of progress could be realized. The point of view advocated by Marx and his followers and classical modernity equated the idea of chronological progress with the flow of time as if there was only one road connecting the past to the future and this road would lead us to the future. The rationality of the Enlightenment and the material success of industrialization reinforced the illusion that a better social order could be achieved by following this linear path. Transforming the fabric of time was an intervention that made progress synonymous with the future and claimed that the future would be superior to the present. Modernization has become a normative force. One of the most distinctive features of modernity was the consciousness of change, the effort to control the direction and speed of change. An accepted motivation developed to see everything that stood in the way of this effort as resistance that had to be broken. Even a new discipline, called social engineering, was designed to rein in the problems created by this endless innovation and the constant urge to compete and to level the obstacles it faced. Social engineering was closely linked to Taylorism, which emerged from efforts to rationalize business processes. The basic principle of Taylorism, which also shapes today's perceptions, was to see actions as items to save time by breaking down, measuring, and optimizing (Nelson, 2020). This method has been effective not only in the scientificization of management but also in the instrumentalization of science in the field of social sciences.

Western thought, which played a role in the shifting of the world's axis during the Second World War, lost its historical consciousness and humanitarian mission. A new philosophy developed from its ashes, arguing that destruction and the aftermath are the beginning, not the end. This process also revealed some managerial concepts that promised to make politics through post-war restructuring. Theoretical topics such as game theory, computational sciences, rational choice theory, cybernetics, operations research, and systems analysis have been adapted from the conflict arena to the construction of civil society. The promise of these concepts was associated with the Western utopia of balancing global powers that dominated the post-war era; regulating, and controlling humanity, and transforming social institutions and the world into an efficient machine for building a solid society. The destruction caused by the war resulted in the understanding of managing the future with rational and scientific methods (Nelson, 2020).

The common aspect of this framework was the effort to rationalize politics and rein in, plan, organize, control, and shape the future with decisions taken from today. According to this approach, in order to dominate the future, the here and now must be reduced to a controllable scenario and strategically managed. Instead of the Enlightenment's ideal of perfecting humanity, its scientific approach and disciplines turned into an effort to limit an open-ended and dangerous future. In order to plan and make decisions, diversity and complexity had to be broken down into measurable chunks, reduced to factors that could be controlled, in the here and now. As a result, the focus shifted from the mind to regulation and feedback control. The war had created new opportunities for those who wanted to actively reshape and rein in society by reducing uncertainties and effectively controlling the future (Nelson, 2020). In that period, the observation of the effects of systems approach and complex structures in social sciences accelerated the modernization process of management science.

According to Luhmann, if modern society would have become overly complex, it was possible to reduce and systematically manage all possible futures by the process of defuturization. Since the future is a gray area due to lack of information, this uncertainty can be systematically reduced by applying binary code with defuturization. For this reason, the method of accepting future events as possible or impossible by coding them as 0s and 1s has been adopted. Prognosis and forecasting made possible by developments in computational sciences, especially mathematics and statistics, would come to the fore. The concept of cybernetics was developed during the Second World War as a method for directing current actions to desired results in the future. Its purpose was to define the goals and the path to those goals through a feedback process. Computational scientific attempts to prevent a nuclear war by polarizing actors and calculating the future eventually became an important part of the dominant power structure (Nelson, 2020). As a result of the adaptation of computational fields such as game and rational choice theories to politics and administration in determining the balance of power, the impact of the modern paradigm on society has increased, and social progress has begun to be evaluated as a process that can be formulated through industrial indicators, especially in the Western approach.

Cybernetic thinking, which suggested that control could be adjusted retrospectively once the target was set, developed the practice of dividing the future into manageable segments to gradually correct deviations. According to the theory of cybernetics, systems are essentially self-sustaining or autopoietic. An autopoietic system is not based on linearity between past, present, and future. The self-regulation process lasts from the moment the system becomes unbalanced to the moment it regains balance. This method brought with it the idea of predicting all stable processes and controlling all unstable processes for those eager to build society. The purpose of self-regulating systems theory is no longer to set a roadmap and exclude possibilities for change. In this societal paradigm, technocratic officials take the helm as individuals with the ability or legitimacy to monitor and regulate the possibilities for change, including the system itself (Nelson, 2020).

In this context, authorities and the actors interacting with them rely on, invest in, and bet on computational methods that remove undesirable futures in their efforts to balance power structures and the economy to reduce risks and increase utility. Goals set for the future work like a kind of feedback loop, that is, calculated predictions are considered correct not because they are ultimately correct, but because all resources are channeled to make them a reality. However, such a process is prone to risks such as a virus that cannot be predicted, calculated, and included in the system or cannot be controlled.

The professionalization of sports in the 20th century hindered the developmental perspective that appealed to the public. In this sense, the search for an Olympic culture and sport's place in human nature and society, which gained strength at the end of the last century, is a resistance and a post-industrial move against the perception of sport deformed by modernity.

Social and Psychological Effects of Pandemic Process

The COVID-19 pandemic causes a series of problems in people's psychological health as well as showing physiological symptoms. While individuals are coping with problems such as fear of contracting the disease and death, uncertainty and related future concerns, social isolation, restrictions in education and professional fields, this process has caused problems such as the lack of social support and alienation from relationships, loneliness, and harmony (Troyer et al., 2020). The great change in the way of life and the anxiety brought about by this change greatly affect the psychological well-being of individuals negatively (Lee, 2020). COVID-19 causes social isolation tendency and hopelessness in people, the need for psychological support increases especially in this period (Banerjee, 2020), and the pandemic has serious negative socio-psychological effects even in healthy people (Tian et al., 2020). Studies have shown that a quarter of the general population has symptoms of post-traumatic and psychological stress from the pandemic (Cooke et al., 2020). In addition, studies have been conducted on the stress and psychological problems in parents and children associated with COVID-19 (Brown et al., 2020; Lee, 2020). Especially children and the elderly may feel more anxiety, fear, and uneasiness than adults in terms of their psychological resilience levels (Kluge, 2020). The stress observed among children is thought to be caused by the changing behaviors of parents and society, such as the closure of schools, staying home, wearing masks, measuring body temperature frequently, and strict quarantine procedures such as mandatory hand washing (Danese et al., 2020). Long-term post-traumatic stress disorder is observed in approximately one-third of children isolated or quarantined due to health problems (Sprang & Silman, 2013). It is known that negative childhood experiences negatively affect those who try to continue their lives. Specifically, long-term effects include increased risk of mental and physical illness (Felitti et al., 1998), developmental and cognitive impairments (Neamah et al., 2018), poor quality of life (Norman et al., 2012), social problems (Bowen, 2015), and reduced life expectancy by up to 20 years (Brown et al., 2009). In studies on COVID-19, it has been determined that there is a significant and negative relationship between anxiety and social support and being with family in young people (Cao et al., 2020).

In addition, limiting peer contact at an early age may negatively affect the development of children and adolescents in the future (Gifford-Smith & Brownell, 2003; Oberle et al., 2010). For this reason, there is a need for channels and media suitable for the situation where remote communication and interaction can be established, especially between children and young people. In this process, unlike the usual leisure time activities, it is seen that children are trying to adapt to the process with reshaped activities adapted to the current situation in children's rooms and over the internet. According to this approach, children take part as social actors who are shaped in the here and now and contribute to the social environment in which they live (Mayall, 2002).

Digitalization and Electronic Gaming Habits during Pandemic Period

COVID-19 has digitalized individuals' social, cultural and commercial events and activities which is its most important effect on people's daily lives. In this context, it is necessary to supply remote access solutions with online support for performance sports as in the fitness industry. Beyond that effect, a door has been wide opened for the exergaming and esports sector, which has made great progress in the last two decades. The fact that the future of all sports activities, especially football, is uncertain for now, has increased the interest in esports. It is known that esports is spreading rapidly in different countries of the world. Today, the International Esports Federation is a global sports organization with national member federations in many countries and has a huge community with millions of athletes and billions of viewers (IESF, 2020).

Following the 8th Olympic Summit, the IOC updated its stance on esports (Webb, 2019). While the IOC previously declared that competitive video games can be "considered sports", a statement from that year's summit stated that the Olympics were not prepared to support non-traditional sports-based games. Instead, the IOC said they wanted to encourage esports professionals and regular players to participate in sports and develop habits that support physical and mental health. Esports, which is expected to be intertwined with modern sports organizations in the long run, may become a part of the Olympic Games in the near future, depending on the interest it attracts. Esports organizations have already come to the fore as a side event in the 2024 Paris Olympic Games (Schaffhauser, 2019). Esports economy, which gathers games played on desktop and laptop computers, consoles, and phones under the same roof, has peaked after the coronavirus epidemic all over the world and is known to reach approximately $250 billion. Nowadays, factors such as the fact that athletes have started to train in virtual and electronic environments, the simulation training of many regular sports activities can be done with technological equipment, and wide awareness of epidemic diseases will pave the way for esports. Under current conditions, sports people, athletes, families, recreation, and sports sector gain have many important experiences. It will not be a surprise that these experiences quickly coincide with the phenomenon of esports and that radical changes in sports practices and philosophy come to the agenda. The rapidly rising popularity of esports and the reality created by the epidemic will result in sports managers to follow the opportunities provided by this field more closely.

On the other hand, psychologists state that the problems of today's children and adolescents may be due to changes in social models in the last 40 years. These changes include an increase in divorce rates, reduced time spent by parents with their children, and the widespread and negative impact of technology (Shapiro, 1998). It is observed that weakened family systems cause loneliness and socialization problems in adolescents (Johnson et al., 2001). Studies in the field generally examine negative effects, especially the effects of violent video games on aggression (Prescott et al., 2018). Moreover, Mehroof and Griffiths (2010) found a positive relationship between online game addiction and neuroticism, sensory seeking, aggression, state, and trait anxiety as a result of their research with university students. A significant negative relationship was found between prolonged exposure to violent computer games and empathy level (Funk et al., 2003). In a study conducted by Houghton et al. (2004), it was concluded that computer games increase dopamine secretion in the brain, increase the temporal dopaminergic activities of children, and this situation may lead to hyperactivity disorder in children. Studies show that there is a significant increase in the rate of playing computer games (Thalemann, 2010). Researches found that students with low school success have high computer game addiction levels (Gentile et al., 2011; Brunborg et al., 2014). As Yao and Zhong (2014) stated in their studies, as individuals become detached from social environments, their virtual addiction increases, and individuals become more lonely and isolated. In the literature, as many studies mention, it has been determined that male students have higher addiction levels than female students (Griffiths & Davies, 2005; Gentile, 2009). On the other hand, Hong and Liu (2003) found that professional video players use more strategic ways of thinking, and novices use more ways of trial and error. Another study revealed that the language course associated with games improves the speaking and writing skills of the players (Kim et al., 2013). During the pandemic, these phenomena were seriously affected by the increase in online interaction and esports activities connected from home.

Economic, social, political, and cultural lives were deeply affected in this radical transformation process, in which psychological and mental power with information and communication technologies at its center became a strategic resource. While the changes and developments in social dynamics have affected the structure of the organizations and society, the understanding of management, the technologies used, and the employees, the institutions had to redesign their functions (Uslu, 2017). It was determined that physical inactivity, which was at the level of one-fifth in children and adolescents before the pandemic, increased up to two-thirds of this population during the pandemic process, and this increase also negatively affected mental states (Xiang et al., 2020). It is also thought that increasing the daily physical activity amount of students after the pandemic process will facilitate healthy development and play an important role in improving social health (Chen et al., 2020). Society should not turn the physical inactivity experienced during the pandemic into a habit of behavior, and this process should be turned into an opportunity to direct people to activity in order to increase social resistance (Hall et al., 2021).

The Characteristics of Virtual Video Games and Esports

Virtual video games have become one of the most popular entertainment activities not only among children and adolescents but also among adults today (ESA, 2014). Virtual video games are played by millions of people today, and it is seen that especially open world games are arranged in the form of metaverses. Almost everyone has the hardware and technological tools to access virtual worlds in most parts of the world. While virtual sports games in this new world are not considered by some authorities as sports events, others oppose this approach. In this context, it is a long-debated issue whether philosophical approaches and video games are accepted as sports activities. The ethical issues of this discussion regarding the addiction level of players entering virtual worlds are also discussed because the level of attachment to games can be so risky that some people get away from daily life while playing video games. Whether video games can be considered sports activities in the traditional sense is still unclear (Eroğlu & Uslu, 2019: 39). However, video game tournaments called esports are becoming more and more common and an increasing number of esports viewers follow video games.

At the beginning of the 2000s, playing video games and competing online became a professional identity and turned into a professional career option for some players in the competitive gaming world (Faust et al., 2013; Griffiths, 2017). This new type of professional video game activity has been described as electronic sports (esports). Esports is a new field in thousands of years of gaming culture and has become one of the most important and popular parts of video game communities, especially among children and adolescents. While defining the sport, it is stated that it is an institutional and autonomous organization that includes physical activity, requires skill, has rules and stability, and has a competitive nature (Rodgers, 1977; Suits, 2007). While discussing whether esports is a real sport in sports sciences, it is defined as a sports field by referring to it requires skill, is competitive by nature, has a structured format (e.g. leagues, teams, coaches, sponsors, and fans), rules and record keeping (Jenny et al., 2017; Keiper et al., 2017; Funk et al., 2018; Hallmann & Giel, 2018). However, due to the scattered and multi-disciplinary nature of sports sciences, it is not possible to reach a clear judgment about the existence of sports. In terms of sports management, the concept of esports has become an important study in the relevant literature due to its industrial effect (Eroğlu & Uslu, 2019: 40). In the field of information technologies, esports means spending more leisure time with online and virtual tools for entertainment, non-physical competition, and recreation.

Also, it is imperative to distinguish between sports video games and esports. Sedentary sports video games are video games that mimic real-life sports and in which the athletes in the game are controlled by a controller but do not involve physical activity (Kim & Ross, 2006). On the other hand, esports by definition is not limited to a particular game genre or category. In fact, the best esports competition games today are not about real-life sports, but focus more on augmented reality fantasy worlds that increase the competitiveness, excitement, and feel of flow.

The concept of esports has already taken its place as a commodity in the sports industry (Eroğlu & Uslu, 2019: 41–42). Defining the concept of esports is complex due to the relative innovation of the industry and the convergence of technology, culture, sports, gaming, and business. Unlike traditional sports like football, esports takes place by connecting multiple platforms. Sometimes described as synonymous with video games, esports is a complex phenomenon that combines computers, games, media, and sporting events (Jin, 2010). In the literature, esports is expressed as "an umbrella term describing organized and sanctioned video game competitions and tournaments" (Whalen, 2013). According to this meaning and similar definitions, electronic sports are a special way of participating in the game through video games and multimedia as an alternative to other sports (Adamus, 2012). From another perspective, esports is defined as "an area of sports activity that develops and trains mental or physical abilities in the use of information and communication technologies" (Wagner, 2007; Martoncik, 2015). Although at the end of the 20th-century esports was seen as a competitive way of playing computer games in a professional setting, it was argued that at the time the concept was too narrowly defined (Wagner, 2006). In these years, esports was defined as a field of sports activity where people improve their mental or physical abilities by using information and communication technologies. In this form of definition, it seems that such activities are incompletely paired with information and communication technologies rather than organized, electronic, and competitive (Eroğlu & Uslu, 2019: 40–41). On the other hand, to gain "sport status", games need to be recognized as a sport worldwide (Witkowski, 2012; van Hilvoorde & Pot, 2016) and are currently considered sports in around 100 countries (IESF, 2020). In this case, it is seen that esports should be internationally accepted and even transnationally recognized as well as electronic.

Esports also have a large pool of followers and customers through online streaming platforms like Twitch and YouTube. Such activities can also be played over a local area network (LAN) connection between local computers, events can be watched in the arena for payment, are sponsored by sponsors, bets can be made, and may include competition-based commentary, spectators, and large cash prizes for top players (Adamus, 2012; Lopez-Gonzalez & Griffiths, 2016). Esports tournaments can also be viewed remotely by followers (fans and other players) by purchasing tickets or as online members.

There are different definitions in the literature about what types of esports consist of and which categories they fall into. In addition, it is especially emphasized in related studies that professional esports players are different from ordinary players (Eroğlu & Uslu, 2019: 53–55). An esports player is a professional gamer who plays the game for competition, not for fun and/or relaxation, and defines it as work. Ordinary players play to entertain themselves and spend their free time (Ma et al., 2013). From this perspective, casual gamers include video games as a recreational activity, while gaming for esports is a professionally managed business (Eroğlu & Uslu, 2019: 40–41). Based on the modern "sport" definitions of Guttman (2004) and Suits (2007), esports is considered a sport because especially online competitive games (i.e. a voluntary, self-motivated activity) involve a specific reward with a winner and a loser and require skills.

It is stated that esports tournaments, game systems, and rules, seasons and matches, evaluations, and broadcast rules are similar to traditional sports and that the characteristics, activities, attitudes, and behaviors (e.g. strict schedules, training and preparation programs of players and teams, physical, psychological and mental states, emotions and excitements, motivations for success and reward) of professional esports players can be compared with professional athletes (Taylor, 2012). However, according to some researchers, in order for esports to be classified as a professional sport, two of Guttmann's (2004) criteria for the definition of sport need to be further elaborated (Jenny et al., 2017). The first criterion in this classification concerns physical performance and the degree of skillful and strategic use of the player's body. However, there are many branches where only certain body parts are used when competing in various sports (eg darts, billiards, shooting), so this criterion in itself does not preclude esports from being classified as a true sport. The second criterion concerns institutional stability. This criterion means that for esport to be recognized as a sport and not just as a leisure recreational activity, it must be regulated by governance and autonomous rules for stability (Jenny et al., 2017). However, different types of esports games, which have become brand specific to software companies and have certain characteristics, make it difficult to ensure institutional stability. However, today, in terms of management, there are global sports organizations such as the International Esports Federation (IESF), federative structures that support the recognition of esports as professional sports and provide an institutional basis for regulations and stability (IESF, 2020).

However, not all scholars support the concept of viewing esports as a sports activity. These researchers argue that some characteristics of playing video games negatively affect people and society, after these digital games, which took place as a leisure activity in the early period, became a task and a business activity with competitive power. Caillois (2001) identified six different game-playing characteristics (free, discrete, ambiguous, unproductive, regular, and fictional). Therefore, when esports becomes a work activity, it compromises recreational amateur spirit and some of the game characteristics. The current game activity becomes a part of working life and negatively affects the fact that playing games is a free leisure activity (Eroğlu & Uslu, 2019: 40). Based on this approach, Brock (2017) argues that by playing video games, esports motivates the pursuit of extrinsic rewards as opposed to internal ones (Ryan & Deci, 2000; Ryan et al., 2006). However, some research shows that esports players can be motivated to become professionals through both external and internal rewards (Kim & Thomas, 2015). Also, simply playing video games more competitively is not enough to define it as a business or recreational activity. This discussion suggests that esports is a serious leisure activity that players enjoy, and that some players can improve themselves in the process of becoming professional players (Martoncik, 2015; Seo, 2016).

According to the criteria of Guttman (2004) and Suits (2007), which define the field as sports, there are many similarities (eg ways of training, practices, skill acquisition, work commitment, and discipline) between the players who play video games professionally and the players defined as athletes. In addition, in Taylor's (2012) studies, professional players and professional athletes in traditional branches can overlap the same tournament rules with the same conditions and practices, including the preparation, broadcasting, and evaluation of the players (mentally and physically) for the competitions. International sports organizations define a sport according to five basic criteria (Sport Accord, 2016). The proposed sport should include an element of competition. The sport must not contain any chance factors specifically incorporated into that sport. The branch must not pose an undue risk to the health and safety of its athletes or participants. The recommended sport should not harm any living thing. Sport should not rely on infrastructure and equipment provided by a single supplier. In fact, the most important aspect of esports that is discussed starting from brands is related to executive ownership in this last criterion. In esports, too, due to the nature of competition, skill requirements, physical precision and ethical compliance are essential. However, the compelling criterion for esports supporters is the requirement that "sports should not be based on infrastructure and equipment provided by a single supplier". Esports, on the other hand, relies on a branded commercial game and commodity, always managed by an executive. This situation will continue to raise various issues related to the identity and status of the phenomenon in terms of industrial sports, depending on the environment in the cultures and societies it is in. However, due to its business volume and economic value, it will continue to grow by creating new identities and brands for institutions, clubs, professional esports players, casual players, and spectators (Eroğlu & Uslu, 2019: 57). For example, although the mobile apps of well-known sports brands in recent years are not designed as health promotion interventions, their systems aim to attract new users and help them stay physically and mentally active, and by doing so, increase sales of sportswear and provide financial benefits to companies. These sports apps use sensors to monitor physical activity and combine it with game elements, including personalized feedback, individual and team-level challenges, social interaction and support, as well as status levels (Thin & Gotsis, 2013: 472).

With the development of digital technologies, exergames or active video games used for professional purposes have gained a structure that can be used in schools and workplaces that appeal to society and sub-communities (Baranowski et al., 2014; Chamberlin and Maloney, 2013; Maddison et al., 2013) and have begun to be integrated with different mobile virtual reality applications.

Healthcare, Electronic Sports and Exergames

At the beginning of the 21st century, it is seen that the level of physical activity has decreased, and the risk of obesity and diabetes has increased due to greater dependence on technology (Hu, 2003). On the other hand, in terms of community health, exercise, and recreation disciplines, esports has the potential to engage otherwise inactive or sedentary people in sport and physical activity. Some researchers also state that technology can be a tool to make people more active (Garney et al., 2017). Esports events and competitions can also play a role in the society's orientation toward physical activity and gaining a sports culture (Heere, 2018). Although esports competitions and game options often involve sedentary behavior, alternatives to physical activity are increasing as virtual video games evolve. Especially recently, it has been found that active gaming (exergame training), which requires participants to move physically while playing video games and even participate in the game through sensors, motion detectors, and controllers placed on the body, provides physical benefits for both young and old (Biddiss & Irwin, 2010; Larsen et al., 2013). Studies show that playing video games at home that include physical activity significantly improves well-being, flexibility, balance, lower extremity muscle strength, braking force, heart rate, maximum oxygen capacity and calorie expenditure (Li et al., 2016; Nitz et al., 2009; Rodrigues et al., 2018; Roopchand-Martin et al., 2015), plays an important role in active aging and can be as effective as conventional exercises (Guimarães et al., 2018; Li et al., 2018; Maillot et al., 2014; Monedero et al., 2015; Strand et al., 2014; Toulotte et al., 2012; Vázquez et al., 2018). Active video games, virtual reality and exergaming based balance systems have been demonstrated to be an effective additional intervention for rehabilitation programs, including balance rehabilitation for the elderly, during the COVID-19 pandemic (Siddiqi & Azim, 2021). Also, research has shown that players develop psychological and mental self-regulation skills and a developmental mindset as a result of their competitive performance in the game (Himmelstein et al., 2017). In fact, these skills are often sought after not only for esports performance but also in social interactions and the business world, which can be transferred to other fields of work as well (Eroğlu & Uslu, 2019: 42). For this reason, the coming years will make esports an application that can be used not only for entertainment purposes for professional players but also as a tool in social life, preventive health, rehabilitative interventions, education, and business processes. Moreover, it is clear that there are many potential new digital avenues to explore to develop more effective forms of health promotion interventions (Thin & Gotsis, 2013: 472). For example, in recent years, exergamers who regularly exercise by playing electronic games in their living spaces for entertainment and health purposes have emerged. Exergamers are individuals who regularly play electronic games that require physical effort and performance exceeding the level of sedentary activity, the outcome of which is determined by the bodily movements related to strength, balance or flexibility, in order to improve or maintain physical fitness, health and wellness.

Exergames are defined as a bodily interactive digital game format that includes activities related to strength, balance and flexibility, exceeds the level of sedentary activity and requires more physical effort during the act of playing than traditional video games, in which targeted movements are performed (Kari, 2017: 15). In health research, terms such as interactive video games, motion video games, active video games, physical play, fitness games, dance simulations, and kinesthetic video games are used for exergames (Oh & Yang, 2010).Electronic Sports at the Breakpoint of New and Digital Consumption Trends

Games and sports, as a part of human nature and active life, are an individual need and an important social and cultural tool for civilization (Esen & Uslu, 2021: 87). In the last century, it is seen that with the widespread use of sportive practice for the middle and lower classes in the society, mass interest has increased and the said practice has become widespread, and professionalization has become dominant in the sports branches followed by the middle and lower classes. Moreover, the rapid spread of the internet, as well as communication and transportation technologies in the last quarter-century, will play an important role in remembering the current period as a transition period in the future. In this process, while traditional consumer approaches and marketing styles leave their place to proactive consumers with new media, these intermediaries formed in this context can be enriched in a way that can create a more holistic but at the same time alternative to face-to-face communication and have the ability to bring the brand and service directly with the consumer. The current period tends to leave the place of classical production and marketing methods to online media planning strategies in line with today's rising trends, brand and commodity management (Uslu & Çubuk, 2015: 91).

Each stage of human and social development and perceptual expansion will help us make sense of consumer behavior and how consumption decisions are made. In order to solve the consumer, it is useful to remember the changing socio-economic conditions and breakpoints of each period and to make a definition according to the spirit of the time. In this context, the definition of consumer identity makes it possible to analyze the stages of change in humanity and to construct consumer identity in this way. In this process, consumption and production relations essentially constitute the main focus of this paradigm shift. Especially in the period following the industrial revolution, it has enabled the conscious individual to discover that change is parallel to his own transformation and at the same time, the individual's freedom of choice in the stages of technological development and industrialization. In today's conditions, it points to a paradigm-shifting period from the approach of "I sell what I produce" or "I produce what the market needs", where the consumer says "I must have what I want, marketing techniques should act according to my level of expectation". In the conceptual framework, the historical development and change processes cover an area ranging from the development of the individual to the stages of marketing techniques, and the effect of marketing made through "traditional" and "new media" on consumer behavior. In today's society, the individual's relationship with the internet and networks has also determined his/her own identity (Sarı & Uslu, 2012: 2672). In the second half of the 20th century, technology also affected cultural elements and lifestyles, the universal and the local began to live together in a postmodern way. Intercultural interaction is also important for marketing communication because interaction can cause a meaningless product, service, or idea in a market to gain meaning over time, and as a result of interactions, the demands of consumers in the market can become similar or diversify in a certain focus (Eroğlu & Uslu, 2019: 43).

The variables that distinguish the new postmodern consumer identity from previous groups are related to demographic and socio-economic as well as personal preferences and internal dynamics. The common point of the new groups is the place and importance of consumption in their lives. Consumption patterns such as the fan group or football team one is a member of, the type of game preferred, the music listened to, the TV series watched, and the clothes used indicate the basic elements that determine who is a member of a group or not (Bocock, 1993). The postmodern consumer, who acts to control her life independently and individually, consumes in a way that has unique characteristics different from other individuals, and the consumption patterns and preferences show different features of his/her own personality. For this reason, the necessity of taking into account the group, society and trends together with the customers in the postmodern marketing approach, ensuring integration with the environment, has turned the primary purpose of the organization into increasing the value of the intangible assets in the long term and fertility for the consumer instead of the profitability and mass growth. For this reason, organizations aim to achieve sustainability by increasing diversity by reaching different customer groups. Video games have also taken their share of this postmodern approach. New games are also associated with the awareness and lifestyle that develops with the understanding of freedom discovered and gained as a result of the increase in mobility and tools that provide easy access to alternatives (Eroğlu & Uslu, 2019: 44–45).

In this context, in today's conditions and structuring, being able to offer the best and most different alternatives to the isolated individual is a prerequisite for success. Organizations that care about their relations with target communities position the individual consumer in the center (who is also behind the camera), and the demands and expectations of each customer are interactively met in integrated marketing communication (Uslu et al., 2016). In particular, the metaverse provides an environment where they can offer educational, entertainment, cultural and social dimensions together for organizations that want to offer integrated services to this new consumer profile that demands a much broader, layered, and personalized content. The social dimensions of the metaverse also have commercial implications. Many practitioners and metaverse users (Smart et al., 2007: 20) state that the leadership and collaboration skills required in virtual environments are increasingly appropriate for excelling in the business world. Joining a quest-oriented adventure in the virtual world or winning in serious entrepreneurial strategy games can be just as effective tools for executive education as sports team leadership or other traditional experiences.

Self-Perception Dimension of Exercise and Sports among Young People

Regular physical activity has important effects on mental processes and cognitive functions. It has been suggested that physical exercise makes a difference in the central nervous system, increases the release of endorphins and bodily strength, and leads to improvement in an emotional state. It is stated that regular physical activity integrates body image and mood, increases self-confidence, reduces anxiety, regulates sleep, and contributes to learning to live with stress (Korkmaz & Uslu, 2020: 2). Today, the need for movement and body image are not the only reasons that push people to do sports. Motivations such as the desire to bond with other people, the anxiety of being alone, and the need to be a social individual are as effective as the desire to be a sportive and healthy individual. Motivations such as the desire to bond with other people, the anxiety of being alone, the need for socialization, and being a social individual are as effective as the desire to be a sportive and healthy individual (Korkmaz & Uslu, 2020: 3). In addition to these, sport is an effective concept in personal and social development as well as in identity development and personality by transforming destructive, aggressive, hurtful, and deviant behaviors in the instincts of the individual, and by strengthening intuitions such as self-control, determination to win, and desire to progress (Baumann, 1986). Studies have shown that there is a decrease in stress and depression levels in individuals who do sports, and accordingly, there is an increase in self-esteem and self-perception (Berger, 1983). It is emphasized that self-esteem is important in terms of gaining autonomy, having a fulfilling life, being active for a purpose, establishing healthy and continuous communication with other people, showing a high level of harmony, developing value systems, being successful, and planning the future (Aşçı, 1999). It has been shown that participation in physical activity increases the physical ability and fitness level of the individual, and this increase causes a positive change in the individual's self-perception (Aşçı, 2004). It is stated that individuals who have reached the age of puberty and are engaged in regular sports are less incompatible with their parents, show less signs of depression and substance addiction, and are more successful in education (Field et al., 2001). It has been determined that physical activity has positive effects on self-esteem, depression, anxiety, and behavioral disorders in children and adolescents (Ekeland et al., 2005). Studies show that participation in physical activity and especially sports activities at a young age has an effect on self-perception and therefore identity formation and social identity.

In the last 25 years, the use of technology, computer, and internet is also associated with psychological factors such as role-related self-efficacy, anxiety, and identity formation. The relationship of the individual with the virtual environment and multiple realities has become an important identity element. In the field research, it is found that there are differences in internet and computer self-efficacy and anxiety according to gender, age, experience, and duration of use. There is a negative relationship between computer-internet self-efficacy and technopolitical stress, and a positive relationship between experienced anxieties and technopolitical stress. Computer technology, cyber problems, and internet concerns increase technopolitical stress. These concerns cause individuals to react to change over time through this stress (Uslu et al., 2012). These findings show that the self-efficacy of using new media tools is effective on both the psychological attitudes and social identity of the person.

Recent research on social identity shows that members of a particular community identify with the social identity of the community, along with certain small circles of friends with whom they interact frequently. Identity consists of three interrelated parts (Bagozzi & Dholakia, 2006: 58); the consumer's being a member of a particular community (cognitive identification), the development of feelings of commitment and membership with the community (emotional commitment), and awareness of the importance of community membership (collective or group-based self-esteem).

Recent research on social identity shows that members of a particular community identify with the social identity of the community, with particular small circles of friends with whom they often interact. Identity consists of three interrelated parts (Bagozzi & Dholakia, 2006: 58): the membership in a particular community (cognitive identification), the development of feelings of belonging and community membership (affective commitment), and awareness of the importance of community membership (collective or group-based self-esteem). From this point of view, they developed the concepts of personal, relational and collective identity that connect organizations and consumers (Bagozzi et al., 2012: 63–64). This categorization in the formation of social identity can describe the process of forming the identities of the eplayers in the gaming universe. This model can be used to explain the motivational process of players in esports, including the cognitive development of personal identity while playing, the emotional commitment that results from experience and relationships in the game, and the collective value of membership in the game.

Physical Activity and Wellness during the Pandemic Period

Sports and exercise are indispensable for human life and local identity as they are fundamental rights. In this context, leisure time and recreational activities will create an environment and opportunities where people can be fed physically and spiritually from their habitus, and will produce material and moral values that they can contribute to the development of this environment (Esen & Uslu, 2021: 87). But even before the pandemic period, most people lived a sedentary life due to the hectic pace of work life and the planned flows in their family and social circles. For these reasons, an individual who leads a sedentary life becomes physically weak in middle age and faces many health problems in later life. On the other hand, the most effective way to live a fit life and stay healthy is to keep the body active and exercise at regular intervals to keep the body vigorous at all times. People who lead an active life, exercise habits or regularly do low and moderate sports feel good thanks to the endorphin hormone secreted by the body. This allows individuals who do sports and exercise to lead a fitter and healthier life (Korkmaz & Uslu, 2020: 16).

Ironically, it can be assumed that the pandemy period and social restrictions will also be effective in changing the lives of sedentary individuals who move away from active life by producing projections for the future in this process. Contrary to the fictional rational human perspective, our future is not born from the present, it is derived from the present. That is, the current flow is set up as if looking back, based on projections for the future. The vision of the future is reinvented over and over again toward a specific horizon to shape the present and set missions for our reality. Essentially, the vision of the future here is just one of the possible or desired futures, not the actual future. In this sense, the future is an abstraction of the present world, an ideal to be realized. The hallmark of the cultural unconscious of the Western world is the lack of clarity or acceptance for the future. The future is not embraced as it is, it is something created and planned for someone's benefit (Nelson, 2020). From this point of view, whether esports is a sport or not is a futile debate carried on by those who want to shape the future, it does not really accept or describe the flow of the process. The debate that esports should be defined categorically is a perspective imposed by modernity. From this point of view, discussion and proposals may need to be more acceptable and dignified rather than imposing in order to understand the nature of the phenomenon.

It is seen that the physical activity levels of children, adolescents and undergraduate students have decreased with both technological and other developments. In addition, the limitations brought by the pandemic process have caused the physical activity levels to be affected more, especially in this age group, and it is thought that it leads to a decrease in the quality of life of the students and to the formation of various depressive symptoms. Studies published in the literature during the pandemic process show that physical inactivity is an important problem that affects the whole society both mentally and physically (Sabiston et al., 2019; Chen et al., 2020; Xiang et al., 2020; Hall et al., 2021). It is thought that during and after the pandemy, playing interactive physical games in kindergartens and increasing students' daily physical activities during school hours by supporting them with digital games will increase physical, mental and psychological resistance, facilitate the development of healthy children and young people, and play an important role in improving social health. This process will also ensure that digital activities such as esports, electronic and virtual social games are used as tools in informing and training the public, in the development and awareness of individuals, and in the active participation of citizens in public processes.

Sports and exercise are activities that should be done for human fitness at all ages and under all conditions (Esen & Uslu, 2021: 87). The effect of the pandemy on the exercise and sport environment has been discussed in many studies. The scientists considered moderate-intensity aerobic exercise (such as brisk walking) to be a viable alternative to exercise, with particular attention to maintaining a safe distance from other individuals and surfaces in open spaces. The dangers of high-paced exercise in public gyms and crowded environments are greater during the pandemy and it is emphasized that it should be avoided (Halabchi et al., 2020). However, today, doing sports and exercising in the same gyms and crowded environments with people is not just a leisure time activity or a means of protecting physical health. At the same time, it is seen that there is a positive and significant relationship between socialization and self-esteem, especially in exercise and sports, and that the increase in the level of socialization in sports raises self-esteem (Korkmaz & Uslu, 2020: 1).

In order to lead a mentally and physically healthy life, it is recommended to do light and moderate exercises instead of heavy training, to spare time for fitness sports to increase the quality of life, and to do sports by regularly planning in accordance with the flow of life. Another reason that directs individuals in modern society to fitness and makes fitness centers the focal point for physical activity in city life is that fitness is not just a single movement or routine, but consists of a combination of many movements done at certain intervals in a certain time period. Similar to this pattern, a regular flow and leisure time management should be valid for esports activities during and after the pandemy in order to strengthen mental stability and psychological resilience and to support the well-being of the individual. It is seen that regular fitness training reduces body fat, increases physical movement capacity, strengthens the immune system, accelerates blood circulation and increases the oxygen level to the brain (Korkmaz & Uslu, 2020: 16). In the upcoming period, both physical and mental exercises will be delivered to customers as a more satisfying and continuous service by integrating exercise and fitness with virtual game-based physical activities and applications.

Motivations of Esports Players: The Meaning of Journey and Experience in the Gaming Universe

Research on esports to date focuses on the differences and similarities between electronic sports and traditional sports (Jenny et al., 2017; Schaeperkoetter et al., 2017), but this is not the main issue for those who are consumers of sports other than professional athletes and sports scientists. Essentially, having mobility competence is an important determinant of physical activity and play behavior in young people (Rudd et al., 2017). A physically active lifestyle improves resilience to mental, social and physical illness. Through esports, it is possible to help children and adolescents to develop basic movement skills by making use of adventure-based stages, immersive environments and sensor technology (Bisi et al., 2017). Mastering a range of motor skills through playing esports can help overweight children or individuals with limited access to gain confidence in their mobility while participating in a wide range of physical activities, which will eventually contribute to the improvement of overall community health. For these reasons, besides the physical and institutional comparisons, the psychological similarities of the players show that sports psychology practices and interventions can also be applied to the field of esports (Eroğlu & Uslu, 2019: 54–55).

In addition to participating in the event as a hobby, when video games turn into a profession and career where players lead a financial life, the motivation to play may also change (Griffiths, 2017). In various studies, player motivations were examined and some common motivational patterns were found even though the video game genres examined were different. For example, empirical studies have found that the most basic elements underlying the motivation of the players are interaction and competition (Vorderer, 2000). Interaction is an opportunity to communicate and collaborate with other players online, while competition is a mechanism for players to compare themselves with others (Eroğlu & Uslu, 2019: 55). This process is instrumental in creating unique subgroups with their own histories and cultures in the context of the games players are involved in and the communities and teams within the game.

As people become attached and enslaved to the technology that surrounds them (Rheingold, 2003), the constant online presence of individuals causes the concepts of leisure and work to change meaning again, and two separate entities that were previously separated are now intertwined. This situation coincides with the concept of heterotopic space (Bryce, 2001) which is based on the principle that more than one space comes together and the boundaries merge. According to the definition of Stebbins (1982), video games and professional recreational sports are defined as serious leisure activities (Seo, 2016). The concept of serious entertainment can be defined as an intermediate activity (such as participation in amateur sports) between everyday leisure and work activity, which has beneficial consequences such as self-acquisition and identity development during the activity. It is stated that the main elements that attract professional esports players to a career in esports are the pursuit of self-development, the praise of their mastery and abilities, respect, justice, equality and reciprocity (Seo, 2016). It is seen that the journey of esports players and the acquisition of a professional career give them the opportunity to experience high self-confidence, success and social recognition. While esports is a serious leisure activity, even professional gamers find it fun and motivating.

The costs of not playing games compared to the benefits for children include developmental delay, poor physical fitness, poor mental health, poor socialization and poor creativity (Bateson, 2014:105). Instincts such as the opportunity for self-development, competition and superiority while playing games constitute the motivation behind the fields such as art, science, law and commerce in the future life (Huizinga, 1949/2003). Stating that esports players have gained a professional player identity, Seo (2016) identified three stages on the analogy of Campbell's (1965) hero's journey. According to the narratives of esports players, in the first phase of the "call for adventure", players see games as a daily leisure activity (playing for fun, getting to know the player community). But meanwhile, they begin to form the first perceptions and gain interpersonal relationships in the social world of esports. The second phase, "on the way to competition", is the personal transformation process that transforms game participants into esports players. Players are improving their knowledge and skills on gameplay and mechanics, their behavior is changing in terms of playing games, and they are starting to participate in esports applications more regularly. In the last stage, the "master of two worlds" stage, professional players gain a new esports player identity. This new identity then creates opportunities in other important areas of their daily life and to validate their concept of being a global athlete.

Conclusion

To minimize the effects of the epidemic and to determine the most appropriate time to start sports activities again, to protect the health of the sports sector, athletes and spectators, to perform sports activities safely and to participate in sports at all levels, national public health institutions, epidemiologists, all researchers and practitioners working in the field of athlete health, sports organizations, sports federations and sports clubs should cooperate (Corsini et al., 2020; Timpka, 2020). From the medical sector perspective, electronic game-based interactive applications are influencing large-scale positive health behavior change throughout society and guarantee a comprehensive research and development program. Based on an empowerment approach to health promotion and utilizing game worlds and mechanics, mobile devices, sensors, social media and health data to create transformative experiences, carefully designed digital supportive virtual environments appear to have significant potential for both service access and cost effectiveness (Thin & Gotsis, 2013: 476). Alternative sports skill training (small area kinesthetic ball training, visualization, technical assistance with virtual and augmented reality, video analysis and theoretical training) should be organized by focusing on the deficiencies and needs of the athletes during and after the pandemy, and by making use of technological tools (Jukic et al., 2020). This process brings with it the need to develop augmented sports activities (acquiring exercise habits with portable sensors and stimuli, developing mental exercises and implicit skills with esports) where real and virtual worlds can be integrated and goal-oriented.

With the pandemy and its social restrictions, new opportunities have emerged, especially in terms of the use of virtual worlds. Due to the features of esports events suitable for multi-user virtual worlds, it is seen that in this period, they have turned from being end-user products into processes that are constantly evolving and offering new experiences to players. In the information age, it is imperative that the communication be structured in such a way as to convey the right message to the receiver in the shortest way. However, when it comes to the sale of a product or the provision of a service, as in virtual video games and esports, the most intense and enriched information load for the consumer comes into play not with the shortest way, but with impressive visuals, colors and design arrangements (Eroğlu & Uslu, 2019: 46–55). The virtual gaming phenomenon has been identified as a problematic area due to the increasing popularity, attractiveness, economics and psychology of esports, as well as the lack of physical activity and sedentary nature (van Hilvoorde & Pot, 2016), intense and excessive time spent (Griffiths, 2017). However, due to the limited field research in the literature, more theoretical and empirical studies are needed before solid conclusions can be drawn about esports psychology.

In the coming years, ergogenic aids in traditional sports such as nutrition, rest, physiotherapy and mental training in professional branches will increase their importance in esports. For these reasons, competitive esports teams need to work with more preventive sports professionals, child psychologists, counseling and guidance services for adolescents compared to traditional sports. In the field of esports, where the pandemy has increased the interest, the number of followers and investments have increased exponentially, it can be said that the most critical issue in the coming years will be the awareness of the family about the health of athletes and child protection.

It is seen that the coronavirus outbreak causes social isolation and hopelessness in people, and the need for psychological support increases (Banerjee, 2020). Although multi-user social video games and esports activities in particular serve as a serious leisure activity and psychological resilience tool during the pandemy, this new habit also prepares the infrastructure for the formation of new communities, subcultures, fandoms and social networks. As multi-user social media emerges in virtual worlds and social experiences in the gaming world more popularly spread to gaming platforms, the distinction between gaming and social worlds for goal-oriented gaming is blurring. In the coming years, this distinction may narrow further as the interoperability of open world games and social networks and multi-user virtual world integrations emerge (Smart et al., 2007: 7). This situation creates unique worlds and local communities within their own universes, especially in team matches, seasonal games and leagues. Multiplayer online worlds are spontaneously transforming into metaverses with long-term and constant connections of consumers.

Considering the nature, function and social role of the game, electronic sports games appear as archetypes of different digital cultures (eplayers, exergamers etc.) and living spaces (metaverses) in the near future. Class variation and the habitus of those who participate in sports is the most basic determinant of the meaning of any sportive practice and the gains to be obtained from this activity. Therefore, even if individuals with different habitus do the same sport, their opinions, participation motivations, expectations from that activity or their execution patterns will change (Bourdieu, 1984). Those who follow a particular esports event and participate in the game as a leisure activity often develop a personal player identity within this metaverse through the professional esports players they follow or the specific small circles of friends they interact with and the influencers of that group. Thus, autochronous worlds and local communities with their own codes, hierarchies and cultures begin to develop in game universes. Consumers maintain their roles and social identities unique to these autochronous worlds, mostly by realizing their existence on these platforms through their digital characters, avatars and teams. Even within the same game, different digital native communities and indigenous clans emerge depending on the language they speak, the country and culture they live in. The competitive environment in esports events, the mobility in multiplayer virtual worlds, and the social creativity in games updated and modded by eplayers have created a second nature in an online dimension. The rich and satisfying nature of esports creates an important motivation on identities of individuals. This nature is a combination of a dynamic social structure, characteristics and behaviors. This structure creates social groups, organizational behaviors, habitus, habits and social identities that affect the lives of individuals, where they maintain their online and face-to-face relationships in a heterotopic space.

In the light of that fact, there is a need not only for new standards and integrations, but also for complementary structures to go beyond existing metaverse and to enable players to maintain their inherent characteristics and unique social identities together. To ensure that players are accountable to the unique rules of each world they belong to, more advanced and collective systems are needed for user identity, group unofficial rules, trust and reputation (Smart et al., 2007: 7). The pandemy has made personalities, relationships, subgroups and collective identities of young people more visible in the digital environment in accordance with their habitus. On the other hand, this process did not offer a similarly generous environment for physical activity. Thus, psychological problems and physical inactivity experienced by children and young people, especially during the pandemy period, should not turn into a habit of behavior and chronic stress. In addition, studies show that exergames are also effective in the participation of different groups in active life. For this reason, esports activities involving social interaction and multi-user virtual worlds should be increased with digital physical activity rewards (such as pedometer goals, enhanced experience through information gathered by sensors and interfaces, and choices for physical participation in the cybernetic systems) and turned into a tool to lead people to an active life and socialization experience. This post-humanistic process brings a more integrated cybernetic active life for individuals, communities and organizations that are connectionless of the grid but coherent, or consistent in a connected network structure.

References

Adamus, T. (2012). Playing computer games as electronic sport: In search of a theoretical framework for a new research field. J. Fromme, & A. Unger (eds.), *Computer games and new media cultures: A handbook of digital games studies.* Dordrecht: Springer Netherlands, 477–490.

Aşçı, F. H. (1999). Benlik Kavramı ve Spor [Self Concept and Sport]. Spor Psikolojisi, Ankara: Bağırgan.

Aşçı, F. H. (2004). Benlik Algısı ve Egzersiz [Self-Perception and Exercise]. *Spor Bilimleri Dergisi,* 15(4), 233–266.

Bagozzi, R. P., & Dholakia, U. M. (2006). Antecedents and purchase consequences of customer participation in small group brand communities. *International Journal of Research in Marketing,* 23, 45–61.

Bagozzi, R. P., Bergami, M., Marzocchi, G. L., & Morandin, G. (2012). Customer–Organization relationships: Development and test of a theory of extended identities. *Journal of Applied Psychology,* 97(1), 63–76.

Banerjee, D. (2020). The COVID-19 outbreak: Crucial role the psychiatrists can play. *Asian Journal of Psychiatry,* 50, 102014. https://doi.org/10.1016/j.ajp.2020.102014

Baumann, S. (1986). *Praxis der Sportpsychologie.* München: Blv Buchverlag.

Baranowski, T., Maddison, R., Maloney, A., Medina, Jr. E., & Simons, M. (2014). Building a better mousetrap (exergame) to increase youth physical activity. *Games Health Journal,* 3(2), 72–78. https://doi.org/10.1089/g4h.2014.0018

Bateson, P. (2014). Play, playfulness, creativity and innovation. *Animal Behavior and Cognition,* 1(2), 99–112. https://doi.org/10.12966/abc.05.02.2014

Berger, B. G., & Owen, D. R. (1983). Mood alteration with swimming-Swimmers really do "feel better." *Psychosomatic Medicine,* 45, 425–433.

Biddiss, E., & Irwin, J. (2010). Active video games to promote physical activity in children and youth: A systematic review? *Archives of Pediatrics & Adolescent Medicine,* 164(7), 664–672.

Bisi, M. C., Panebionco, P., Polman, R., & Stagni, R. (2017). Objective assessment of movement competence in children using wearable sensors: An instrumented version of the TGMD-2 locomotor subset. *Gait & Posture,* 56, 42–48.

Bocock, R. (1993). *Consumption.* London: Routledge.

Bourdieu, P. (1978). Sport and social class. *Social Science Information,* 17(6), 819–840.

Bourdieu, P. (1984). *Distinction: A social critique of the judgement of taste.* Cambridge, MA: Harvard University Press.

Bowen, E. (2015). The impact of intimate partner violence on preschool children's peer problems: An analysis of risk and protective factors. *Child Abuse & Neglect,* 50, 141–150. https://doi.org/10.1016/j.chiabu.2015.09.005

Brock, T. (2017). Roger Caillois and e-sports: On the problems of treating play as work. *Games and Culture,* 12(4), 321–339.

Brown, D. W., Anda, R. F., Tiemeier, H., Felitti, V. J., Edwards, V. J., Croft, J. B., & Giles, W. H. (2009). Adverse childhood experiences and the risk of premature mortality. *American Journal of Preventive Medicine*, 37(5), 389–396. https://doi.org/10.1016/j.amepre.2009.06.021

Brown, S. M., Doom, J. R., Lechuga-Peña, S., Watamura, S. E., & Koppels, T. (2020). Stress and parenting during the global COVID-19 pandemic. *Child Abuse & Neglect*, 110, 104699. https://doi.org/10.1016/j.chiabu.2020.104699

Brunborg, G. S., Mentzoni, R. A., & Frøyland, L. R. (2014). Is video gaming, or video game addiction, associated with depression, academic achievement, heavy episodic drinking, or conduct problems? *Journal of Behavioral Addictions*, 3(1), 27–32.

Bryce, J. (2001). The technological transformation of leisure. *Social Science Computer Review*, 19(1), 7–16.

Caillois, R. (2001). *Man, play and games*. Chicago, IL: University of Illinois Press.

Campbell, J. (1965). *Hero with 1000 faces*. New York: World.

Cao, W., Fang, Z., Hou, G., Han, M., Xu, X., Dong, J., & Zheng, J. (2020). The psychological impact of the COVID-19 epidemic on college students in China. *Psychiatry Research*, 287, 1–5. https://doi.org/10.1016/j.psychres.2020.112934

Chamberlin, B., and Maloney, A. (2013). Active video games: Impacts and research. K. E. Dill (ed.), *The Oxford Handbook of Media Psychology*. New York: Oxford University Press, 316–333.

Chen, P., Mao, L., Nassis, G. P., Harmer, P., Ainsworth, B. E., & Li, F. (2020). Returning Chinese school-aged children and adolescents to physical activity in the wake of COVID-19: Actions and precautions. *Journal of Sport and Health Science*, 9(4), 322–324. https://doi:10.1016/j.jshs.2020.04.003

Cooke, J. E., Eirich, R., Racine, N., & Madigan, S. (2020). Prevalence of posttraumatic and general psychological stress during COVID-19: A rapid review and meta-analysis. *Psychiatry Research*, 292, 113347. https://doi.org/10.1016/j.psychres.2020.113347

Corsini, A., Bisciotti, G. N., Eirale, C., & Volpi, P. (2020). Football cannot restart soon during the COVID-19 emergency! A critical perspective from the Italian experience and a call for action. *British Journal of Sports Medicine*, 54(20), 3–6. https://doi.org/10.1136/bjsports-2020-102306

Danese, A., Smith, P., Chitsabesan, P., & Dubicka, B. (2020). Child and adolescent mental health amidst emergencies and disasters. *The British Journal of Psychiatry*, 216(3), 159–162. https://doi.org/10.1192/bjp.2019.244P

Deloitte (2020). Understanding the Impact of COVID-19 on the Sports Industry. UK. Retrieved from https://www2.deloitte.com/content/dam/Deloitte/uk/Documents/sports-business-group/deloitte-uk-understanding-the-impact-of-covid-19-on-the-sports-industry.pdf

Ekeland, E., Heian, F., & Hagen, K. B. (2005). Can exercise improve self esteem in children and young people? A systematic review of randomised controlled trials. *British Journal of Sports Medicine*, 39(11), 792–798.

Eroğlu, Y., & Uslu, T. (2019) Espor Endüstrisinde Tüketici, Marka ve Kimlik Etkileşimi [Consumer, Brand and Identity Interaction in Esports Industry], Sporda Dijital Devrim Espor, Güler, C. and Çakar, D.B. (eds.), Gazi Kitabevi, ISBN: 9786057805911

ESA (2014). Essential facts about the computer and video game industry. *Entertainment Software Association*. Retrieved from https://time.com/wp-content/uploads/2015/03/esa_ef_2014.pdf

Esen, E. (2019). Turkey's growing esports community crowned by new venue, Hürriyet Daily News, January 18. Retrieved from https://www.hurriyetdailynews.com/turkeys-growing-esports-community-crowned-by-new-venue-140609

Esen, S., Or, E., & Uslu, T. (2019). Destruction or creative destruction? Investigation of the relationship between coach change and team performance in football. *Journal of Health and Sport Sciences*, 2(1), 7–14. ISSN: 2651-5202

Esen, S., & Uslu, T. (2021). Smart urban transformation in the context of active cities: Evaluation of outdoor exercise parks in different districts of İstanbul in terms of social municipalist. *Fenerbahce University Journal of Sport Science (FBU-JSS)*, 1(2), 75–92. e-ISSN: 2791-7096

Faust, K., Meyer, J., & Griffiths, M. D. (2013). Competitive and professional gaming: Discussing potential benefits of scientific study. *International Journal of Cyber Behavior, Psychology and Learning*, 3(1), 67–77.

Felitti, V. J., Anda, R. F., Nordenberg, D., Williamson, D. F., Spitz, A. M., Edwards, V., Koss, M. P., & Marks J. S. (1998). Relationship of childhood abuse and household dysfunction to many of the leading causes of death in adults: The adverse childhood experiences (ACE). *American Journal of Preventive Medicine*, 14, 245–258. https://doi.org/10.1016/s0749-3797(98)00017-8

Field, T., Diego, M., & Sender, C. E. (2001). Exercise is positively related to adolescents relationships and academics. *Adolescence*, 36, 105–110.

Funk, J. B., Buchman, D. D., Jenks, J., & Bechtoldt, H. (2003). Playing violent video games, desensitization, and moral evaluation in children. *Journal of Applied Developmental Psychology*, 24(4), 413–436.

Funk, D. C., Pizzo, A. D., & Baker, B. J. (2018). eSport management: Embracing eSport education and research opportunities. *Sport Management Review*, 21, 7–13.

Garney, W. R., Wendel, M., McLeroy, K., Alaniz, A., Cunningham, G., Castle, B., Ingram, M., & Burdine, J. (2017). Using a community health development framework to increase community capacity: A multiple case study. *Family & Community Health: The Journal of Health Promotion & Maintenance*, 40(1), 18–23. https://doi.org/10.1097/FCH.0000000000000135

Gentile, D. A. (2009). Pathological video-game use among youth ages 8 to 18. *Psychological Science: A Journal of the American Psychological Society*, 20(5), 594–602.

Gentile, D. A., Choo, H., Liau, A., Sim, T., Li, D., Fung, D., & Khoo, A. (2011). Pathological video game use among youths: A two-year longitudinal study. *Pediatrics*, 127(2), 319–329. https://doi.org/10.1542/peds.2010-1353

Gifford-Smith, M. E., & Brownell, C. A. (2003). Childhood peer relationships: Social acceptance, friendships, and peer networks. *Journal of School Psychology*, 41, 235–284. https://doi.org/10.1016/S0022-4405(03)00048-7

Griffiths, M. D. (2017). The psychosocial impact of professional gambling, professional video gaming & eSports. *Casino & Gaming International*, 28, ss. 59–63.

Griffiths, M. D. and Davies, M. N. O. (2005). Videogame addiction: Does it exist? In J. Goldstein & J. Raessens (Hrsg.), *Handbook of computer game studies*. Boston, MA: MIT Press, 359–368.

Guimarães, A. V., Barbosa, A. R., & Meneghini, V. (2018). Active videogame-based physical activity vs. aerobic exercise and cognitive performance in older adults: A randomized controlled trial. *Journal of Physical Education and Sport*, 18(1), 203–209. https://doi.org/10.7752/jpes.2018.01026

Guttmann, A. (2004). *From ritual to record: The nature of modern sports.* New York: Columbia University Press.

Halabchi, F., Mazaheri, R., Sabeti, K., Yunesian, M., Alizadeh, Z., Ahmadinejad, Z., Aghili, S. M., & Tavakol, Z. (2020) Regular sports participation as a potential predictor of better clinical outcome in adult patients with COVID-19: A large cross-sectional study. *Journal of Physical Activity and Health*, 1–5. https://doi.org/10.1123/jpah.2020–0392

Hall, G., Laddu, D. R., Phillips, S.A., Lavie, C. J., & Arena, R. (2021). A tale of two pandemics: How will COVID-19 and global trends in physical inactivity and sedentary behavior affect one another? *Progress in Cardiovascular Diseases*, 64, 108–110. https://doi.org/10.1016/j.pcad.2020.04.005

Hallmann, K., & Giel, T. (2018). eSports-Competitive sports or recreational activity?. *Sport Management Review*, 21(1), 14–20. https://doi.org/10.1016/j.smr.2017.07.011

Heere, B. (2018). Embracing the sportification of society: Defining e-sports through a polymorphic view of sport. *Sport Management Review*, 21, 21–24.

Himmelstein, D., Liu, Y., & ve Shapiro, J. L. (2017). An exploration of mental skills among competitive league of legend players. *International Journal of Gaming and Computer-Mediated Simulations*, 9(2), 1–21.

Hong, J. C., & Liu, M. C. (2003). A study on thinking strategy between experts and novices of computer games. *Computers in Human Behavior*, 19(2), 245–258.

Honoré, C. (2005). *In praise of slowness: How a worldwide movement is challenging the cult of speed.* San Francisco, CA: HarperCollins.

Houghton, S., Milner, N., West, J., Dougles, G., Lawrence, V., Whiting, K., Tannock, R., & Durkin, K. (2004). Motor control and sequencing of boys with Attention Deficit/Hyperactivity Disorder (ADHD) during computer game play. *British Journal of Educational Technology*, 35(1), 21–34.

Hu, F. B. (2003). Sedentary lifestyle and risk of obesity and type 2 diabetes. *Lipids*, 38(2), 103–108.

Huizinga, J. (1949/2003). Play and Contest as Civilizing Functions. *Homo ludens: A study of the play-element in culture.* London: Routledge & Kegan Paul.

IESF (2020). International Esports Federation Members, Retrieved from https://iesf.org/about/members

Jenny, S. E., Manning, R. D., Keiper, M. C., & Olrich, T. W. (2017). Virtual(ly) athletes: Where eSports fit within the definition of 'sport'. *Quest*, 69(1), 1–18

Jin, D. (2010). ESports and television business in the digital economy. In D. Jin (ed.), *Korea's online gaming empire.* Cambridge, MA: MIT Press, 59–79.

Johnson, H. D., Lavoie, J. C., & Mahoney, M. (2001). Interparental conflict and family cohesion: Predictors of loneliness, social anxiety, and social avoidance in late adolescence. *Journal of Adolescent Research*, 16(3), 304–318.

Jukic, I., Calleja-González, J., Cos, F., Cuzzolin, F., Olmo, J., Terrados, N., Njaradi,. N, Sassi, R., Requena, B., Milanovic, L., Krakan, I., Chatzichristos, K., & Alcaraz, A. E. (2020). Strategies and solutions for team sports athletes in isolation due to COVID-19. *Sports*, 8, 56. https://doi.org/10.3390/sports8040056Kari, T. (2017). Exergaming usage: Hedonic and utilitarian aspects. Academic dissertation, University of Jyväskylä, Finland. Retrieved from https://jyx.jyu.fi/bitstream/handle/123456789/52866/978-951-39-6956-1_vaitos11022017.pdf

Keiper, M. C., Manning, D. C., Jenny, S., Olrich, T., & Croft, C. (2017). No reason to LoL at LoL: The addition of esports to intercollegiate athletic departments. *Journal for the Study of Sports and Athletes in Education*, 11, 143–160.

Kelly, J. R. (2000). Issues at the millennium: A global perspective. In M. C. Cabeza (ed.), *Leisure and human development*. Proposals for the 6th World Leisure Congress. Bilbao, Spain: University of Deusto, 51–57.

Korkmaz, M., & Uslu, T. (2020) Fitness Yapan Bireylerin Benlik Saygısı, Sosyal Görünüş Kaygısı ve Sosyalleşme Düzeyleri Arasındaki İlişkilerin İncelenmesi [Researching Relationships between Socialization Levels, Social Appearance Anxiety and Self-Esteem of Individuals Who Doing Fitness], *Spor Eğitim Dergisi*, 4(3), 1–18. e-ISSN 2602–4756

Kim, P. W., Kim, S. Y., Shim, M., Im, C. H., & Shon, Y. M. (2013). The influence of an educational course on language expression and treatment of gaming addiction for massive multiplayer online role-playing game (MMORPG) players. *Computers and Education*, 63, 208–217.

Kim, S. H., & Thomas, M. K. (2015). A stage theory model of professional video game players in South Korea: The socio-cultural dimensions of the development of expertise. *Asian Journal of Information Technology*, 14(5), 176–186.

Kim, Y., & Ross, S. D. (2006). An exploration of motives in sport video gaming. *International Journal of Sports Marketing & Sponsorship*, 8(1), 34.

Kluge, H. H. P. (2020). Physical and mental health key to resilience during COVID-19 pandemic. Retrieved from https://www.euro.who.int/en/health-topics/health-emergencies/coronavirus-covid-19/news/news/2020/3/mental-health-and-psychological-resilience-during-the-covid-19-pandemic

Larsen, L. H., Schou, L., Lund, H. H., & Langberg, H. (2013). The physical effect of exergames in healthy elderly-a systematic review. *Games for Health: Research, Development, and Clinical Applications*, 2(4), 205–212.

Lau, A. L., Chi, I., Cummins, R. A., Lee, T. M., Chou, K. L., & Chung, L. W. (2008). The SARS (Severe Acute Respiratory Syndrome) pandemic in Hong Kong: Effects on the subjective wellbeing of elderly and younger people. *Aging and Mental Health*, 12(6), 746–760. https://doi.org/10.1080/13607860802380607

Lee, S. A. (2020). Coronavirus anxiety scale: A brief mental health screener for COVID-19 related anxiety. *Death Studies*, 44(7), 393–401.

Li, J., Theng, Y.-L., & Foo, S. (2016). Effect of exergames on depression: A systematic review and meta-analysis. *Cyberpsychology, Behavior and Social Networking*, 19(1), 34–42. https://doi.org/10.1089/cyber.2015.0366

Li, J., Erdt, M., Chen, L., Cao, Y., Lee, S.Q., & Theng, Y.L. (2018). The social effects of exergames on older adults: Systematic review and metric analysis. *Journal of Medical Internet Research*, 20(6). https://doi.org/10.2196/10486

Lieberman, D. A., Fisk, M. C., & Biely, E. (2009). Digital games for young children ages three to six: From research to design. *Computers in the Schools*, 26, 299–313. https://doi.org/10.1080/07380560903360178

Lopez-Gonzalez, H., & Griffiths, M. D. (2016). Understanding the convergence of markets in online sports betting. *International Review for the Sociology of Sport*. https://doi.org/10.1177/1012690216680602Maddison, R., Simons, M., Straker, L., Witherspoon, L., Palmeira, A. & Thin, A.G. (2013). Active video games: an opportunity for enhanced learning and positive health effects? *Cognitive Technology*. 18(1), 6–13.

Maillot, P., Perrot, A., Hartley, A., & Do, M. C. (2014). The braking force in walking: Age-related differences and improvement in older adults with exergame training. *Journal of Aging and Physical Activity*, 22(4), 518–526. https://doi.org/10.1123/japa.2013-0001

Martoncik, M. (2015). e-Sports: Playing just for fun or playing to satisfy life goals? *Computers in Human Behavior*, 48, 208–211.

Mayall, B. (2002). *Towards a sociology for childhood: Thinking from children's lives*. Berkshire: Open University Press.

Monedero, J., Lyons, E. J., & Gorman, D. J. (2015). Interactive video game cycling leads to higher energy expenditure and is more enjoyable than conventional exercise in adults. *PLoS one*, 10(3), 1–12. https://doi.org/10.1371/journal.pone.0118470

Neamah, H. H., Sudfeld, C., McCoy, D. C., Fink, G., Fawzi, W. W., Masanja, H., Goodarz Danaei, G., Muhihi, A., Kaaya, S., & Fawzi, M. C. S. (2018). Intimate partner violence, depression, and child growth and development. *Pediatrics*, 142(1), e20173457. https://doi.org/10.1542/peds.2017-3457

Nelson, C. (2020). No future! Cybernetics and the genealogy of time governance. Partisan analysis of the present. Retrieved from https://illwill.com/no-future

Nitz, J. C., Kuys, S., Isles, R., & Fu, S. (2009). Is the Wii Fit™ a new-generation tool for improving balance, health and well-being? A pilot study. *Climacteric*, 13(5), 487–491. https://doi.org/10.3109/13697130903395193

Norman, R. E., Byambaa, M., De, R., Butchart, A., Scott, J., & Vos, T. (2012). The long-term health consequences of child physical abuse, emotional abuse, and neglect: A systematic review and meta-analysis. *PLoS Medicine*, 9, e1001349. https://doi.org/10.1371/journal.pmed.1001349

Oberle, E., Schonert-Reichl, K. A., & Thomson, K. (2010). Understanding the link between social and emotional well-being and peer relations in early adolescence: Gender-specific predictors of peer acceptance. *Journal of Youth and Adolescence*, 39, 1330–1342. https://doi.org/10.1007/s10964-009-9486-9

Oh, Y., & Yang, S. (2010). Defining exergames & exergaming. *Proceedings of the Meaningful Play*. East Lansing, MI: MSU Serious Games Program, 1–17.

Prescott, A. T., Sargent, J. D., & Hull, J. G. (2018). Metaanalysis of the relationship between violent video game play and physical aggression over time. *Proceedings of the National Academy of Sciences*, 115(40), 9882–9888. https://doi.org/10.1073/pnas.1611617114

Reardon, S. (2015). Ebola's mental-health wounds linger in Africa. *Nature*, 519, 13–14. https://doi.org/10.1038/519013a

Rodgers, B. (1977). Rationalizing sport policies: Sport in its social context. *International Comparisons*. Council of Europe: Strabourg.

Rodrigues, G. A. A., Rodrigues, P. C., da Silva, F. F., Nakamura, P. M., Higino, W. P., de Souza, R. A. (2018). Mini-trampoline enhances cardiovascular responses during a stationary running exergame in adults. *Biology of Sport*, 35(4), 335–342. https://doi.org/10.5114/biolsport.2018.78052.

Roopchand-Martin, S., Nelson, G., Gordon, C., & Sing, S. Y. (2015). A pilot study using the XBOX Kinect for exercise conditioning in sedentary female university students. *Technology and Health Care*, 23(3), 275–283. https://doi.org/10.3233/THC-150899

Rudd, J., Barnett, L., Farrow, D., Berry, J., Borkoles, E., & Polman, R.C.J. (2017). Effectiveness of a 16 week gymnastic curriculum at developing movement competence in children. *Journal of Science and Medicine in Sport*, 20(2), 164–169.

Ryan, R. M., & Deci, E. L. (2000). Intrinsic and extrinsic motivations: Classic definitions and new directions. *Contemporary Educational Psychology*, 25(1), 54–67.

Ryan, R. M., Rigby, C. S., & Przybylski, A. (2006). The motivational pull of video games: A self-determination theory approach. *Motivation and Emotion*, 30(4), 344–360.

Sabiston C. M., Pila E., Vani M., & Thogersen-Ntoumani C. (2019). Body image, physical activity, and sport: A scoping review. *Psychology of Sport and Exercise*, 42, 48–57. https://doi.org/10.1016/j.psychsport.2018.12.010

Sarı, A. Ş., & Uslu, T. (2012). Yeni Medya ile Geleneksel Pazarlama Yöntemlerinin Tüketici Tutumları Üzerindeki Etkisinin Nicel ve Nitel Olarak İncelenmesi. *Proceedings Book of International Symposium on Language and Communication: Research Trends and Challenges (ISLC)*, Izmir University, Mega Press, Erzurum, ISSN: 978-605-86867-0-0, 2671-2686.

Schaeperkoetter, C. C., Mays, J., Hyland, S. T., Wilkerson, Z., Oja, B., Krueger, K., Christian, R., & Bass, J. R. (2017). The 'new' student-athlete: An exploratory examination of scholarship eSport players. *Journal of Intercollegiate Sport*, 10, 1–21.

Schaffhauser, D. (2019). Esports Joining Olympics in 2024. Steam Universe. Retrieved from https://steamuniverse.com/articles/2019/07/30/esports-joining-olympics-in-2024.aspx

Seo, Y. (2016). Professionalized consumption and identity transformations in the field of eSports. *Journal of Business Research*, 69(1), 264–272. http://doi.org/10.1016/j.jbusres.2015.07.039

Shapiro, L.E. (1998). *EQ für Kinder. Wie Eltern die Emotionale IntelligenzIhrer Kinder Fördern Können*. München: dtv.

Shigemura, J., Ursano, R. J., Morganstein, J. C., Kurosawa, M., & Benedek, D. M. (2020). Public responses to the novel 2019 coronavirus (2019-nCoV) In Japan: Mental health consequences and target populations. *Psychiatry and Clinical Neurosciences*, 74(4), 281–282. https://doi.org/10.1111%2Fpcn.12988

Siddiqi, F.A. & Azim, M.E. (2021). Elderly and Balance Rehabilitation: Current Dynamics and Future Possibilities for Pakistan. *Foundation University Journal of Rehabilitation Sciences*, 1(1), 1–2.

Smart, J. M., Cascio, J., & Paffendorf, J. (2007). Metaverse Roadmap Overview: Pathways to the 3D Web. A Cross-Industry Public Foresight Project, Retrieved from https://metaverseroadmap.org/MetaverseRoadmapOverview.pdf

Sport Accord (2016). Definition of Sport, Organization Homepage, Retrieved from http://www.sportaccord.com/about/membership/definition-of-sport.php

Spor İstanbul (2021). İBB Spor Okulları E-Spor Eğitimi [İBB Sports Schools E-Sports Training]. Retrieved from https://spor.istanbul/ibb-spor-okullari-e-spor-egitimi/

Sprang, G., & Silman, M. (2013). Posttraumatic stress disorder in parents and youth after health-related disasters. *Disaster Medicine and Public Health Preparedness*, 7(1), 105–110. https://doi.org/10.1017/dmp.2013.22

Suits, B. (2007). The element of sport. W. Morgan (Ed.), *Ethics in sport*. Champaign, IL: Human Kinetics, 9–19.

Strand, K. A., Francis, S. L., Margrett, J. A., Franke, W. D., & Peterson, M. J. (2014). Community-based exergaming program increases physical activity and perceived wellness in older adults. *Journal of Aging and Physical Activity*, 22(3), 364–371. https://doi.org/10.1123/japa.2012-0302.

Stebbins, R. A. (1982). Serious leisure: A conceptual statement. *Pacific Sociological Review*, 25(2), 251–272.

Taylor, T. (2012). Raising the stakes: E-sports and the professionalization of computer gaming. Cambridge, MA: The MIT Press.

Thalemann, C. (2010). Pathologische Computernutzung bei Schülern verschiedener Schultypen der 8. und 10. Klassenstufe. Dissertation. Aus dem Institut für Medizinische Psychologie der Medizinischen Fakultät Charité – Universitätsmedizin Berlin.

Thin, A. G., & Gotsis, M. (2013). Game-based interactive media in behavioral medicine: creating serious affective-cognitive-environmental-social integration experiences. *Design, User Experience, and Usability. Health, Learning, Playing, Cultural, and*

Cross-Cultural User Experience. Berlin Heidelberg: Springer-Verlag, 470–479. http://doi.org/10.1007/978-3-642-39241-2_52

Tian, F., Li, H., Tian, S., Yang, J., Shao, J., & Tian, C. (2020). Psychological symptoms of ordinary Chinese citizens based on SCL-90 during the level I emergency response to COVID-19. *Psychiatry Research*, 288, 112992. https://doi.org/10.1016/j.psychres.2020.112992

Timpka, T. (2020). Sports health during the SARS-Cov-2 pandemic. *Sports Medicine*, 50(8), 1413–1416. https://doi.org/10.1007/s40279-020-01288-7

Toffler, A. (1980). *The Third Wave*, London: Collins.

Toulotte, C., Toursel, C., & Olivier, N. (2012). Wii Fit training vs. Adapted Physical Activities: Which one is the most appropriate to improve the balance of independent senior subjects? A randomized controlled study. *Clinical Rehabilitation*, 26(9), 827–835. https://doi.org/10.1177/0269215511434996

Troyer, E. A., Kohn, J. N., & Hong, S. (2020). Are we facing a crashing wave of neuropsychiatric sequelae of COVID-19? Neuropsychiatric symptoms and potential immunologic mechanisms. *Brain, Behavior, and Immunity*. 87, 34–39. https://doi.org/10.1016/j.bbi.2020.04.027

Uslu, T. (2017). Agile intrapreneurship in volatile business environment: Changing roles of financial managers and risk takers according to Schumpeterian approach. *Risk management, strategic thinking and leadership in the financial services industry: A proactive approach to strategic thinking, part V, Springer Contributions to Management Science Series*. Switzerland: Springer International Publishing AG. ISBN: 978-3-319-47171-6, 323–343.

Uslu, T., & Çubuk, D. (2015) Post-Modern ile Geleneksel Pazarlama Yöntemlerinin Tüketici Tutumları Üzerindeki Etkilerinin Nitel ve Nicel Yöntemlerle İncelenmesi [Investigation of the Effects of Post-Modern and Traditional Marketing Methods on Consumer Attitudes with Qualitative and Quantitative Methods], *Uluslararası Ekonomi Yönetimi ve Pazar Araştırmaları Kongresi*, 4–5 December 2015, Istanbul, 91–92.

Uslu, T., Çubuk, D., & ve E. İşbilen (2016). Yeni Medya Kullanıcıları ile Geleneksel Tüketiciler Arasındaki Farklar [Differences between New Media Users and Traditional Consumers], 20. *Türkiye'de İnternet Konferansı İnet-Tr'15*, 1–3 Aralık 2015, İstanbul Üniversitesi, İstanbul, 63–67.

Uslu, T., Rodoplu Şahin, D., & Çam, D. (2012). Yaş ve Kuşak Farklılıklarına Göre İnternet ve Bilgi Teknolojileri Kullanımının Düzeyi, Yarattığı Tekno-Politik Stres ve Sonuçları [Level of Techno-Political Stress and Use of Internet and Information Technologies by Age and Generational Differences], The *Journal of Knowledge Economy & Knowledge Management*, VII(I), Spring, 76–93. ISSN: 1308–3937

van Hilvoorde, I., & Pot, N. (2016). Embodiment and fundamental motor skills in eSports. *Sport, Ethics and Philosophy*, 10(1), 14–27. https://doi.org/10.1080/17511321.2016.1159246.

Vázquez, F. L., Otero, P., García-Casal, J. A., Blanco, V., Torres, Á. J., & Arrojo, M. (2018). Efficacy of video game-based interventions for active aging. A systematic literature review and meta-analysis. *PLoS one*, 13(12), e0208192. https://doi.org/10.1371/journal.pone.0208192

Vorderer, P. (2000). Interactive entertainment and beyond. D. Zillman & P. Vorderer (eds.), *Media entertainment: The psychology of its appeal*. Mahwah, NJ: Lawrence Erlbaum Associates, 21–36.

Wagner, M. G. (2006, June). On the scientific relevance of esports. Symposium conducted at 2006 international conference on Internet computing & conference on computer games development, Las Vegas, NV. Retrieved from http://ww1.ucmss.com/books/LFS/CSREA2006/ICM4205.pdf

Wagner, M. G. (2007). Competing in MetagameGamespace: eSport as the first professionalized computer metagames. F. von Borries, S.P. Walz, M. Bèottger, D. Davidson, H. Kelley, & J. Kücklich (eds.), *Space time play*. New York: Springer, 182–185.

Webb, K. (2019). Games like 'League of Legends' and 'Fortnite' Dominate the World of Esports, but they won't be Showing up at the Olympics Anytime soon. Business Insider. Retrieved from https://www.businessinsider.com/esports-olympics-ioc-pro-video-games-2019-12

Whalen, S. J. (2013). Cyberathletes' Lived Experience of Video Game Tournaments. Doctoral Dissertation, University of Tennessee.

Witkowski, E. (2012). On the digital playing field: How we "do sport" with networked computer games. *Games and Culture*, 7(5), 349–374.

Xiang, M., Zhang, Z., & Kuwahara, K. (2020). Impact of COVID-19 on children and adolescents' lifestyle behavior larger than expected. Elsevier Public Health Emergency Collection. https://doi.org/10.1016/j.pcad.2020.04.013

Yao, M. Z., & Zhong, Z. J. (2014). Loneliness, social contacts and internet addiction: A cross-lagged panel study. *Computers in Human Behavior*, 30, 164–170.

Chapter 8

Innovation in Sports Competitions during the COVID-19 Era

Mustafa Selçuk Özaydın and Cem Tinaz

Introduction

The outbreak of the COVID-19 pandemic, or coronavirus pandemic, is the defining global health crisis of our time, and it may be considered the most significant global challenge since World War Two. The pandemic has triggered the most severe economic recession in nearly a century, which may prove worse than the financial and economic crisis of 2008–2009. The fast and dramatic changes due to COVID-19 are far from over, with great uncertainty about the future. The world has already witnessed significant changes in both the employment and consumption patterns of individuals. The pandemic normalized remote work as well as remote leisure. Individuals stopped going to gyms, courts, and pitches as well as cinemas and theaters. It is very likely that some of the changes in individuals' habits are going to be permanent. The degree to which individuals, organizations, and institutions can adapt will determine whether societies succeed in managing this crisis or continue to have more problems with adverse long-term effects.

But what is undoubtedly clear is that the post-pandemic world will be different socially, economically, and health-wise. Due to the pandemic, almost all governments decided to stop social activities, including sports. As contemporary sports consumption is highly dependent on live sporting events, these closures and cancellations have had broad disruptive effects. The coronavirus crisis is somewhat different from previous global crises and has had real and tangible impacts on the sports industry. The COVID-19 pandemic has seen a move away from indoor sports facilities toward outdoor facilities, trails, and other recreational areas. Digital transformation and innovation in sports have accelerated dramatically during the pandemic. Innovation and digitalization in sports competitions have many advantages, such as decreasing costs and time consumption.

On the other hand, it is difficult to say that consuming sports through digitalized mediums offers a comparable experience to live gatherings. As a result, the social aspect of sports may come to gain more value in the future. Although fans can consume sports digitally, the athletes cannot feel the presence of the fans. It is a well-known and documented fact that live audiences enhance teams' and athletes' performance (Rhea et al., 2003; Epting et al., 2011); therefore, the absence of fans at sporting events is of no minor consequence.

DOI: 10.4324/9781003253891-8

This chapter's scope is confined to examining how innovation and digitalization in sports competitions have changed during the COVID-19 era and discussing the impacts and offerings of these initiatives on athletes and fans. This chapter aims to identify and review various innovative applications in different sports, and sports competitions, including leagues, championships, and circuit events from different world regions.

The Interruption of Sporting Events due to the Pandemic

On December 31, 2019, Wuhan Municipal Health Commission publicly revealed its coronavirus cases for the first time (WHO, 2020). Although the official statement was made in December 2019, there is a possibility that COVID-19 had been circulating in China for a few months before the official statement was made (Pekar et al., 2021). Even though China was able to control the local transmission of the disease by April 2020, there were reported cases in more than 100 countries by then, which meant that coronavirus had already spread all around the globe and the world was facing a global pandemic (LaFee, 2021).

The use of face masks and other protective gears has been highly encouraged if not enforced to prevent the spread of the coronavirus. In almost all countries, numerous precautions were taken to halt public events and mass gatherings and prevent people from coming together, which meant that sporting events were also canceled or postponed.

The first two international sporting events to be canceled due to the pandemic – both in China – were the Men's Alpine Skiing World Cup in the Yanqing District of Beijing in February 2020 (BBC, 2020) and the World Indoor Track and Field Championship, which was scheduled to be held in Nanjing in March 2020 (Dutch, 2020). Following the postponement of two international championships, the Chinese Super League (football) and Chinese Basketball Association League were also postponed due to the coronavirus pandemic. In the United States, the 2019/20 NBA regular season had 259 games left when it was suspended on March 11, 2020 (Christina Gough, June 1, 2021, Statista). The overall revenue losses for the leagues because of these cancellations were estimated to be between 350 and 450 million US dollars (USD) (Gough, 2020, Sport & Recreation). NBA managers decided to resume the league in a "bubble" at Walt Disney World's ESPN Wide World of Sports Complex in Orlando. Less than two months later, the 2020–2021 NBA season began in December 2020, with each team's regular season shortened to 72 games. Only seven clubs have played all their home games in front of spectators since the season began, even though people were allowed back into the arenas for this season. NCAA, which handles college sports, followed the professional league's lead and canceled all its remaining winter and spring championships, including the men's basketball tournament known as "March Madness." The event's television and marketing rights themselves are worth 867.5 million dollars, all of which were thrown into chaos when the tournament was canceled for the first time since its beginning in 1939. This cancellation potentially led to a loss of 933 million USD in television rights, ticket sales, and sponsorships. On March 24, 2020, the International Olympic Committee (IOC) decided to postpone the 2020 Tokyo Olympic Games, scheduled for July–August 2021. The financial cost to the host country is enormous: the new Olympic Stadium in Tokyo alone cost 277 million USD, and Japan has pledged a total of 13.4 billion USD to the event's organization (David Lange, November 26, 2020). Although the IOC has insurance in case of cancellation, the tournament's postponement to 2021 created numerous logistical and financial problems for all parties involved. Table 8.1 presents the information regarding the status of other major sporting events in the world.

Table 8.1 The Impact of COVID-19 Pandemic on Major Tournaments

Tournament	Postponement Date	Initial Verdict	Final Decision
Premier League	March 13, 2020	Postponed until the beginning of April.	Resumed on June 17.
La Liga	March 12, 2020	Matchdays 28 and 29 are postponed.	Resumed on June 11.
Bundesliga	March 13, 2020	Postponed until the beginning of April.	Resumed on May 16.
Ligue 1	March 13, 2020	Suspended until further notice.	Did not resume and registered with current standings.
Serie A	March 9, 2020	Suspended until further notice.	Resumed on June 20.
NBA	March 11, 2020	Suspended until further notice.	Resumed on July 30.
NFL	March 16, 2020	Postponed offseason training activities.	The season was delayed.
MLB	March 12, 2020	Canceled pre-season activities.	The season was delayed and shortened.
NHL	March 12, 2020	Suspended until further notice.	Playoffs resumed on August 10.
MLS	March 12, 2020	Suspended for 30 days.	Resumed on July 8 with fewer teams.
Formula 1	March 13, 2020	Postponed the races in March and April.	Resumed on July 5.
Tennis	March 12, 2020	ATP, WTA and ITF suspended all tournaments until mid-April.	Resumed with 2021 Australian Open on February 2021.
Olympics	March 30, 2020	Postponed to July 2021.	Started on July 23, 2021.
Golf	March 12, 2020	PGA Tour canceled all the tournaments.	Resumed on June 11.
Esports	March 13, 2020	Suspended all live events.	Still no live events.

Source: Compiled by the authors.

Despite being disregarded in the early stages of the pandemic, as the number of cases increased worldwide, effectively all sporting events were postponed or canceled. The events resumed with strict measures against the pandemic, such as playing without fans or forcing players and other stakeholders to have regular coronavirus tests. Numerous athletes missed competitions and games due to testing positive or travel restrictions, and fans could not attend any events. The revenue lost due to the lack of fans has serious adverse effects on sports, leading organizations to explore new ways of generating revenues. The physical restrictions of the pandemic forced the clubs, organizations, and policymakers to digitalize and innovate.

In addition to the cancellation of all amateur and professional competitions, sports establishments were shut down in almost all the countries in the world during the lockdown. Football pitches, basketball and tennis courts, swimming pools, and gyms were all closed. Individuals were not able to participate in almost all kinds of sports due to the unavailability of facilities. Millions of people developed new routines for engaging in sports from their homes. Fitness equipment sales grew by more than 170% during the lockdown (Research and Markets, 2020). Thousands of trainers started streaming online fitness, yoga, and dance sessions, which have been watched by millions of people. Hundreds of exercise applications have been launched for home workouts. In addition to fitness, sporting activities which can be performed at home with appropriate equipment such as rowing, running, and cycling have also become hugely popular. The home-fitness revolution is very likely to continue even after the pandemic is completely over and the extent to which it has changed people's sporting habits is yet to be witnessed.

The following section presents the stakeholders in the sports industry and discusses how these stakeholders were affected during the global pandemic.

Stakeholders of the Industry

As in any industry, the sports industry has multiple stakeholders that are involved in the production and consumption process. Especially in the lockdown period the industry almost completely stopped. The stakeholders in sports include governing bodies, administrators, coaches, athletes, spectators, and fans. In order to overcome the adverse impact of the pandemic, all the stakeholders tried to adapt to the "new normal," attempting to come up with solutions to the problems that arose and innovate to mitigate their losses.

Governing Bodies and Administrators

After the cancellation of the sporting events worldwide, the governing bodies' and administrators' primary responsibility was to determine how the events could be resumed without jeopardizing the athletes' and spectators' health. After the initial lockdown period, most sporting events resumed behind closed doors, as presented in Table 8.1. Although the spectators were not at risk, the athletes were, and therefore almost all the governing bodies in sports issued event protocols to ensure the safe return of sports.

The standard protocols included continuous monitoring and testing of players, hand sanitization, physical distancing, risk awareness, tracing contacts, and isolating and treating people with COVID-19 symptoms (FIFA, 2020). The athletes were not allowed to shake hands, and they were obliged to keep their physical distance during the events. Any other officials who were not athletes were required to wear face masks at all times, including the coaches, trainers, and medical personnel. Athletes who tested positive could be in quarantine for up to ten days and were only allowed to resume their activities if they managed to test negative twice in PCR tests after the sixth day of their initial diagnosis (Anthes & Petri, 2021).

At the same time, the sporting world witnessed some of the most exciting events in the history of world sports. For instance, the remainder of the NBA season was played in a bubble constructed in Disney World in Orlando. Twenty-two teams very invited to play based on their current rankings, and they stayed in three different hotels. Players had the freedom to refuse to play due to the pandemic, although they had binding contracts. Fans were not allowed into the bubble, but players were allowed to watch other teams play, and anyone who wanted to get into the bubble had to go through a 48-hour quarantine and test negative on a PCR test. Each night, everybody in the bubble was tested and all were obliged to wear face masks in common areas unless they were eating or training (Ward-Henninger & Maloney, 2020). The extreme measures succeeded, and there were no cases of COVID-19 in the bubble – with the season completed without any other interruption. The teams who were invited to the bubble were checking in at least for six weeks. For the two teams qualifying for the playoff final, that period would be almost three months therefore the players and staff had to be made comfortable. All residents had to be made feel at home to overcome the adverse psychological effects of the lockdown in and around the bubble. Players were provided with player-only lounges, amusement arcades, barbers, hairstylists, and manicurists in addition to the counselors provided by the NBA (ESPN, 2020).

The Ultimate Tennis Showdown (UTS) is another important innovation that emerged during the pandemic. UTS is an alternative tennis tournament that consists of four quarters of eight minutes with some additional rules. UTS was created by Patrick Mouratoglou, the well-known tennis coach, and aims to attract younger generations with its dynamic gameplay and shortened duration. Furthermore, the prize money is shared 70:30 between the winner and the loser of the game, enabling the lower-ranked players to generate income and prize money from the ITF and ATP tournaments. The first UTS tournaments featured several top 10 and 20 players since the ITF and ATP tournaments had not resumed yet (UTS, 2020). The third and fourth UTS events were not as popular as the first two because of the resumption of regular events. Although the impact of UTS on tennis and its popularity among fans is still a matter of question, it is for sure an innovative and bold enterprise.

Another innovative step in tennis is the collaboration between the Women's Tennis Association (WTA) and KPMG which is s a global network of professional firms providing audit, tax, and advisory services. WTA designed an application to enhance communication and the tracking and monitoring of players with the help of KPMG (Cohen, 2021). In addition to players' vaccination status and test results, the application provides present and past data about tournaments and performance insights. Providing such additional information encourages players to download and use the application.

Amazon and NFL extended their contract for the live streaming rights of the NFL through the popular live streaming service Twitch. Amazon was already providing additional features such as on-demand replay and a selection of commentators for the games. This year, they have added the data-tracking x-ray tool, enabling streamers to access real-time player tracking data (Lemire, 2021). Enhancing the streaming experience is extremely important for both the broadcasters and the consumers. Despite the growing popularity of online streaming services, there are still consumers reluctant to use such services. Providing additional features as such might encourage people to use online streaming services rather than TV broadcasts.

Although the COVID-19 pandemic is not over yet, it has remained imperative for the sports industries to continue in whatever guise possible. The global pandemic showed the sporting industry's dependence on "hot money" which signifies the currency that quickly and regularly moves between financial markets. Governing bodies, organizations, clubs, and athletes all rely on sporting events, and many would be unlikely to survive another lockdown. The governing bodies in the sporting industry are thrilled with the resumption of sporting events, but health authorities in the world are concerned. The World Health Organization (WHO) issued guidelines reports for the public health authorities, explicitly sporting events. WHO strongly recommends that the governing bodies coordinate the decision-making process, reconsider the need for travel and mass events, use a risk-based approach and enhance public health and social measures (WHO, 2021).

Coaches and Athletes

In the initial stages of the pandemic, athletes were also in lockdown like everybody else. Although it was not sure when the sporting events might resume, the athletes were obliged to keep themselves in good shape, and since they were not able to train with their teammates and trainers, it meant that they had to train on their own. Before discussing how athletes' training schemes have transformed during the pandemic, it is essential to mention the probable dangers athletes faced before the events resumed.

First, due to a lack of or decrease in training during the early stages of the pandemic, athletes were most likely to lose their strength and endurance, which would have increased the risk of injuries when competitions resumed (Paoli & Musumeci,

2020). In addition to the risk of injury, Baggish and his colleagues (2020) argue that detraining during the pandemic has been a threat to athletes' cardiac safety when they start competing again. Finally, it should be mentioned that the permanent adverse effects of COVID-19 are yet to be discovered. Like anyone else, athletes still face the risk of getting infected and developing severe symptoms even if they are vaccinated. Evidence suggests that lung functions decrease in post-infection COVID-19 patients (Torres-Castro et al., 2020); therefore, getting infected with COVID-19 is also a significant threat that athletes face. Vaudreuil and his colleagues (2021) found that NBA players who have recovered from COVID-19 performed significantly worse in the matches played in the "NBA bubble" than those who did not get infected.

As presented in Table 8.1, in March 2020, all sporting events were canceled or postponed worldwide. Despite the uncertainty of the events' resume date, the athletes had to keep training. The two main types of training during the initial lockdown that come forward, were synchronized online training and unsynchronized online training (Tjønndal, 2020). In synchronized online training, athletes and trainers come together through a visual gathering app. It could be a one-to-one session or a group session, depending on the sport the athlete is training for. In unsynchronized online training, athletes train by themselves using online training material such as videos and programs. It is essential to mention that these trainings are mostly strength and endurance training, due to equipment limitations. Although online training strategies have been used for a while, the main target for these strategies was amateurs who wanted to train with personal trainers; however, with the coronavirus pandemic, professional athletes started using online training programs. In another study, Teodorescu and his colleagues (2021) argue that coaches have to change their training targets. During the lockdown, most coaches focused on the physical aspect of training to keep their athletes in good physical shape. Due to the nature of some sports, it can be immensely difficult to train for strategies while training alone. The tactical preparations diminished significantly due to self-training, whereas more emphasis has been put on theoretical training. Furthermore, the study presents findings regarding mental challenges faced by athletes and the loss of their motivation. Washif and his colleagues (2021) also studied the adverse training effects on athletes' mental health during the lockdown. The authors conclude that athletes were suffering from motivation loss and emotional stress, which have adverse effects on training performance. The NBA created an application to check players' mental well-being. Two simple questions were asked to the players twice every week: "How are you doing?" and "What can we do to make your day better?" (Avidon, 2020). Especially in North American professional leagues – where players have had to stay away from home for a few months during the playoffs due to the isolation measures – players' mental health has been seriously threatened. This application enables the NBA officials to be proactive, meaning that they can act before a player is mentally distressed.

Although the lockdown disrupted athletes' training routines and teams, it also meant extra time to revise their routines. One team that made good use of this was the Toronto Raptors. The analysts put down several dozens of clips for offensive and defensive plays, which enabled coach Nick Nurse and his staff to study their plays throughout the season, something that would not have been possible without the lockdown (Arnovitz, 2020). After each game, the analysts and coaching staff prepare for the next game by analyzing the opponent rather than their plays.

Athletes already used smart devices and wearable technology to track their progress, measure their performance and control their physical health. These smart tools have long been in the process of integration with sports equipment. Whether kicking a football, throwing a javelin, or shooting a basketball, the smart equipment can detect the correctness of any range of techniques. The sensors in the smart equipment collect data for each kick, throw, or shot (Delgado, 2015). This smart gear has become more critical than ever, especially during the lockdown, where athletes trained themselves. Both the coaches and the athletes relied heavily on the smart equipment to track their training performance and their physical condition. Especially since fever is one of the main symptoms of the coronavirus, regular temperature checks are essential to keep the athletes and the ones around them safe against the coronavirus, which can be done efficiently with the correct device.

Finally, it is essential to mention the social burden athletes' have carried during the pandemic. Athletes, like many other celebrities, have people looking up to them. They are obliged to set an example to society for the greater good – and often athletes publicly advocate social movements. In the early phases of the pandemic, an NBA player, Rudy Gobert, mocked the coronavirus measures and expressed his disbelief around the COVID-19 pandemic. A few days later, he tested positive and apologized for his reckless behavior (Leng & Phua, 2020). Today, the most important channel of communication between fans and athletes is social media platforms. Fans are able to get in touch with athletes, coaches, and even the presidents of clubs and organizations. Celebrities in the sports industry are able to set trends, and influence people or brands. Especially during times like this, athletes should encourage the adoption of safety measures so as to be good role models.

Spectators and Fans

Stadiums are a central feature of the sports world. While they are obviously the place where the magic happens, they are the homes to unforgettable memories for people. Live sport is a central and critical part of the lives of millions of people. Watching a match is not just about supporting teams but is also about coming together in a commonplace and sharing an identity. Sports fandom is one of the strongest forms of modern identity and many people define themselves through the teams they support. Organizations and clubs provide a commonplace for the fans and in return they generate significant revenue.

In addition to being a vital source of revenue for sports clubs and organizations, fans are an essential part of any competition. Fans might enjoy a sporting event by seeing it live at the venue, on TV at home or in public, or by livestreaming it – but the dedicated fans mostly prefer live crowds. The atmosphere is crucial while enjoying a live sporting event. That is why most football broadcasters in Europe provided crowd noise in the background while broadcasting the games when the leagues resumed without fans in the stadiums. The director of BBC Sport, Barbara Slater, states that "artificial noises improve the enjoyment of football fans watching games on TV or a mobile device" (Kelly, 2020). From boxing to basketball, baseball to tennis, only a tiny proportion of the fans are ever lucky enough to attend the events. In contrast, the majority of fans watch the games on TV or through online streaming services. The enjoyment of the fans that are not at the stands is perhaps more important than those at the stands, which is why broadcasters have been trying to please them. The artificial crowd noise is just one of the many innovative solutions to enhance their enjoyment during the pandemic.

A less technological innovation came from Germany, where the fans of Borussia Mönchengladbach placed cardboard scale models on the stands to make the players feel better (Majumdar & Naha, 2020). An interesting and somewhat bizarre attempt came from the Korean football team Seoul FC. Stadium officials placed a couple of dozens of sex dolls on the stands with jerseys to make the players feel "at home," which received huge criticism from the public and a record fine from the Korean Football Federation (McCurry, 2020). A Danish football club, AGF Aarhus virtually brought thousands of fans to the stadium using 556 Zoom meetings on a huge screen which was built in the stadium (Lauletta, 2020). Fans were able to watch the game together over Zoom and players were able to feel the presence in the stands. Another Danish team, Midtjylland set up big screens in the parking lot outside the stadium so that fans could watch the match taking place inside. The club also partnered with a local radio station to enable the fans to listen to the game on their car radios (Wright, 2020). A drive-in football experience was offered to the fans and thousands of people attended the event.

As mentioned earlier, feeling the presence of fans is crucial for the athletes, and in the English Premier League, clubs make sure the players are feeling the support. During the Premier League games, players could see the fans watching the games at home through the screens in the stadiums (SportsMedia, 2020). Although fans were not physically at the stadium, players were still made aware of their presence. Fans are a critical element of the home advantage, and unsurprisingly evidence shows that home advantage significantly decreased during the pandemic when the games were played behind closed doors (McCarrick et al., 2021). In addition to contributing to home advantage, keeping the fans digitally in the stands makes sure that the bond between the fans and their team stays strong. Being digitally present is a priceless memoir for the fans which can be turned into a revenue stream for the clubs. In most of the major tournaments, fans are allowed to attend the events, therefore there is no need for screens anymore. Still, clubs and organizations can offer fans the chance to be broadcasted on screens in the stadiums during the events as another means of generating income. To keep the bond strong during the lockdown and the offseason, teams in North American professional leagues have hosted virtual events to bring the fans and the athletes together. These digital events aim to get the fans excited about the upcoming season and increase their overall engagement (Avidon, 2020).

Having no fans on the stands is, of course, an adverse effect of the COVID-19 pandemic. However, there are some upsides to it, such as in the case of the NBA. The most desired and paid tickets in basketball games are for the courtside seats, and since these seats were empty in the NBA 2020 playoffs, these tickets were sold virtually. Cameras were set up in the place of the courtside seats, and fans could enjoy the game from that angle if they were willing to pay extra (Schmidt & Fühner, 2020). Teams were able to recover some of the lost revenue, and a select few fans' enjoyment of watching the games was enhanced. Organizations and clubs from many different sports are trying to enhance the pleasure of watching sporting events. Virtual stadium tours, customized watching experiences, virtual meetings, and social media polls are just the beginning of the digitalization in watching sports. The fans are sure to witness much more soon.

Broadcasters will probably change their formulaic approach to the sport due to COVID-19. Broadcasters started showing videos of fans at home at appropriate moments during games in the lockdown period. The fans on the couch may indeed replace the fans in the stands, which again are generally shown on TV broadcasts. The broadcaster does not need to put cameras in public places to broadcast fan emotions. Almost all the fans have smartphones and internet data packages that enable them to record, send, or livestream their reactions and emotions during the events. Along with every other type of demographic, an essential proportion of sports fans has become digitalized over the past decade, generating and sharing content over the internet (Pegoraro, 2013). We might see mobile applications that enable fans to send videos directly to the broadcaster in the coming years. The broadcaster will select a number of them to stream during or after the event. This has been already done with text messages and tweets. Commentators and experts in the broadcasts have for some time now been answering viewer questions during and after events to make the events more interactive. Videos might replace the text in the future, and the fans at home would start to feel more involved (Majumdar & Naha, 2020).

Concluding Remarks

The coronavirus pandemic is probably one of the biggest social and economic challenges in the history of humankind, and in many ways, it is going to permanently change daily living. Thanks to developing technologies and the improving means of communication, people are able to work from home, shop from home and even socialize from home. Like all other aspects of social life, sporting events have been severely affected by the pandemic. Sports organizations were already going through a digital transition due to changing consumer demands, and undoubtedly the pandemic has accelerated the transition. Clubs, organizations, coaches, and athletes must adapt to the changing environment and become more innovative.

All of the stakeholders in the industry have been affected by the pandemic in one way or another. On many occasions, stakeholders came together to respond to the changing circumstances. The communication and collaboration between organizations, clubs, athletes, and coaches have reached an all-time high. The clubs', organizations', and coaches' control over the athletes has increased significantly. Athletes are being monitored not only during their trainings but also in their daily lives and even in their sleep thanks to the improving technology. In a professional sense, such control can be beneficial for performance but in terms of ethics, it remains a gray area. Being constantly monitored might have adverse effects on athletes' mental health. The COVID-19 pandemic accelerated the existing trend in remote work and caused the boundaries between personal and professional lives to become massively blurred. Many employees complain about higher workloads and inconsiderate behavior from their superiors. Similar effects might be present in the sports industry, which is very likely to have adverse effects on athletes.

It is also essential to be mindful of the adverse economic effects of the pandemic. All the organizations and clubs have lost vast amounts of revenue due to the cancellation of events and due to the lack of fans in the early stages of the pandemic. The decrease in revenues has canceled transfers, delayed infrastructural investments and in a very unique case, caused the loss of a superstar. The bond between Lionel Messi and FC Barcelona seemed unbreakable at least it looked like it can't be broken with money. The Argentine star had a release clause of 700m € which wouldn't have been paid by any club in the World. It is quite ironic that his departure from Barcelona was related to finances. Due to the floating salary cap rule in La Liga, which was introduced in 2013, clubs are obliged to keep their salary/revenue ratio below 70%. The drastic decrease in Barcelona's revenues due to the pandemic made it impossible for Barcelona to pay Messi's wages (Borg, 2021), which led to his transfer to the French giant Paris Saint-Germain (PSG). His departure is perhaps one of the harshest economic consequences of the global pandemic in sports How Messi's departure will affect Barcelona and PSG is still a matter that needs to be answered, but it will inevitably have immense effects. Although not all clubs lost their superstars, all have suffered from the adverse effects of the pandemic. The employees on the other hand went through similar difficulties. Athletes, coaches, and other staff either lost their jobs or experienced pay cuts. Both governments and intergovernmental organizations have been subsidizing various industries to help to overcome the adverse economic effects. Due to its unique nature, the sports industry is often seen as a luxury rather than a necessity. However, it should be kept in mind that – for better or worse – the sports industry is crucial to the economic well-being of millions of people worldwide.

The growth of professional sports has been rather unsustainable in the previous decade. The increasing commercialization of sports caused sports to grow distant from their ethical and cultural roots. Corruption, doping, and competitive imbalances have all led to the questioning of sports' relevance and true meaning.

In many cases, fans have become reduced to consumers or investors that are being used to finance sports organizations and clubs. The financial distress the sports industry went through during the pandemic might be a wake-up call for the whole industry to rely less on hot money. Clubs are organizations that are already looking for new and innovative ways to get back on their feet.

So far, we have seen several innovative solutions to the problems at hand, but it does not mean that things will go back to normal when or if the pandemic is truly over. The changing consumer needs, rapid digitalization of the world, and different demands of the younger generations are challenging the existing mechanisms in sports. The long-run winners will be those sports, organizations, and clubs that can innovate during this period and adapt to this challenge.

References

Anthes, E., & Petri, A. (2021, July 21). *Olympics virus cases raise tricky questions about testing.* Retrieved from NYtimes.om: https://www.nytimes.com/2021/07/21/health/coronavirus-olympics-testing.html

Arnovitz, K. (2020, July 2). *How NBA coaches are preparing for the bubble in Orlando as restart nears.* Retrieved from ESPN.com: https://www.espn.com/nba/story/_/id/29375147/how-nba-coaches-preparing-bubble-orlando-restart-nears

Avidon, E. (2020, October 1). *Pandemic speeds up digital transformation in sports.* Retrieved from SearchBusinessAnalytics.com: https://searchbusinessanalytics.techtarget.com/news/252489982/Pandemic-speeds-up-digital-transformation-in-sports

Baggish, A., Drezner, J., Kim, J., Martinez, M., & Prutkin, J. (2020). The resurgence of sport in the wake of COVID-19: Cardiac considerations in competitive athletes. *British Journal of Sports Medicine, 54*(19), 1130–1131.

BBC. (2020, January 29). *Coronavirus: World Cup alpine skiing events in China cancelled Last updated on.* Retrieved from BBC – Sport: https://www.bbc.com/sport/winter-sports/51293035

Borg, S. (2021, August 15). *Why did Lionel Messi leave Barcelona? Explaining what happened between Messi and La Liga club.* Retrieved from SportingNews.com: https://www.sportingnews.com/us/soccer/news/why-did-lionel-messi-leave-barcelona-explain-what-happened/1dwtnwr31kcox1qki0fueupe64

Cohen, A. (2021, October 5). *WTA partners with KPMG to design health and safety app.* Retrieved from Sporttechie.com: https://www.sporttechie.com/wta-partners-with-kpmg-to-design-health-and-safety-app/

Delgado, R. (2015, January 20). *Sports training gets smart: How new technology helps athletes reach the next level.* Retrieved from Social Media Today: https://www.socialmediatoday.com/content/sports-training-gets-smart-how-new-technology-helps-athletes-reach-next-level

Dutch, T. (2020, January 29). *World indoor championships postponed in response to coronavirus outbreak.* Retrieved from Runners World: https://www.runnersworld.com/news/a30706482/world-indoor-championships-coronavirus-outbreak/

Epting, K., Riggs, K., Knowles, J., & Hanky, J. (2011). Cheers vs. Jeers: Effects of audience feedback on individual athletic performance. *North American Journal of Psychology, 13*(2), 299–312.

ESPN. (2020, October 8). *Everything that happened in the NBA bubble*. Retrieved from ESPN. com: https://www.espn.com/nba/story/_/id/30055011/everything-happened-nba-bubble

FIFA. (2020, October 1). *Bureau of the FIFA Council approves International Match Protocol and adapts rules on release of players*. Retrieved from FIFA.com: https://www.fifa. com/tournaments/mens/worldcup/qatar2022/media-releases/bureau-of-the-fifa-council-approves-international-match-protocol-and-adapts-rule

Kelly, R. (2020, June 24). *Premier League crowd noise: Why it is used, how to turn it on or off & can players hear?* Retrieved from Goal.com: https://www.goal.com/en/news/premier-league-crowd-noise-why-how-to-turn-it-on-off-can-players-/1fn9xscokj38t10ssltv3ve7tg

LaFee, S. (2021, March 18). *Novel coronavirus circulated undetected months before first COVID-19 cases in Wuhan, China*. Retrieved from UC San Diego Health: https:// health.ucsd.edu/news/releases/Pages/2021-03-18-novel-coronavirus-circulated-undetected-months-before-first-covid-19-cases-in-wuhan-china.aspx

Lauletta, T. (2020, May 29). *A soccer team in Denmark brought thousands of fans into their stadium through Zoom and people can't decide if it's clever innovation or something out of 'Black Mirror'*. Retrieved from Insider: https://www.insider.com/ danish-superliga-zoom-agf-aarhus-fans-2020–5

Lemire, J. (2021, October 4). *Amazon to infuse data-tracking X-ray tool on its thursday night NFL football streams*. Retrieved from Sporttechie.com: https://www.sporttechie.com/ amazon-to-infuse-data-tracking-x-ray-tool-on-its-thursday-night-nfl-football-streams

Leng, H. K., & Phua, Y. X. (2020). Athletes as role models during the COVID-19 pandemic. *Managing Sport and Leisure, 27*(1–2), 1–6.

Majumdar, B., & Naha, S. (2020). Live sport during the COVID-19 crisis: Fans as creative broadcasters. *Sport in Society, 23*(7), 1091–1099.

McCarrick, D., Bilalic, M., Neave, N., & Wolfson, S. (2021). Home advantage during the COVID-19 pandemic: Analyses of European football leagues. *Psychology of Sport and Exercise, 56*, 1–10.

McCurry, J. (2020, May 21). *South Korea football league imposes record fine on FC Seoul over sex dolls outrage*. Retrieved from The Guardian: https://www.theguardian.com/world/2020/may/21/ south-korea-football-league-imposes-record-fine-on-fc-seoul-over-sex-dolls-outrage

Paoli, A., & Musumeci, G. (2020). Elite athletes and COVID-19 lockdown: Future health concerns for an entire sector. *Journal of Functional Morphology and Kinesiology, 5*(2), 1–3.

Pegoraro, A. (2013). Sport fandom in the digital age. In P. Pedersen (ed.), *Handbook of Sport Communication* (pp. 248–258). London: Routledge.

Pekar, J., Worobey, M., Moshiri, N., Scheffler, K., & Wertheim, J. (2021). Timing the SARS-CoV-2 index case in Hubei province. *Science, 372*(6540), 412–417.

Research and Markets (2020, April 28). Fitness equipment grows 170% during coronavirus lockdown. Retrieved from ResearchandMarkets.com: https://www.researchandmarkets. com/issues/fitness-equipment-grows-170pct?utm_source=dynamic&utm_medium= BW&utm_code=m6djfc&utm_campaign=1386770++Fitness+Equipment+Sales+ Grow+by+170%25+During+Coronavirus+Lockdown&utm_exec=joca220bwd

Rhea, M., Landers, D., Alvar, B., & Arent, S. (2003). The effects of competition and the presence of an audience on weight lifting performance. *Journal of Strength and Conditioning Research, 17*(2), 303–306.

Schmidt, S., & Fühner, J. (2020, November 18). *How COVID is pushing tech to revamp sports*. Retrieved from Harvard Business School: https://digital.hbs.edu/innovation-disruption/ how-covid-is-pushing-tech-to-revamp-sports/

SportsMedia. (2020, June 16). *Premier League closed-doors return to feature fans on live video wall*. Retrieved from SportsMedia.com: https://www.sportspromedia.com/news/premier-league-restart-live-fan-video-wall-celebration-camera/

Teodorescu, S., Bota, A., Popescu, V., Mezei, M., & Urzeala, C. (2021). Sports training during COVID-19 first lockdown – A Romanian Coaches' experience. *Sustainability*, *13*(18), 1–27.

Tjønndal, A. (2020). #Quarantineworkout: The use of digital tools and online training among boxers and boxing coaches during the COVID-19 pandemic. *Frontiers in Sports and Active Living*, *2*, 8–19.

Torres-Castro, R., Vasconcello-Castillo, L., Alsina-Restoy, X., Solis-Navarro, L., Burgos, F., Puppo, H., & Vilaró, J. (2020). Respiratory function in patients post-infection by COVID-19: A systematic review and meta-analysis. *Pulmonology*, *27*(4), 328–337.

UTS. (2020). *Frequently asked questions*. Retrieved from UTSLive.tv: https://utslive.tv/faq/frequently-asked-questions/

Vaudreuil, N., Kennedy, A., Lombardo, S., & Kharazzi, D. (2021). Impact of COVID-19 on recovered athletes returning to competitive play in the NBA "Bubble". *Orthopaedic Journal of Sports Medicine*, *9*(3), 1–5.

Ward-Henninger, C., & Maloney, J. (2020, July 30). *NBA Disney World rules: Details of how the bubble will work with league set to resume play in Orlando*. Retrieved from CBSSports.com: https://www.cbssports.com/nba/news/nba-disney-world-rules-details-of-how-the-bubble-will-work-with-league-set-to-resume-play-in-orlando/

Washif, J., Kassim, S., Lew, P., Chong, C., & James, C. (2021). Athlete's perceptions of a "Quarantine" training camp during the COVID-19 lockdown. *Frontiers in Sports and Active Living*, *2*, 1–8.

WHO. (2020, April 27). *WHO Timeline – COVID-19*. Retrieved from World Health Organization: https://www.who.int/news/item/27-04-2020-who-timeline---covid-19

WHO. (2021, May 28). *Sporting events during the COVID-19 pandemic considerations for public health authorities*. Retrieved from euro.who.int: https://www.euro.who.int/__data/assets/pdf_file/0005/502853/sporting-event-considerations-COVID-19.pdf

Wright, C. (2020, June 2). Drive-in football! Fans watch at stadium from comfort of cars, limos and quad bikes. Retrieved from ESPN.com: https://www.espn.com/soccer/blog-the-toe-poke/story/4105206/drive-in-football!-fans-watch-at-stadium-from-comfort-of-carslimos-and-quad-bikes

Chapter 9

Economic Impacts of COVID-19 on Sports Sector

A Review of the Developments of Sports Events, Audience and Emerging Sectoral Trends

Burcu Turkcan

Introduction

The world has experiencing a new era with the emergence of COVID-19 pandemic. The recent pandemic has given rise to transformations in all economies. Many sectors have negatively been affected by lockdowns, border bans and other precautions related to the pandemic. Trade, tourism, sportive and cultural events have been the most affected sectors on the global scale (UNWTO, 2020). Downturns in these sectors have dragged the global economy into a brand-new economic crisis and re-reading the global economy has become a necessity. Sectoral analyses have become more important than ever before. In this respect, this chapter tries to shed light on the recent developments in the sports sector and its near future with emerging sectoral trends.

The sports sector is a substantial but sometimes underestimated sector in the global economy. It has several interlinkages with manufacturing (through sports products and sports brands), tourism (through mega and major sports events) and cultural (creative) activities (through media). It contributes to the balance of payments by the courtesy of major sports events. It also creates employment and income in domestic markets. United Nations (2020) underlines that sports activities contribute to the Sustainable Development Goals (SDGs) with their socio-economic impacts. However, the COVID-19 pandemic has affected this sector in many aspects. It has created a deep and staggering crisis in all sports and related activities all over the world. Most of the mega and major sports events have been postponed or canceled during 2020. Some of the events have been organized and played behind closed doors. No audience has been allowed to attend the events. Teams and clubs have faced many financial challenges. Athletes have experienced low morale and declining physical conditions. Audience has been faced with low morale and the loss of community networks. All these developments have pushed the sports sector to a quick transformation in terms of esports activities. In this context, this study aims to review the economic impacts of COVID-19 on the sports sector and to offer a framework for policy formation for the post-COVID era. In this respect, the main contribution of this study is expected to be on the point that a brief review of the economic impacts of

DOI: 10.4324/9781003253891-9

COVID-19 on sports activities would help to take effective policy actions for the new era. In this context, after a brief introduction, the first section is devoted to the short history of the global economic crisis, driven by the pandemic. Then, the second section is dedicated to the economic impacts of COVID-19 on sports events and audiences. Lastly, the third section is attributed to emerging trends in sports activities and conclusions summarize some policy recommendations for the emerging post-COVID era.

COVID-19: Not only a pandemic but also a global economic crisis

The global economy has been experiencing a new economic crisis since the identification of COVID-19 pandemic at the beginning of 2020. A new form of SARS-Cov2 virus has transformed the whole world. This transformation has different facets with its health-related, economic and sociological outcomes. When the short history of the pandemic is examined, it's observed that the primary impacts of the pandemic have been health-related impacts. The virus has spread quickly all around the world. The number of COVID-19 cases and COVID-related deaths increased drastically. At this stage, the priorities of humankind were the diagnosis and treatment of infections and preventing the spread with some precautions like lockdowns, border bans and social distancing implementations. However, severe impacts of the pandemic emerged from the economic side as well. The next priority of mankind has been to remedy the economic downturn.

COVID-19 pandemic has directly affected both global Gross Domestic Product (GDP) and employment. Unemployment increased and hence labor income decreased during 2020 on the global scale. International Labour Organisation (ILO) (2020) estimated that labor income declined approximately 11% in the first three quarters of 2020. Moreover, Organisation for Economic Cooperation and Development (OECD) (2020) estimated that global GDP declined by 4.2% in that year. World Tourism Organisation (UNWTO) (2020) underlined that this sharp decline in real GDP has been experienced because of sharp declines in trade and tourism activities. This brand-new global crisis has been compared to the previous global economic crisis in 2008 and it's underlined that the emerging crisis has been more severe than the global financial economic crisis (UNWTO, 2020: 1–3). In this context, recovery has been the key concept after the first shock of the pandemic. OECD (2021) has projected global GDP to grow by 5.7% in 2021 and by 4.5% in 2022. It has also underlined that although recovery is on track for GDP, there are still gaps in output and employment compared to pre-pandemic levels as of 2021.

By the second half of 2021, new virus variants (such as the Delta variant and Omicron variant) have slowed the positive impacts of vaccination in many countries and this situation has negative impacts on global supply chains and logistic costs. Not only shipping costs but also uncertainties of the pandemic have been fostering global inflation. What is more critical is that inflation has become severe and sustained on the global scale. Especially, the USA, Canada, the UK and emerging markets have experienced sharp increases in consumer price indexes. In this respect, a resilient recovery following the period of the pandemic, has been the key issue for the new era. As an example, the European Economic and Social Committee (2020) has underlined that only a comprehensive recovery plan could save the common destiny of European countries. As another example, World Bank (2021) has pointed out that a resilient recovery should be dynamic and inclusive. Also, such a recovery should have a framework for a green economy.

Economic impacts of COVID-19 on the sports sector: A review of sports events and audience

COVID-19 pandemic has dragged the sports sector to an unforeseeable and deep crisis. Both precautions of pandemic and global economic crisis have redounded on the sports sector. Not only demand-side but also supply-side impacts have occurred and reciprocal relationships between the economy and the sector have deepened the situation. COVID-19 pandemic has introduced new rules and implications at regional, national and international levels. Lockdowns and border bans have been the first actions that have been implemented all over the world. Restricting human mobility was the first attempt to decelerate the spread of the virus. However, this attempt has caused significant downturns in several sectors such as trade, tourism, entertainment and sports. With the rise of the pandemic, most of the sports events have been postponed or canceled; international tourist mobility has been restricted; border bans and lockdowns have caused the international trade to decline; and most of the entertainment events have been canceled.

As the number of COVID-19 cases and COVID-19-related deaths have increased, many restrictions have been implemented all around the world. The basic purpose of the restrictions was to prevent mass gatherings. Social distancing has been one of the fallouts of the pandemic. Hence, some sectors have directly been affected by lockdowns. As mentioned before, the sports sector has been one of those sectors affected by lockdown. Not only local and regional sports events but also national and international major sports events have been postponed or canceled. China was the first country which suspended the Chinese Super League (Tovar, 2021: 69). As the virus has spread to other countries, they have also reacted with postponements and cancelations. For example, the Olympic Games and the European Soccer Championship planned for 2020 were postponed to next year. The sports events that have not been canceled or postponed, have been played behind closed doors (Drewes et al., 2021: 126–127). Some of the sports events which were conducted under the aegis of Tipico were Bundesliga in Austria, Fortuna Liga in Czechia, 3 F Superliga in Denmark, Premier League in England, Bundesliga in Germany, Premier Liga in Russia, La Liga in Spain, Raiffeisen Super League in Switzerland and SPORTOTO Superlig in Turkey have been played behind closed doors. Such events have been called 'ghost games' in some sources (Drewes et al., 2021: 126).

Organizing and delivering major and mega events include different stakeholders. Without a pandemic, organizing a major event contains lots of risks and sunk costs on its own (Ludvigsen & Hayton, 2020: 2–3). What is more, the COVID-19 pandemic has worsened the situation and made things difficult. It's evident that mass gatherings in major sports events cause higher infection rates in contagious diseases. For example, the 2002 Winter Olympics and 2006 FIFA World Cup have both increased influenza infection rates respective years (Gundlapalli et al., 2006; Schenkel et al., 2006). Consequently, the unique option during a pandemic has been in organizing events without the mass gathering of the audience.

At this point, it should be noted that the pandemic has not only impacted sports events in terms of audience, but it has also impacted the audience itself. In this respect, the impacts of COVID-19 on the sports audience are multifaceted. The recent pandemic-driven economic crisis has resulted in financial burdens on spectators' budgets. Also, networked communities have been deteriorated because of both ghost games and canceled events. Moreover, the atmosphere of sports events has been lost due to the lack of audience during the pandemic and its positive impacts on well-being, happiness and community identity have also been lost (Bond et al., 2020: 1–3).

The lack of audience in sports events has also several impacts on the clubs and teams. First of all, they cannot earn money through tickets without an audience. The financial burdens that spectators are faced with have threatened the future and survival of some sports clubs and events. As an example, it's estimated that US National Basketball Association has lost approximately 650 million US dollars in revenue because of the postponement of the league (Parrish & Lam, 2021: 138). With a wider outlook, global estimates indicate that the loss of revenue in the sports industry was approximately 8 billion US dollars during the pandemic (Alam & Abdurraheem, 2021: 3). Second, field researches have indicated that spectators influence players' performances, referees' decisions and match scores (Grix et al., 2021: 3). Consequently, it's obvious that the pandemic has had several negative impacts on the audience and also several negative impacts on sports events and clubs due to the lack of audience. To sum up, the COVID-19 pandemic has caused some negative impacts on the audience and these negative impacts have caused new and deeper impacts on teams and sports events. Figure 9.1 visualizes all these aforementioned impacts.

Emerging trends in sports activities

Since the introduction of vaccines, the pandemic has slowed down and the global panic atmosphere has faded out. Globally, more than 3 billion people have been fully vaccinated as of November 2021.[1] However, the number of cases is still high due to new Sars-Cov2 variants. In this respect, the near future of the pandemic has still full of uncertainties. This complex nature of the pandemic has created some trends in sports activities. There are two fundamental emerging trends such as 'accelerating esports applications and events' and 'virtualization of sports

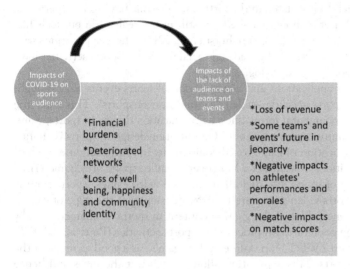

Figure 9.1 Impacts of COVID-19 on sports audience and impacts of the lack of
audience on teams and events.
Source: Author's own design.

activities'. Virtualization of sports activities and events is actually a form of esports
activities but it has its own development routes with the acceleration of some
technological breakthroughs in recent years.

Virtualization of sports events has emerged by the courtesy of online networks
and augmented reality (AR) applications. The rise of globalization and the spread
of web technologies have accelerated the attention on networks since the 1990s
(Möller & Svahn, 2004: 2020). Networks are the structures in which numerous
units are tied to each other with specific threads. The complex interactions between these units enhanced over time and networks are the aggregate of all these
transforming interactions (Hakansson & Ford, 2002: 133). The rise of social networks has added new dimensions to the understanding of networks and it has
created new values. Social networks have been constructed on the idea that social
interactions in networks create opportunities for individuals due to the fact that
these network-based interactions form social entities and they are more important than individual behaviors and attitudes (Wasserman & Galaskiewicz, 1994:
xii). In this respect, today lots of activities can be fictionalized through social
networks.

Augmented reality (AR) and virtual reality (VR) applications are also the
fruits of the technological breakthroughs of this century. AR has three fundamental properties. Firstly, it bands together reality and virtual content. Secondly,
it interactively works in real time. And lastly, it's recorded with three-dimensional
properties (Azuma, 1997). AR is the enhanced form of VR applications and both
of them are used effectively today. The basic difference between AR and VR is

that a VR user feels fully isolated in the virtual world while having an experience. However, an AR user realizes that she/he is still in the real world but feels like experiencing the virtual world (Billinghurst et al., 2015). These applications widened the range of activities on the web and social networks. Sports activities have also benefited from these technologies.

Emerging sports applications and virtualization of sports events have brought a new trend in esports activities called "gamification of sports". This emerging trend has three fundamental forms, such as gamification design in sports, gamified sports, and gaming content in sports. Gamification design in sports is characterized by the application of game-based components in sports activities such as rankings, competitions, rewards, etc. Moreover, gamified sports are characterized by the conversion of sports into digitally enhanced video games. Sports gaming simulators and sports video games are two basic examples of this type of gamification. The last one, which is the gaming content in sports, is characterized by the use of gaming content in all processes of sports activities (Pu et al., 2021: 3). A novel application ZWIFT – an online cycling game – is a good example of the gamification of sports. This application allows to connect the bikes and hence makes it possible to make physical training. Moreover, it follows the performances of users with sensors and hence it becomes possible to compete with other users in an online sports event (Westmattelmann et al., 2021: 119).

The second trend, the acceleration of esports events and their applications, has also occupied a substantial place in the new era. It should be noted that esports activities have some basic forms. They can be listed as: (i) athletes' esports competitions, (ii) crossover esports competitions, (iii) esports Pros' competitions, (iv) esports fans' competitions, (v) virtual game simulations, and (vi) esports bettings (Pu et al., 2021: 7). Athletes' esports competitions are live sports events between athletes. E-Premier League Invitational Tournament[2] and NBA 2K Players Tournament[3] are two examples of such events. Crossover esports competitions are video game competitions combining the activities of different fields such as music and art, with sports activities. Madden NFL 20 Celebrity Tournament[4] is an example of such events. Esports Pros' competitions are the tournaments of professional esports gamers. esports fan tournaments are game tournaments organized for sports fans. Moreover, virtual game simulations are simulations to predict game results. The Finnish Ice Hockey Virtual League[5] is an example of using these simulations to make projections about the results. Lastly, esports betting is betting on esports competitions. The volume of all these activities has significantly increased following the recent pandemic. In 2021, esports market revenue has reached approximately US$ 1.1 billion and it's estimated that the esports market size will reach US$ 6 billion as of 2028 (Fact.MR, 2018; Statista, 2021).

Conclusions

COVID-19 pandemic has dragged the global economy into a deep crisis with full of sectoral transformations. Lots of sectors have negatively been affected by the pandemic with loss of revenue and employment. The sports sector has been one of these sectors, too. With its significant contributions to GDP and employment, the sports sector has always been an important sector for all economies worldwide. What is more is that the significant sectoral declines during the pandemic have underlined the economic importance of this sector one more time. Today, it's quite important to examine the situation of the sector and the emerging sectoral trends in forming good policy options and taking suitable policy actions. In this respect, this chapter reviews the developments in major sports events, audiences and emerging sectoral trends. The main purpose of this chapter is to provide a framework for policy formation for the post-COVID era.

The pandemic has added several burdens on sports events, activities and audiences. Several events have been postponed or canceled during 2020. An increase in the overall unemployment and decrease in labor incomes have caused the audience and fans not to spend on sports activities as usual they do. The number of ghost games and esports events have increased. Virtualization of sports activities has accelerated. Emerging trends exhibit that transformations in the sports industry have been relying on technological breakthroughs. Web-based technologies, VR and AR applications, social networks and mobile applications are at the core of emerging trends. Although emerging trends have a promising future for the sector, it is still facing some problems to overcome in the post-COVID era.

Deloitte Center for Technology, Media & Telecommunications (2021) underlines that the sports industry has to face three critical issues following the pandemic. These issues are: (i) reshaping and expanding revenue generation models, (ii) rethinking the role of sports in societies, and (iii) redefining relationships with sports fans. Under the context of the first critical issue, it seems that sports organizers and teams should enhance the potential of sports arenas, stadiums and gymnasiums. In the post-COVID era, fans and audiences will demand to feel safe while they are watching games and it's expected that this attitude will be persisting in the medium and long terms. Consequently, investments to provide better and safer experiences for the audience will bring more revenue for teams and clubs. What is more, is that digital infrastructure should be enhanced and data monetization should be provided for better audience experiences and higher revenues. As the second critical issue, the role of sports activities should be revisited in all societies. It's observed that sustaining the mental health and keeping the physical conditions have been struggling issues during the lockdown implications. Consequently, it seems critical to manage both expertise and relationships. These are not only important for the mental and physical health of the audience but also substantial for the health of athletes. Lastly, the third critical issue is a multifaceted issue. Redefining relationships with fans and audience has several aspects such as physical, emotional, financial and digital. Physical conditions should provide safer experiences for the audience; the emotional well-being of spectators should be sustained during sports activities; economic and financial concerns of fans and audience should be considered; and personal information of the audience should be secured (Deloitte, 2021: 3–8).

All these explanations point out that post-COVID sports policy actions should be multidimensional. Public and private partnerships at both national and international scales can help to form and implement effective policies. Analyzing demand and supply conditions, and blending them with emerging sectoral trends will be the key issues in near future. It seems that the post-COVID era will serve different and enhanced sports experiences for both athletes and audiences. Sports teams, clubs and mega events' organizers who will be able to analyze and interpret the sectoral developments, will survive in the next period. The rest will experience natural selection in the evolution of the sports sector. Moreover, with a wider outlook, regional and national economies that will be able to analyze and interpret the sectoral developments will be able to quickly overcome the global economic crisis and take competitive advantages in international markets.

Notes

1 For more information, please visit: https://covid19.who.int/
2 For more information, please visit: https://www.premierleague.com/epl-invitational
3 For more information, please visit: https://www.nba.com/news/nba-2k-players-tournament-official-release
4 For more information, please visit: https://espnpressroom.com/us/press-releases/2020/04/espn-announces-madden-nfl-20-celebrity-tournament-featuring-snoop-dogg-deandre-hopkins-katie-nolan-and-more/
5 For more information, please visit: https://www.helsinkitimes.fi/themes/themes/sports/18119-finnish-ice-hockey-league-heating-up-again-in-2020.html

References

Alam, Md. M., & Abdurraheem, I. I. (2021). COVID-19 and the financial crisis in the sports sector around the world. *Sport in Society*. https://doi.org/10.1080/17430437.2021.1979964

Azuma, R. T. (1997). A survey of augmented reality. *Presence: Teleoperators and Virtual Environments*, 6(4), 355–385. https://doi.org/10.1162/pres.1997.6.4.355

Billinghurst, M., Clark, A., & Lee, G. (2015). A survey of augmented reality. *Foundations and Trends in Human-Computer Interaction*, 8(2–3), 73–272. https://doi.org/10.1561/1100000049

Bond, A. J., Cockayne, D., Ludvigsen, J. A. L., Maguire, K., Parnell, D., Plumley, D., Widdop, P., & Wilson, R. (2020). COVID-19: The return of football fans. *Managing, Sport and Leisure*. https://doi.org/10.1080/23750472.2020.1841449

Deloitte. (2021). *2021 outlook for the US sports industry*. https://www2.deloitte.com/us/en/pages/technology-media-and-telecommunications/articles/sports-business-trends-disruption.html

Drewes, M., Daumann, F., & Follert, F. (2021). Exploring the sports economic impact of COVID-19 on professional soccer. *Soccer & Society*, 2(1–2), 125–137. https://doi.org/10.1080/14660970.2020.1802256

ESPN. (2020, April 16). *ESPN announces Madden NFL 20 Celebrity Tournament featuring Snoop Dogg, DeAndre Hopkins, Katie Nolan and more*. https://espnpressroom.com/

us/press-releases/2020/04/espn-announces-madden-nfl-20-celebrity-tournament-featuring-snoop-dogg-deandre-hopkins-katie-nolan-and-more/

European Economic and Social Committee. (2020). *Building a resilient and inclusive European economy after the COVID-19 crisis – the views of organised civil society*. https://www.eesc.europa.eu/sites/default/files/files/qe-01-20-678-en-n.pdf

Fact.MR. (2018). *Market research report*. https://www.factmr.com/report/217/e-sports-market?utm_source=adwords&utm_medium=ppc&gclid=Cj0KCQiAtJeNBhCVARIsAN-JUJ2Fg95snYoHmU83BwpKBGOki9FPrp75VKIUSIT1O_hTDu6zsScFqwmQaAiE-TEALw_wcB

Grix, J., Brannagan, P. M., Grimes, H., & Neville, R. (2021). The impact of COVID-19 on sport. *International Journal of Sport Policy and Politic*, 13(1), 1–12. https://doi.org/10.1080/19406940.2020.1851285

Gundlapalli, A. V., Rubin, M. A., Samore, M. H., Lopansri, B., Lahey, T., McGuire, H. L., Winthrop, K. L., Dunn, J. J., Willick, S. E., Vosters, R. L., Waeckerle, J. F., Carroll, K. C., Gwaltney, J. M., Hayden, F. G., Elstad, M. R., & Sande, M. A. (2006). Influenza, winter olympiad, 2002. *Emerging Infectious Diseases*, 12(1), 144–146. https://doi.org/10.3201/eid1201.050645

Hakansson, H., & Ford, D. (2002). How should companies interact in business networks? *Journal of Business Research*, 55(2), 133–139. https://doi.org/10.1016/S0148-2963(00)00148-X

Helsinki Times. (2020, September 29). *Finnish ice hockey league heating up again in 2020*. https://www.helsinkitimes.fi/themes/themes/sports/18119-finnish-ice-hockey-league-heating-up-again-in-2020.html

ILO. (2020). *ILO monitor: COVID-19 and the world of work*. 6th Edition. https://www.ilo.org/

Ludvigsen, J. A. L., & Hayton, J. W. (2020). Toward COVID-19 secure events: Considerations for organizing the safe resumption of major sporting events. *Managing Sport and Leisure*. https://doi.org/10.1080/23750472.2020.1782252

Möller, K., & Svahn, S. (2004). Crossing east-west boundaries: Knowledge sharing in intercultural business networks. *Industrial Marketing Management*, 33(3), 219–228. https://doi.org/10.1016/j.indmarman.2003.10.011

NBA. (2020, April 1). *NBA players go head-to-head in 1st 'NBA 2K Players Tournament'*. https://www.nba.com/news/nba-2k-players-tournament-official-release

OECD. (2020). *OECD economic outlook*. No 108. http://www.oecd.org

OECD. (2021). *OECD economic outlook, interim report September 2021 – Keeping the recovery on track*. http://www.oecd.org

Parrish, C., & Lam, M. (2021). Impact of the COVID-19 pandemic on a community soccer organization in the United States: The case of Asheville City Soccer Club. *Soccer & Society*, 22(1–2), 138–151. https://doi.org/10.1080/14660970.2020.1797495

PREMIER LEAGUE. (2021, May). *ePremier league invitational 5–9 May*. https://www.premierleague.com/epl-invitational

Pu, H., Kim, J., & Daprano, C. (2021). Can esports substitute traditional sports? The convergence of sports and video gaming during the pandemic and beyond. *Societies*, 11(4), 129. https://doi.org/10.3390/soc11040129

Schenkel, K., Williams, C., Eckmanns, T., Poggensee, G., Benzler, J., Josephsen, J., & Krause, G. (2006). Enhanced surveillance of infectious diseases: The 2006 FIFA World Cup experience, Germany. *Eurosurveillance*, 11(12), 15–16. https://doi.org/10.2807/esm.11.12.00670-en

Statista. (2021). *Esports market revenue worldwide from 2019 to 2024*. https://www.statista.com/statistics/490522/global-esports-market-revenue/

Tovar, J. (2021). Soccer, World War II and Coronavirus: A comparative analysis of how the sport shut down. *Soccer & Society*, 22(1–2), 66–74. https://doi.org/10.1080/14660970.2020.1755270

UN. (2020). *Sport and SDG indicators – category 1 indicators v4.0 draft*. https://thecommon-wealth.org/sites/default/files/inline/Sport%20and%20SDG%20Cat1%20indicators%20%28v4.0%29.pdf

UNWTO. (2020). *World tourism barometer*. 18(7), 1–36. https://www.e-unwto.org/doi/epdf/10.18111/wtobarometereng.2020.18.1.7

Wasserman, S., & Galaskiewicz, J. (1994). *Advances in social network analysis*. Sage Publishing.

Westmattelmann, D., Grotenhermen, J- G., Sprenger, M., & Schewe, G. (2021) The show must go on – Virtualisation of sport events during the COVID-19 pandemic. *European Journal of Information Systems*, 30(2), 119–136, https://doi.org/10.1080/0960085X.2020.1850186

WHO. (2022). *WHO Coronavirus (COVID-19) dashboard*. https://covid19.who.int/

Worldbank. (2021). *Recovering growth – Rebuilding dynamic post-COVID-19 economies and fiscal constraints*. https://openknowledge.worldbank.org/bitstream/handle/10986/36331/9781464818066.pdf?sequence=11&isAllowed=y

Chapter 10

The Effect of COVID-19 and Innovation on World Sports Tourism

H. Neyir Tekeli

Introduction

Tourism has been placed on the agenda of the world, especially after the 1950s, for being a source of income for businesses, for providing foreign currency inflow and employment for countries, for providing services that can meet human needs with its contributions to other sectors that are directly or indirectly related. From the 1950s to the present, tourism has differentiated in terms of definition and diversity, and has been divided into many market segments.

Although tourism is a sector whose economic and socio-cultural importance has been increasing and developing since the 1950s, humans have always traveled in order to sightsee, to find healing and to participate in religious and social activities beginning from the early ages (Başol, 2012: 351). It is known that the act of traveling in the historical process emerged with the history of humanity. The tourism industry has developed rapidly as a result of the development of civilizations, the enrichment of societies, the need for people to take a vacation caused by intense work tempo, the diversification and proliferation of transportation vehicles and the development of their systems, the increase in people's spare time day by day, technological development and the introduction of natural and historical values and beauties in various geographies of the world over time. With the end of World War II, tourism movements have begun to develop, especially in today's developed countries, Western societies. Since its economic importance has been understood over time, it has been the fastest-growing sector in the global economy of the 21st century along with telecommunications and information technologies. Today, tourism is seen as one of the most important sources of economic growth and development in many developed and developing countries (Diamond, 1977: 539; Britton, 1982: 332; Copeland, 1991: 515; Hao, Var & Chon, 2003: 33).

In the 20th century, the tourism sector was able to provide the greatest contribution to the development of countries in terms of economic and socio-cultural aspects (Önen, 2008: 2). While 25 million people participated in tourism activities in 1950, this number reached 683 million in 2000 and 980 million in 2011.

According to the United Nations World Tourism Organization (UNWTO) data, in 2011, the United States has the highest share in the world tourism

DOI: 10.4324/9781003253891-10

revenues as in previous years. Turkey's share is at the level of 23 billion dollars. The point that draws attention is that Turkey makes a significant contribution to employment and economy by increasing tourism revenues every year provided that it maintains its stable economic development and that there are no negative external factors. Today, the main factors that increase the importance of the tourism sector are its effects on increasing employment, providing income to the country, contributing to sustainable economic development with the names "open air factory", "environmentally friendly industry" and "smokeless factory", contributing to world peace and being the locomotive of the changing world. In addition to being a service sector, the tourism sector also shows flexibility.

As in all other service sectors, crises that have negative consequences also arise in the tourism sector, and these crises occur for many different reasons such as terrorist acts, financial problems, careless use of the natural environment, and political indecision (Yılmaz, 2004: 72–73). For example, it is stated that tourism infrastructure has deteriorated and the number of visitors has decreased at a high rate in South, Southeast and North Asia due to natural disasters, health events and terrorist events in Asia-Pacific (Richardson, March, Lewis, & Radel, 2015: 152).

The COVID-19 Pandemic and Its Effects on Tourism Sector

With the emergence of the COVID-19 pandemic, it is observed that the results, first in the human dimension and then in the economic dimension, have caused greater damage than any crisis so far. The tourism sector plays an important role in the development of countries. The tourism sector, which keeps social, political and economic relations alive on an international scale, is affected very quickly by the developments in the world. There are some factors that affect tourism negatively, as well as features such as destination attractiveness, price, advertising and promotion that revitalize tourism. Events such as terrorism, war and natural disasters occurring in the world adversely affect the tourism movements of countries. One of them is epidemic diseases. Cases such as SARS virus, MERS virus, Ebola, Cholera and Swine Flu, which emerged in the past years, had a negative impact on the tourism of the countries. Crises that cause a number of negative effects can be defined as unexpected events. Along with the crises that occur within the enterprise, larger-scale crises that have an impact on the sectors may also occur. Natural disasters, economic turmoil, terrorist incidents and political/political events can be counted among the causes of crises that have an impact on the tourism sector. However, pandemics can also be considered as a cause of the crisis. The pandemic that occurs in the destination can create a crisis environment and cause the region to lose its attractiveness to tourists. As a result of a crisis affecting the tourism sector, it can be predicted that the demand for the destination will fall and the income will decrease.

A new epidemic disease emerging today is the COVID-19 virus. Short-term and infrequent events such as epidemics, natural disasters, and political and economic crises may adversely affect tourism development in the short or long term. Among these, epidemic diseases reduced the volume of tourism in the regional sense before COVID-19, SARS was effective in the Far East in 2003, and MERS was effective in the Middle East and Arabian Peninsula. Unlike SARS and MERS epidemics, COVID-19 spread rapidly all over the world after China, and the center of the epidemic first moved to Europe and then to the United States. As of March 11, 2020, it has been declared a pandemic by the World Health Organization. Undoubtedly, tourism is one of the industries where the negative effects of the pandemic are seen the most. Travel restrictions and social isolation were among the first measures taken to control COVID-19. With the start of voluntary and mandatory quarantine practices all over the world, travel movements have ended, and the tourism industry has experienced a sudden pause. Against this pause, various measures were taken to overcome the crisis in tourism, and with the decrease in the number of cases, some flexibility in travel restrictions began to be offered. Tourism, as an industry with intense human interaction, will undoubtedly witness some long-term transformations after COVID-19.

As of July 2020, the number of people caught in COVID-19 disease worldwide reached 11,284,997 and the number of those who lost their lives reached 530,946 people. In the last 24 hours, 2,537 people died and 102,421 people got the disease (WHO, 2020). It is seen that the pandemic continues even though it loses its virulence, and in addition to the humanitarian damage, the social and economic damage is gradually increasing. For this reason, in countries where the initial rapid increase in the number of Corona cases and the number of people who lost their lives from this disease was curtailed, quarantine bans and decisions to close international borders began to be gradually relaxed. Although the humanitarian dimension of the pandemic has very heavy costs, the fact that economic effects encountered in many sectors in the world are very worrying is the most important factor in these decisions.

The effects of COVID-19 on sectors are generally seen at different levels depending on the countries' unpreparedness for the pandemic and their ability to manage the crisis. With the effect of the emerging crisis being related to human health, activities in sectors such as pharmaceutical industry, medical equipment, protective masks, protective gloves and clothing, medical devices, cologne and disinfectant materials are increasing. The tendency of people to use digital technology tools in compulsory situations such as meeting the basic needs of people and the application of the remote working model in business life during the peak quarantine bans has led to a positive effect on the digital economy. However, the tourism sector, where the most negative effects were experienced due to the pandemic, is one of the sectors whose activities were completely stopped within the scope of the measures deemed necessary to minimize the damages of COVID-19. Because the borders between countries were closed, airlines and all other means of transportation were stopped, and in short, travel was prohibited.

The pandemic crisis started with the prohibition of travel and tourism to China in the first few months, when there was not enough information about the course and severity of the coronavirus epidemic. Then, it became global with the closure of international borders with the emergence of the virus spreading in other countries. In addition, depending on the increase in the number of cases encountered in countries, a process in which urban public transportation and intercity transportation were restricted has begun.

In the analysis of the annual changes in tourism development in the international tourism sector in the world, the extremity of the downward trend increasing with the effect of COVID-19 is seen. The tourism sector, which grew by 7% in 2017 and 6% in 2018, decreased by 4% in 2019, but this rate decreased by −40% at the end of the first four months of 2020. With the effect of the downward trend in the number of international tourists, it is estimated that international tourism revenues may decrease by 1 trillion dollars by the World Tourism Organization. While the decreases in international travel are announced by the World Tourism Organization, the difference between international tourism and other sectors is emerging with the effect of COVID-19 (UNWTO, 2020). Turkey reached the highest number of visitors in its history with approximately 52 million visitors in 2019. In the same year, it earned tourism income that is approximately 35 billion dollars (TUIK, 2020). Even before the COVID-19 epidemic started to be seen in Turkey, cancelations started, especially in the Far East market and Anatolian tours, and the fact that the epidemic occurred at a time when early reservations were made resulted in canceling or delaying holiday plans of consumers (TUIK, 2020). Tourism has also been one of the first and most affected sectors by this epidemic. Travels have completely stopped due to quarantine practices, and individuals who are psychologically affected have postponed or canceled their vacation plans.

The tourism sector, which has both national and international trade and labor capacity in different fields, has a very high share of global trade and employment. At the same time, according to the World Health Organization (WHO), the total contribution of travel and tourism to GDP is quite high in the countries which are worst affected by the impact of COVID-19 on tourism (WTTC, World Tourism and Travel Council, 2020). The pandemic is characterized as an unprecedented crisis for the tourism economy. The Organization for Economic Cooperation and Development (OECD) estimates that there will be a 45% decline in international tourism in 2020 due to COVID-19. If the recovery is delayed until September 2020, it is predicted that this rate may increase to 70%. Domestic tourism is also heavily affected by restriction measures, but a faster recovery is expected in domestic tourism after the recovery phase (OECD, 2020).

Sport Tourism and Its Economic Effects

Sport is basically defined as the phenomenon that people do to stay healthy, have fun and spend their free time (Saatçioğlu, 2013;5). The concept of tourism, on the other hand, has been expressed as all of the relationships and events that occur during people's travels and stays other than their permanent work and residence (Kozak et al., 2001: 2–3). From this point of view, sports and tourism are known as complementary concepts. As the name suggests, sports tourism aims to directly participate in the trip. Again, the concept of recreation, which is an indispensable concept in tourism, is closely related to sports and tourism (Karaus, 1977: 5). Like most approaches to sports and tourism, many approaches to sports define sports tourism as an activity and generally as tourism movements that occur as a result of people leaving the region for the purpose of watching sports or participating in sports (Stevenden & Knop, 1999: 15).

If we look at the definitions in the literature, sports tourism is defined as non-commercial travel for the purpose of attending or watching sports activities away from home (Weed, 1997: 5). Sports tourism is a type of tourism that consists of travels that take place with the active or passive participation of people in predetermined sports activities (Turco, Riley, & Swart, 2002: 6). Sports tourism is defined as the travels of people to watch or participate in sports activities by leaving the place where they live for fun (Gibson, 1998: 46). Sports tourism is travel and experiences made to do or watch sports-related activities (Ross, 2001: 3).

The increase in the popularity of sports in the 1970s, the establishment of sports consciousness and habits worldwide as a result of the investments made in the sports sector, the acceptance of sports as an indispensable habit of life and the desire of people to continue their daily sports life during their travels have led to the fusion of the tourism sector and sports. These developments have revealed a symbiotic relationship between sports and tourism. However, the relationship between sports and tourism is not unidirectional. In other words, not only do sports support tourism, but tourism also contributes to the development of sports by using its natural or man-made resources (Sağcan, 1986: 15; Karakoç, 2011: 20). Sports and tourism are seen as two complementary concepts. It is known that on sports tourism, which is still popular and which is a current topic, the first study establishing the connection between sports and tourism was the work of Victor Balck, who is accepted as the father of modern Swedish sports, and the relationship between "Tourism and Sports" was defined in a part of his book dealing with different sports (Ross, 2001: 3).

When we look at the development of sports tourism in the historical process, we again encounter the Olympic Games which started in the 8th century BC in the city of Olympia in the Peloponnesian Peninsula of Greece. These athletic-oriented games were an important element of the ancient Greek lifestyle, and every reputable city in the country had a stadium. In addition, an important aspect or dimension of these sporting events was the round element. The participants were professional athletes and they competed against each other for prizes in the rounds. Moreover, thousands of spectators attended these games to support the athletes and the reputation of their hometown. At that time, an Olympic game could bring in about 40,000 spectators from different parts of Greece. In ancient times, thousands of people did not set out to go to the same place for any reason other than the Olympics. At that time, different from the opportunities that today's tourists have, there was no accommodation facility and people were staying in tents. In addition, it was determined that the first hostel was established in Olympia in the 4th century (İçöz, 2008: 39). In the later periods, people travel for sports purposes like gladiator fights and chariot races held during the Roman Empire. During the Middle Ages and Renaissance, professional knights traveled constantly as athletes as part of their lives, and both elite and spectator tournaments were held in the 16th and 17th centuries, which were specific only to the upper classes of society. It can be said that the 19th century was a century in which sports and tourism made a splash (İçöz, 2008: 38–41). Types of sports tourism are classified under two main headings, according to the purposes of participation and the place where sports are performed. The effects of sports tourism are evaluated under three headings. These are economic, socio-cultural and environmental effects.

Like sports, tourism also depends on many parameters. First of all, tourism is the event of traveling to the chosen destination. Thus, tourism requires the displacement of people. Second, the common feature of sports and tourism is that travel is a temporary activity, as in sports. Third, the main purpose of travel is an important parameter of tourism, and **there are** many reasons for travel in tourism. Thus, tourism, like sports tourism, has both leisure and recreational dimensions, as well as business and commercial dimensions. The World **Tourism** Organization (WTO) has included sports among the activities related to leisure time (WTO, 1995). Although the regions or societies that are open to sports tourism are interested in the visual and in a sense of having a pleasant time dimension, they also attach special importance to this event by giving it different meanings due to the effects of sportive events and the tourism movements created by it, such as increasing the prestige of the region and the community of the region and encouraging visitor expenditures in the region.

There are many positive and negative effects of these organizations on the countries or regions where the sports organization is held, economically, socially, environmentally and about health. While the active or passive participant who comes to the sports organization brings money, ideas and innovations, they expect to be fed, hosted and entertained as a demand from the other party. In addition, the emergence of various job opportunities in the services created by this organization is expressed as a positive effect by some people, while the emergence of social and environmental problems is expressed as an activity that causes negative effects on the social structure by others. Today, organizations organized within the scope of sports tourism are also known as the activities that come to the fore due to their income-generating and foreign exchange-earning features (Alpullu, 2011: 58).

According to the data published by the World Tourism Organization, the total world tourism income in 2013 was 1.159 billion dollars. This income is concentrated in Europe, America, Asia-Pacific region. According to 2013 data, Europe had the highest share of tourism revenues with 489.3 billion dollars and 42.2%. Asia-Pacific region is the second region with 358.9 billion dollars, and America is the third region in terms of world tourism revenues with 229.2 billion dollars. Turkey, on the other hand, provides an important income from tourism, and in 2014, it provided 34.3 billion dollars of income to the country's economy.

The total cost and total profit status of the Olympic organizations on the basis of years and cities of the countries are presented. Accordingly, while the total cost of the Olympic Games held in London in 2012 was 13.9 billion dollars, its total profit was 1.9 billion dollars. While the total cost of the Olympic organizations held in Barcelona in 1992 was 1.6 billion dollars, the total profit was seen as 358 million dollars (Yıldız & Aydın, 2013: 273). It is generally accepted that a significant benefit and welfare increase is achieved by the use of the developed infrastructure by the public, as well as the incomes of the host countries thanks to the organizations. Benefits such as the promotion of host countries, the increase in tourism activities and the acquisition of modern sports facilities are considered rewards at the end of the costs endured. Countries hosting sports tourism organizations offer their facilities, personnel, accommodation businesses and shopping centers to the service of incoming tourists. Therefore, this situation will enable various social and cultural changes to occur by performing cultural exchanges between tourists and local people to a certain extent.

According to the statement made by TURSAB for Turkey in 2014, more than 550 thousand foreign tourists came to Turkey for sports activities and spent over 900 million dollars. The share of sports tourism in Turkey is around 1.5%. Golf and football get the most from this pie. A sports tourist spends twice as much as the average tourist. In other words, the expenditure of foreign sports-loving tourists coming to Turkey is around 1648 dollars. While the number of golf lovers coming to Antalya Belek in Turkey is close to 160.000, the number of football teams camping in Antalya this year (Ross, 2001: 3) is around 1,200. 90% of these teams are foreign football teams. The share of sports in the tourism sector, which reached a size of around 1.2 trillion dollars in the world in 2014, is at the level of 180 billion dollars. While the growth of global tourism is around 4%–5%, this figure rises to 14% in sports tourism.

The most important effects of sports tourism occur economically. According to the TURSAB Sports Tourism Report (2014), sports tourism has an economic size of 180 billion dollars on a global scale and 900 million dollars in Turkey. The economic effects of sports tourism are generally in parallel with the economic effects of tourism. Some of the positive economic effects of sports tourism can be listed as providing income for tourism and non-tourism areas, closing the current account deficit, providing employment, and contributing to regional and national development.

Since the sports tourist spends twice as much money as the average tourist, the income contribution it provides to the country's tourism and the share of closing the current account deficit are important. If the economic contribution of sports tourism to destinations is to be explained with a small example, the 2019 UEFA Super Cup final match was held in Istanbul for only 90 minutes. For one match, Istanbul earned about 100 million euros. The total revenue of the Olympic Games played between 1993 and 2006 is around 107.32 billion dollars. 420,000 tourists visited the region to watch the 2012 London Olympics and each one spent approximately £1300. As a result, the economic effects of sports tourism and sports organizations are formed by the expenditures of people (participants, spectators, managers, etc.) who participate in quality organizations in different forms in that country or region.

Sports tourism can also have negative economic effects. If the cost exceeds expectations, facilities become idle; tax rates increase, opportunity costs are high, the perception of economic return is exaggerated, subcontractors from outside the city are included instead of local stakeholders and the goods and services in the region cost more; economic effects can be seen negatively (Çakıcı & Güler, 2014: 40–41; Scandizzo & Pierleoni, 2018: 5; Güdük, 2019: 23). Negative effects are especially seen in mega-scale sports organizations. Therefore, the costs should be well calculated, especially in mega sporting events investments. Otherwise, a job that is more harmful than profitable for the country will be done, for example, the economic damage to the host country in all of the Montreal (1972), Seoul (1988), Atlanta (1996), Sydney (2000), Athens (2004) and Beijing (2008) Olympics has far exceeded its economic profit. The Athens Olympics held in Greece in 2004 became a burden that would drag the country into a deep economic depression later on. The budget deficit caused by Olympic expenses reached 6.1% of the country's gross product in 2004. The public borrowing to finance Greece's 108 expenses has also increased to 43 billion dollars, exceeding the 35 billion dollars envisaged for 2004. The national debt of the country has increased exponentially since 2004 and reached 469.8 billion dollars (165% of the GDP as of 2013) in 2010 (Tunçdemir, 2013).

The Effects of COVID-19 on the Sports Industry

The sports industry undertakes to supply, produce sports goods for sports institutions or consumers or the process of organizing a sports competition or forming a part of it. The sports industry is considered as an industry that has a direct impact on the economies of societies and offers high added value in economic terms if it is active. (Mullin, Hardy, & Sutton, 2000: 14).

The COVID-19 outbreak has deeply affected the sports industry, as it has affected many industries. The economic dimension of matches without spectators, postponements, and the uncertainty of the fate of many sports organizations has emerged. First of all, when the basic expenditure and income items of football clubs and other sports clubs are examined; it is seen that the income is obtained from broadcasting rights, sponsorship and advertising revenues. In addition, product revenues, ticket sales, operating and stadium revenues constitute other items. The expenditure part consists of athlete's recruitment, equipment, technical team and athlete's wages, official obligations and testimonial obligations. Before the COVID-19 pandemic, sports events to be held in 12 cities in Europe were expected to bring 110 million dollars to Ireland alone. According to UEFA, the EURO 2016 tournament, which was held in France, provided France with an income of 1.3 billion dollars. It can be said that the fact that EURO 2020 is postponed to another date due to the virus, it will be deprived of economic benefit from the budget of billion-dollar sports organizations. It is observed that the GDP of Japan decreased by 1.5% in 2020, because of the fact that the Olympics, which is planned to be held in Tokyo in 2020 and undertaken by SMBC Nikko Securities, one of Japan's famous investment companies, are postponed due to the virus (Koçdemir, 2020).

Sports economics is a field where economic sciences show themselves in practice and it deals with the interaction between economics, sports and sports sciences. It is stated that globalization and rapid developments in communication technologies have had an effect on the increase in the importance of sports in the general economic picture recently (Şimşek, 2011: 393).

Apart from the fact that sports are a leisure time activity and social sharing and entertainment, with the inclusion of its economic value, some economic rules related to sports have emerged and this has enabled sports to become a sector that contributes to the economic structure (Sivrikaya & Demir, 2019: 126). Today, sportive events are compared with their successes or failures based on their economic values (Dever, 2010: 77). In today's current conditions, sports have become an economic institution (Donuk, 2005). Today, only professional sports services reach 150 billion dollars, and the sports industry has a total size of nearly 700 billion dollars, including areas such as sports equipment, licensed products, and health and fitness centers. When we consider sponsorships, broadcasting rights, advertising, legal and illegal bets, the figure reaches unpredictable gigantic proportions. These huge figures reached by the sports industry are more than the national income of 150 countries. According to the Deloitte Football Money League 2020 Report, the sum of the revenues of the 20 highest-earning clubs in the world increased by 11% in the 2018/2019 season compared to the previous period and reached 9.3 billion euros. Barcelona with 840 million euros, Real Madrid with 757 million euros and Manchester United with 711 million euros were the top three clubs. According to research firm Kearney 2019 data, the global sports market has a CAGR (compound annual growth rate) of 5.9%, with a value between $480 billion and $620 billion. This includes infrastructure construction investments, sports equipment, licensed products and live broadcast revenues. In fast-growing economies such as Brazil, Russia, India, and China, and in more mature markets in Europe and North America, the sports industry has been shown to grow faster than gross domestic product. According to the Business Sports Company's Sports Global Market Opportunities and Strategies 2022 Report, the value of the global sports market was expected to increase by approximately 6% annually to $614 billion by 2022. At the 44th UEFA Ordinary Congress held in Amsterdam in March 2020, a total revenue of 3.86 billion euros was announced for the 2018–2019 season, with an increase of 38% compared to the previous year (Devecioğlu, 2020). However, these figures are based on the data prepared without taking into account the impact of the pandemic on world sports, and when these data are taken into account, it is understood that the sports systems of the countries will suffer great destruction.

The COVID-19 pandemic, which affected the world, also seriously influenced the football economy. Due to COVID-19, a 28% loss occurred in the value of football players (www.sporx.com, 2020). Europe's top five football leagues were also hit financially due to COVID-19. It has been reported that the total loss of France (Ligue 1), England (Premier League), Spain (La Liga), Germany (Bundesliga) and Italy (Serie A) will be approximately 4 billion euros due to the COVID-19 outbreak. Economists estimate a loss of 160 billion dollars for the first time in the last 20 years in the sports world (Devecioğlu, 2020).

As of March 2020, during the pandemic process, decisions have been taken to play various sports events without spectators, to postpone or cancel them to a later date in many different countries. However, the matches played until these decisions are taken are considered as "biological bombs" (Gilat & Cole, 2020; Rudan, 2020). In their article, Rudan (2020) and Gilat and Cole (2020) cited a Champions League football match between Italy's Atalanta and Spain's Valencia on February 19 as an example. The Atalanta team is a team from the city of Bergamo with a population of 120,000. As this match was probably the biggest match in the history of the Atalanta team and the local stadium was not big enough for anyone who wanted to watch the match, the match was moved to the San Siro stadium in Milan. The official participation number for this match was announced as 45,792. In this case, it is thought that about a third of Bergamo's population traveled from Bergamo to Milan by bus and roamed the streets of Milan before and after the match. It is reported that around 2,500 Valencia fans also attended the match. Since Atalanta scored four goals in this match, it is thought that a third of Bergamo's population celebrated these goals by hugging at least four times in the cold weather and spent the whole day together. Due to this intense contact, Milan is claimed to be Italy's worst pandemic region. Moreover, it has been reported that at least one-third of the Valencia football team was also infected with the virus and subsequently played with Alaves in the Spanish league, infecting other players of that team. Considering all these, it is seen that a single football match makes a significant contribution to the pandemic process in Spain and Italy (Gilat & Cole, 2020; Rudan, 2020). Although the decisions made by the governments about sports organizations showed various differences in the first days of the COVID-19 pandemic, it was later understood that sports organizations all over the world should be locked. Being aware of this fact, the World Health Organization and governments have first decided to stop sports organizations on different dates one by one from February 2020, and then postpone them to a later date to make a final decision according to the course of the COVID-19 pandemic. These postponements include the postponement of not only local football leagues, basketball and tennis competitions, but even mega events such as the 2020 Tokyo Olympic Games and European Football Championship 2020 (Euro 2020) for more than a year (Parnell, Widdop, Bond, & Wilson, 2020). In addition, despite the silence of bodies such as UEFA and IOC in the early stages of the COVID-19 outbreak, their subsequent decisions on the postponement or postponement of such events (Evans, etc., 2020) have been met with positivity from various stakeholders (Stevens & Prins, 2020). As of May 2020, the COVID-19 pandemic had a very negative economic impact on the sports industry, as it did in all sectors. Many professional leagues around the world have suspended their seasons and hundreds of thousands of people are facing unemployment as public sporting events have been canceled. The analyzes show that the estimated loss of income in terms of sports tourism will be 2.4 billion USD as a result of the postponements and cancelations of sports organizations due to the COVID-19 pandemic, they also reveal the result that there may be a loss of 2.2 billion USD from television broadcasting revenues as a result of the crisis.

Such organizations not only produce significant socioeconomic impacts for the host countries but also provide an opportunity to introduce themselves to the world to the relevant society. However, it also poses great risks to health due to intense transportation and contact. Therefore, it is very important to examine the effects of pandemics such as COVID-19 on mega-sports events. During the current pandemic, early decision-making processes have been observed, and it has been stated that a conflict of opinion suggesting that mega-sports events as a profitable trade industry should be held as planned or canceled has emerged between seeing the "athlete as a tool" and recognizing and promoting the "athlete as a community". On the other hand, it has also been stated that mega sporting events can bring joy and unity in this challenging period if carefully planned (Mann, Clift, Boykoff, & Bekker, 2020).

Innovation After COVID-19 in Tourism and Sports

The concept of innovation, derived from the Latin word "innovatus", means transforming an idea into a salable or improved product or good and service (Tüsiad, 2003: 11). Another source states that the concept of innovation, which is derived from the Latin word "innovore" which means renewal, making new and changing, has been put forward with different perspectives in organizational literature. Innovation is a specific function of entrepreneurship. Innovation is the entrepreneur's generating wealth by creating new resources or increasing the potential for use of existing resources (Drucker, 1998: 112). Innovation is all activities in creating a new product or production process, from scientific research to invention, development and commercialization. (Kamien & Schwartz, 1982).

The removal of economic limits by globalization and the removal of time and space limits by the changes in technology have provided the transition from the industrial economy to the global information economy. This situation has been a transformation that increases the importance of technology and information for businesses. Information is now at the forefront of production factors for businesses and all information sources gain great importance. Globalization and rapid technological change cause the competitive environment to become dynamic (Güleş & Bülbül, 2004: 81).

Tourism is a service industry. Service businesses also need to find, develop and provide new or better service proposals in order to respond to changing conditions. They also have to develop and implement new or better service delivery technologies (Riel & Van, 2005: 79).

Three main features of service innovation are mentioned:

- While there is usually a resultant change in product innovations, service innovation shows continuity. Therefore, it is difficult to determine a specific time period in which innovation is carried out.
- Service innovation demonstrates a strong complementarity between technological and organizational change and technical inputs and human resources. Therefore, unlike product innovation, it does not follow a purely technical process. Thus, service innovation takes the form of finding the right combination of technology and organizational changes and integrating it into existing technology.
- Service innovation requires participatory production. It is difficult to identify the participants, individual contribution levels and users because of the feature of service innovation that is open to everyone's participation in the process.

Turkey's first online food ordering site, "Yemeksepeti.com" is also a service innovation. Orders on the site take place in a fully interactive environment. It is ensured that an order placed on Yemeksepeti.com, which is supported by all the possibilities of information technologies and whose margin of error is close to zero, is delivered to the user in the shortest time and in the most accurate way (Elçi, 2006: 32).

Point Hotel in Istanbul is an example of service innovation and marketing innovation with its distinctive design and service approach. Determining its target audience as business people, the hotel differentiated itself from other hotels by offering "home comfort and office technology" together; by developing a special service concept for business meetings; by establishing an information technology infrastructure suitable for the needs. Again, unlike its competitors, a presentational privilege was created with the interior design in which minimalist details come to the fore (Elçi, 2010: 44).

The most important examples of service innovations in transportation in recent years are airline companies that sell cheap tickets. EasyJet was founded in the UK in 1995 by Greek entrepreneur Stelios Haji-Ioannou. For the first time, the company increased the number of those who preferred the airline with cheap flight tickets. The main reason why these flights are economical is that the prices of the tickets do not include the drinks and food offered to the passengers during the flight. Another important factor in the low ticket prices is that ticket sales are made directly from the branches at the airports or over the internet, without the use of intermediary institutions. In this way, passengers do not give a commission to an intermediary institution. In addition, the company saves significantly on airport taxes by keeping return times limited to an average of 30 minutes. The company, which uses two types of aircraft, also keeps flight times long. EasyJet has made history as an exemplary case for marketing and service innovation. In Turkey, Pegasus followed a similar strategy to Easyjet and soon established itself in Turkish air transportation. Thanks to Pegasus, the plane has become an alternative to the bus in Turkey, and many people who have never been on a plane have become plane passengers thanks to Pegasus.

In the current period, tourism enterprises are experiencing serious economic losses. In addition, they will have to keep up with the changes and innovations and innovation movements that can be experienced in the tourism sector. This also requires an extra cost. It is difficult to predict how businesses will survive this period. However, it is also predicted that businesses will need to postpone tax debts, government incentives and support loans in order to cover this loss, survive, make profits after COVID-19, and adapt to changes.

Providing some innovative initiatives and measures related to sports tourism and the COVID-19 epidemic has become an inevitable reality. National public health institutions, epidemiologists, sports organizations, sports federations, sports clubs, all researchers and practitioners working in the field of athlete health should cooperate in order to minimize the effects of the pandemic, to determine the most appropriate time for the resumption of sports activities and sports tourism, to protect the health of the sports community and spectators, to carry out sports activities safely and to ensure participation in sports at all levels during and after the COVID-19 pandemic (Corsini, Bisciotti, Eirale, & Volpi, 2020: 17; Timpka, 2020: 90).

One of the most important effects of COVID-19 is that it forces social and commercial life to digitalization to a large extent. In this context, it is necessary to produce online supported solutions in performance sports as well as in the fitness sector. Beyond these, a wider door has been opened for the esports industry, which has made great progress in the last 20 years. The Turkish E-Sports Federation was established in 2018 under the Ministry of Youth and Sports in order to gradually develop the gaming industry in our country. It is a global sports organization with national member federations in 61 countries and has a huge community with millions of athletes and billions of viewers (IeSF, 2020). Esports, which is expected to be intertwined with modern sports organization in the long term, may become a part of the Olympic Games in the near future depending on the interest it receives. Esports organizations have already come to the fore as a side event in the 2024 Paris Olympic Games (Morgan, 2019). The economy of esports, which gathers games played on desktop and laptop computers, consoles and phones under the same roof, can be considered as one of the indicators of countries, institutions and even individuals to adapt to the era they are in and the technology that has been reached, with the widespread use of distance education throughout the entire epidemic process (Yamamoto & Altun, 2020: 25). Esports peaked after the coronavirus pandemic in the world and is known to reach approximately 250 billion dollars.

Conclusion

The tourism sector is a sector that is rapidly affected by current fluctuations. The recent COVID-19 (New coronavirus) epidemic has affected the whole world. The studies and reports published by the World Health Organization regarding the new coronavirus, which has spread to the world in a short time since its emergence and mobilized international health authorities due to its effects, are followed with interest and concern by the whole world. Against this new pandemic that spreads from China and threatens international public health, national governments are taking various measures to protect public health and to get rid of the pandemic with the least damage, in line with the instructions of the World Health Organization. However, despite the tightening of the measures, the continuous increase in the area of influence of the pandemic and the death cases due to the pandemic causes serious concerns at the international level. This pandemic, which affects the social and economic structure of the countries, also affects the tourism sector.

Sports and tourism are terms that are no stranger to each other. Travels made by people to participate in sports activities outside the place where they are located are called sports tourism. The periods when the number of participants in sports tourism peaks are mega events such as the Olympics or football world championships. The economic volume it creates is undoubtedly quite high. As of March 2020, during the pandemic process, decisions have been taken to play various sports events without spectators, to postpone or cancel them to a later date in many different countries. The pandemic process, which has seriously damaged the economies of countries, has unfortunately neutralized items that make a great economic contribution to the country's economy, such as sports and sports tourism. One of the sectors most negatively affected by the pandemic so far is the sports sector. The survival of the sports sector, which has reached a gigantic size in the last two decades and which not only has a significant share in the gross national income of all developed/developing countries but also provides a wide range of employment opportunities, is of vital importance for the post-epidemic period.

Since the impact of the COVID-19 crisis is felt in the entire world sports tourism economy, it is understood that a common approach is needed in rescheduling; rescheduling the resconstruction of working models businesses and employees in the sector. Tourism enterprises and their employees benefit from incentive packages across the economy, and many country governments also take tourism-specific measures. In general, the recommendations that are expected to focus on these efforts are as follows:

- Removing travel restrictions – minimizing them and working with businesses to access liquidity supports, implementing new health protocols for safe travel, and helping diversify sports tourism markets;
- Trying to restore trust with new, safe and clean labels for the sector, information applications for visitors, and domestic tourism advertising and promotion campaigns, and to revive demand;

- Preparing comprehensive tourism improvement plans to restructure practices, encourage innovation and investment, and rethink the sports tourism sector.

It is thought that the sports tourism paradigm will need to be established as health-centered, to adopt respect for the environment, to be built with a global vision and only local motives/values, to use digital tools more intensively, to integrate with software, artificial intelligence and robotic technology, to adopt transparency and participation, and to be based on social responsibility as well. It is also clear that COVID-19 has revealed that humanity is on the same boat, and that all plans that will not be based on the general good of the human species were proven to cause harm in the shortest time.

References

Alagöz, M. & Erdoğan, S. (2008). İhracat ile Turizm Gelirlerindeki Değişimin Cari İşlemler Dengesi Üzerine Etkisi. *KMU İİBF Dergisi*, sayı: 14, s. 214–227.

Alpullu, A. (2011). Uluslararası Basketbol Organizasyonlarının Spor Turizmine, Ülke Ekonomisine ve Tanıtımına Katkılarının Değerlendirilmesi, Doktora Tezi, Marmara Üniversitesi, Sağlık Bilimleri Enstitüsü, İstanbul.

Başol, K. (2012) Türkiye Ekonomisi, 11.b., Türkmen Kitabevi, İstanbul.

Brıtton, S. G. (1982) The political economy of tourism in the Third World. *Annals of Tourism Research*, 9, 331–358.

Çakıcı, C. & ve Güler, O. (2014). Büyük Spor Organizasyonlarına Ev Sahipliği Yapmaya Değer Mi? Ekonomik Beklentiler ve Turizm Açısından Bir Değerlendirme, 3. Doğu Akdeniz Sempozyumu, 37–50.

Çeti, B. & Ünlüönen, K. (2019). Salgın Hastalıklar Sebebiyle Oluşan Krizlerin Turizm Sektörü Üzerindeki Etkisinin Değerlendirilmesi. *AHBVÜ Turizm Fakültesi Dergisi*, 22(2), 109–128.

Copeland, B. R. (1991). Tourism, welfare and de-industrialization in a small open economy. *Economica*, 58, November, 515–529.

Corsini, A., Bisciotti, G. N., Eirale, C., & Volpi, P. (2020). Football cannot restart soon during the COVID-19 emergency! A critical perspective from the Italian experience and a call for action. *British Journal of Sports Medicine*. https://doi.org/10.1136/bjsports-2020-102306.17

Devecioğlu, S. (2020). Futbolda Marshall Planı. www.futbolekonomi.com/index.php/haberler-makaleler/genel/125-sebahattin-devecioglu/4815-soccer-and-coronaviruses-futbol-ve-coranavirusuefa-fifa-tff.html, Access Date: April 3, 2020.

Dever, A. (2010). Spor Sosyolojisi: Tarihsel ve Güncel Boyutlarıyla Spor ve Toplum. Başlık Yayınları.77.Dıamond, J. (1977). Tourism's role in economic development: The case reexamined. *Economic Development and Cultural Change*, 25(3), 539–553.

Donuk, B. (2005). Spor Yöneticiliği ve İstihdam Alanları. Ötüken Neşriyat.

Drucker, F. P. (1998). *Innovation and Entrepreneurship*. San Diego, CA: Elsevier Publishers, 112.

Elçi, Ş. (2006). İnovasyon- Kalkınmanın ve Rekabetin Anahtarı. İstanbul: Nova Yayınları, 32.

Elçi, Ş. (2010). İnovasyon Kalkınmanın ve Rekabetin Anahtarı. Ankara: Technopolis Group.44

Gibson, H. (1998). Active sport tourism: Who participates. *Leisure Studies*, 17(2–3), 46–170.

Gilat, R. & Cole, B. J. (2020). Editorial Commentary: COVID-19, medicine, and sports. *Arthroscopy, Sports Medicine, and Rehabilitation*. https://doi.org/10.1016/j.asmr.2020.04.003.

Güdük, T. (2019). Mersin İlinin Spor Turizmi Potansiyelinin Swot Analizi Yöntemiyle İncelenmesi. Yayımlanmamış Yüksek Lisans Tezi. Mersin Üniversitesi Sosyal Bilimler Enstitüsü, Mersin.

Güleş, H. K. & Bülbül, H. (2004). Yenilikçilik. Ankara: Nobel Yayın Dağıtım. 81.

Hao, J., Var, T., & Ve Chon, J. (2003) A forecasting model of tourist arrivals from major markets to Thailand. *Tourism Analysis*, 8, 33–45.

Içöz, O. (2008). Spor Turizmi Pazarlaması ve Futbol Takımlarının Hazırlık Dönemi Kamp Yeri Terc, ihlerini Belirleyen Etkenler. Basılmamış Yüksek Lisans Tezi, Dokuz Eylül Üniversitesi Sosyal Bilimler Enstütüsü, s.45

IESF-International Esports Federation. (2020). https://ie-sf.org/about/members

Kamien, M. I. & ve Schwartz, N. L. (1982). *Market Structure and Innovation*. Cambridge: Cambridge University Press.

Karakoç, B. (2011). 2010 Dünya Basketbol Şampiyonası'nın Spor Turizmi ve Ekonomik Etkileri Açısından İncelenmesi.Yayımlanmamış Yüksek Lisans Tezi, Muğla Üniversitesi, Sosyal Bilimler Enstitüsü, Muğla. 20.

Karaus, R. (1977). *Recration Today; Program, Planning and Leadership*. Santa Monica, CA: Goodyear Publishing, 5.

Koçdemir, B. (2020). Korona Virüsün Türk ve Dünya Futboluna. Etkisihttps://haber.sakarya.edu.tr/korona-virusunun-dunya-futboluna-etkisi-h97419.html, Access Date: April 1, 2020.

Kozak, N., Kozak, A. M., & Kozak, M. (2001). Genel Turizm, Detay Yayıncılık, Ankara.3

Mann, R. H., Clift, B. C., Boykoff, J., & Bekker, S. (2020). Athletes as community; athletes in community: Covid-19, sporting mega-events and athlete health protection. *British Journal of Sports Medicine*. https://doi.org/10.1136/bjsports-2020-102433.

Morgan, L. (2019). Esports is coming to the Olympics after all as Paris 2024 reveal ideas to improve fan engagement. www.insidethegames.biz/articles/1075990/liammorgan-esports-is-coming-to-the-olympics-after-all-as-paris-2024-reveal-ideas-to-improvefan-engagement

Mullin, J. B., Hardy, S., & Sutton, A. W. (2000). *Sport Marketing*. Champaign, IL: Human Kinetics, 14.

OECD. (2020). https://www.oecd.org, Access Date: December 19, 2020.

Önen, M.O. (2008) Dünya'da ve Türkiye'de Turizm, Türkiye Kalkınma Bankası Ekonomik ve Sosyal Araştırmalar Müdürlüğü, Ankara, 2.

Oran, I. B. (2020) Covid-19'un Uluslararası Turizm Üzerinde Diğer Krizlerden Farklı Etkileri, Turkish Studies, Agustos 2020.

Parnell, D., Widdop, P., Bond, A., & Wilson, R. (2020). COVID-19, networks and sport. *Managing Sport and Leisure*, 1–7. https://doi.org/10.1080/23750472.2020.1750100

Richardson, S., March, R., Lewis, J., & Radel, K. (2015). Analysing the İmpact of the 2011 Natural Disasters on the Central Queensland Tourism İndustry. In B. W. Ritchie and K. Campiranon (Eds.), *Tourism Crisis and Disaster Management in the Asia-Pacific*. Boston, MA: Cab International, 152.

Riel, A., & Van, C. R. (2005). Introduction to the special issue on service innovation management. *Managing Service Quality*, 15(6), 79.

Ross, S. D. (2001). *Developing Sport Tourism. An e-Guide for Destination Marketers and Sports Events Planners, National Laboratory for Tourism and e Commerce.* Urbana, IL: Univeristy of illionis at Urbana-Champaing: 3,ss.3–7.

Rudan, I. (2020). A cascade of causes that led to the COVID-19 tragedy in Italy and in other European Union countries. *Journal of Global Health,* 10(1), 55.

Saatçioğlu, C. (2013). Spor Ekonomisi Teori, Politika ve Uygulama, Gazi Kitabevi, Ankara, 5.

Sağcan, M. (1986) Rekreasyon ve Turizm, İzmir: Cumhuriyet Basımevi, 15.

Scandizzo, P. L. & Pierleoni, M. R. (2018). Assessing the Olympic Games: The economic impact and beyond. *Journal of Economic Surveys,* 32(3), 649–682.

Sivrikaya, K. & Demir, A. (2019). Türkiye'de 2001 Yılı Ve Sonrasında Uygulanan Spor Ekonomisi Politikalarına Yönelik Bir Değerlendirme. *Vizyoner Dergisi,* 10(23), 126–136.

Stevenden, J. & Knop, P. (1999). *Sport Tourism.* Champaign: Human Kinetics, 15.

Stevens, V. & Prins, R. G. (2020). Twitterers' sentiments towards the COVID-19 responses of the FIA, UEFA and IOC. Retrieved April 24, 2020 from https://www.mulierinstituut.nl/publicaties/25341/twitterers-sentimentstowards-the-covid19-responses-of-the-fia-uefa-and-ioc/

Şimşek, K. Y. (2011). Erzurum Dünya Üniversitelerarası Kış Oyunlarının Erzurum Şehrine Sosyo-Kültürel veEkonomik Etkisi. *Selçuk Üniversitesi Beden Eğitimi ve Spor Bilimleri Dergisi,* 13(3), 383–393.

T.C. Sağlık Bakanlığı, Halk Sağlığı Genel Müdürlüğü, COVID-19 (2019-n CoV Hastalığı) Rehberi (Bilim Kurulu Çalışması) (2020). T.C. Sağlık Bakanlığı, 25 Şubat 2020. Access Date: November 30, 2020. https://covid19.saglik.gov.tr/TR-66301/covid-19-rehberi.html

Timpka, T. (2020). Sports health during the SARS-Cov-2 pandemic. *Sports Medicine* (Auckland, Nz), 1.90.

TÜİK. (2020). Turizm Geliri, Gideri ve Ortalama Geceleme Sayısı. Türkiye İstatistik Kurumu. tuik.gov.tr

Tunçdemir, C. (2013). Olimpiyat ev sahipliğini kazanmak gerçekten kazandırıyor mu? https://t24.com.tr/yazarlar/cemal-tuncdemir/olimpiyat-evsahipligini-kazanmak-gercektenkazandiriyor-mu, 6423, Access Date: December 12, 2019.

Turco, D. M., Riley, R. S., & Swart, K. (2002). *Sport Tourism.* Indianapolis: Fitness Information Tecnology Inc. 6.

TÜRSAB. (2014). Spor turizmi Sektör Raporu. https://www.tursab.org.tr/apps/OldFiles//dosya/12 195/tursab-spor-turizmi-raporu_12195_5670173.pdf, Access Date: December 20, 2019.

TÜSİAD. (2003). Ulusal İnovasyon Sistemi, Kavramsal Çerçeve, Türkiye İncelemesi ve Ülke Örnekleri. İstanbul: TÜSİAD Yayını, 11.

UNWTO. (2020). International Tourism and COVİD-19. https://www.UNWTO.org/international tourism-and-COVİD-19, Access Date: June 9, 2021

Weed, M. (1997). Influences on sport tourism relations in Britain: The effects of Government Policy. *TourismRecreation Research,* 22(2), 5.

WHO Official Updates – Coronavirus Disease 2019- who.int, Access Date: November 30, 2020.

WTO. (1995). Implications of the WTO/UN Tourism Definitions, Madrid.

WTTC, Dünya Seyahat ve Turizm Konseyi (2020). https://www.turizmgunlugu.com/2020/04/25/Covid-19-sonrasi-turizmde-is-kaybi-wttc/, Access Date: May 13, 2020.

Yamamoto-Telli, G. & ve Altun, D. (2020). Coronavirüs ve çevrimiçi (online) eğitimin önlenemeyen yükselişi. *Üniversite Araştırmaları Dergisi*, 3(1), 25–34.

Yıldız, E. & Aydın, S. A. (2013). Olimpiyat Oyunlarının Sürdürülebilir Kalkınma Açısından Değerlendirilmesi. *Spor Bilimleri Dergisi Hacettepe*, 24(4), 269–282.

Yılmaz, Ö. D. (2004). Turizm işletmelerinde kriz yönetimi ve konaklama işletmeleri yöneticilerinin krizlere ilişkin yaklaşımlarına yönelik bir araştırma (Yayınlanmamış yüksek lisans tezi), Dokuz Eylül Üniversitesi, İzmir.

INDEX

Printed in the United States
by Baker & Taylor Publisher Services